Master Plans and Minor Acts

Master Plans and Minor Acts

Repairing the City in Post-Genocide Rwanda

SHAKIRAH E. HUDANI

The University of Chicago Press

Chicago and London

The University of Chicago Press, Chicago 60637
The University of Chicago Press, Ltd., London
Published 2024
Printed and bound by CPI Group (UK) Ltd, Croydon, CR0 4YY

33 32 31 30 29 28 27 26 25 24   1 2 3 4 5

ISBN-13: 978-0-226-83273-9 (cloth)
ISBN-13: 978-0-226-83272-2 (paper)
ISBN-13: 978-0-226-83274-6 (e-book)
DOI: https://doi.org/10.7208/chicago/9780226832746.001.0001

Library of Congress Cataloging-in-Publication Data

Names: Hudani, Shakirah E., author.
Title: Master plans and minor acts : repairing the city in post-genocide Rwanda /
    Shakirah E. Hudani.
Other titles: Repairing the city in post-genocide Rwanda
Description: Chicago : The University of Chicago Press, 2024. | Includes
    bibliographical references and index.
Identifiers: LCCN 2023037920 | ISBN 9780226832739 (cloth) | ISBN 9780226832722
    (paperback) | ISBN 9780226832746 (ebook)
Subjects: LCSH: Cities and towns—Rwanda—Kigali. | Peace-building—Rwanda. |
    Rwanda—Politics and government—1994–
Classification: LCC DT450.44 .H83 2024 | DDC 967.57104/3—dc23/eng/20230912
LC record available at https://lccn.loc.gov/2023037920

A genocide is not just any kind of story, with a beginning and an end between which more or less ordinary events take place.

BOUBACAR BORIS DIOP[1]

We name this calling into question of my spontaneity by the presence of the Other ethics. The strangeness of the Other, his irreducibility to the I, to my thoughts and my possessions, is precisely accomplished as a calling into question of my spontaneity, as ethics.

EMMANUEL LEVINAS[2]

Contents

Significant Abbreviations

BBTG: broad-based transitional government (set up by the Arusha Accords)
CBD: central business district
CHC: community hygiene club
COK: City of Kigali
CND: Conseil nationale de developpement (earlier name for the parliament building)
CNLG: National Commission for the Fight against Genocide
CSS: Centralized Sewerage System (planned for Kigali)
FAR: Rwandan Armed Forces (under the Habyarimana government)
FARG: National Fund for Genocide Survivors
FDI: foreign direct investment
GOR: Government of Rwanda
HRW: Human Rights Watch
HRZ: high-risk zone
ICTR: UN International Criminal Tribunal for Rwanda
IDP: Rural Integrated Development Program
INMR: Institute of National Museums of Rwanda
MRND: National Revolutionary Movement for Development (Habyarimana's party during the Rwandan second republic)
NISR: National Institute of Statistics Rwanda
NGO: nongovernmental organization
NRM: National Resistance Movement (Uganda)
NST 1: National Strategy for Transformation
NURC: National Unity and Reconciliation Commission
ONAPO: National Office of Population (active in the pre-1994 period)
OSC: one-stop center
Parmehutu: Parti du mouvement pour l'emancipation Hutu (also known as MDR-Parmehutu; Kayibanda's party in the Rwandan first republic)

P P P : public-private partnership

R D F : Rwanda Defense Forces

R G B : Rwanda Governance Board

R P A : Rwandan Patriotic Army

R P F : Rwandan Patriotic Front

S M U : Saemaul Undong (South Korea's New Village Movement)

R T L M : Radio Television Libre Mille Collines (extremist radio station active during the 1994 genocide)

T N A : Transitional National Assembly (name of Parliament building between 1994 and 2003)

W B G : World Bank Group

W D I : World Bank world development indicator

Introduction

Master Plans and Minor Acts is a study of the violence of large-scale spatial planning in traumatized geographies, focused on urban transformation in post-genocide Rwanda. It is a story of how repair and conciliation are enacted, and how political expression and belonging are reconfigured around place. In a terrain starkly delimited by top-down master plans of various orders, spatial repair is an aperture for thinking through a material politics of cohabitation. In other words, I ask what remains unfinished, drawing attention to the politics of reinhabiting the present rather than erasing its vestiges in the physical environment.

The City as a Scale of Repair

This story begins in Rwanda's capital, Kigali, but its narrative threads are not localized in the city alone. Rather, changing urban space and imaginaries of the city form the focal points of this account. In mid-2018 I was sitting in a bureaucrat's office in the diplomatic area of Kigali, discussing the Rwandan positions on issues related to a key international conference: the World Urban Forum, held in Kuala Lumpur, Malaysia, earlier that year. The theme of the conference was "Cities 2030—Cities for All: Implementing the New Urban Agenda," and on the table was the issue of the moment: a call for a global "right to the city," and a training agenda for mainstreaming this vision into the Sustainable Development Goals (SDG). As we conversed, a car blared loud music outside the office building—a rare occurrence. The bureaucrat stared past my chair—past the bookshelf that held selected urban reports, as well as a copy of *From Third World to First*, the autobiography of Singapore's

first prime minister, Lee Kuan Yew—and toward the guards visible outside
the building. The radio was soon silenced.

"A right to the city?" the bureaucrat said. "We in Kigali cannot support an
unconditional right to the city in this country that has been through genocide." He confided that the issue was silently contentious in the upper echelons
of the bureaucracy working to remake urban space in the capital. Rwanda is
often compared to Singapore in the speed and scale of its developmental policy ambitions, and hence this scene in its totality—the blaring music silenced
by guards, the orderly office and its shelved books, and my interlocutor's
statements—appeared to me at that moment to approximate too closely the
often repeated "Singapore of Africa" claims that the global media so frequently
write and reiterate. I left the office thinking about these statements on what I
began to think of as the "right to the city after genocide," or a broader "right to
the city after conflict."

As Henri Lefebvre formulated it, the "right to the city" identifies urban
space as key to cultural expression, economic struggle, and political opportunity, and situates it as a "synecdoche for society," central to the imaginative
geographies of the nation-state and the social mobilities of the citizen (in
Marcuse 2009: 244).[1] As Rwanda's postconflict context discloses to us, the
"right to the city" is not an ubiquitously heralded concept but a contested
one, with multiple local meanings and interpretations. In their plans and
blueprints, Rwandan policy makers are quick to put forth a popularized conception of the "right to the city" as key to their plans for urban design, and
highlight Kigali as an urban space to support innovative design and green city
visions (Republic of Rwanda 2015). Yet, as plans for urban transformation increase displacement and regulation in and around the capital, we must question what happens to urban equity and spatial justice in and around Kigali.
Might a vision of urban change focused on a reparative ethics after conflict
call for renewed reading of the spatiality of repair through and beyond current frames of restorative justice? While Lefebvre's concept situates some of
my questioning, at its core I am more interested in the problematic of urban
repair after conflict. What do urban dispossession and repair mean for rebuilding life in the long aftermath of genocide and civil conflict, and how do
they tie together built and social environments in and beyond the city?

Since 2000, large-scale changes have been underway in the urban space
of Rwanda's capital, Kigali, as part of reordering the city and planning anew
its social and material infrastructures. *Master Plans and Minor Acts* resituates
discussions about post-genocide and postconflict repair and reckoning in the
materiality of the city. I focus on what it means to dislocate the national as the
sole site of redress and to look instead at levels of repair—and dispossession—

that exist at the scale of the city. Decentering the preoccupation with the nation-state as the sole community of collective memory (Halbwachs 1992 [1941]; Renan 2018 [1882]), and thus of collective reckoning, brings into view additional forms of repair. The urban scale permits us to ask new questions about the materiality of social repair (chapter 1). The city condenses socio-material relations and posits shared national futures; it is a central space that conveys the stakes of national visioning and the materiality of the concilia-tion imperative to people living together in close proximity. The foundations for rebuilding in the city, and the shared ties that enable neighbors to forge conciliation and cooperation in relation to the built environment, the neigh-borhood, and the home, invite us to consider spatial relations as templates for the construction of a more inclusive social order. These practices of living with the past push back against and subvert the idea that societies riven with conflict and traumatic pasts can and should use erasure and complete spatial reorganization ("master plans") as a basis for national rebuilding.

This book is inspired by traditions of bridging scholarship between the present temporality of the city and the scalar continuity of work on the post-conflict state, and accordingly speaks to literature in urban studies, human geography, and African studies. I draw on and extend the work of scholars of postconflict space in African cities—such as Danny Hoffman on Monrovia (2007, 2017); Filip De Boeck on Kinshasa (2014); and Claudia Gastrow (2017), Ricardo Cardoso (2016), and Antonio Tomás (2022) on Luanda. I theorize large-scale planning in a postconflict society as a form of erasure that performs different forms of extraordinary violence through the built environment, privi-leging planning over forms of memory and organic remembrance. Planning here serves to reinscribe social memory and unmoor place, following mass violence and attempted cohabitation. Instead, I argue normatively for socio-spatial continuities and small-scale practices of rebuilding ("minor acts") as the basis for an enduring and equitable peace. These minor acts provide a founda-tion for relational repair between and beyond existing governmental structures and the transnational capitalist repurposing of urban terrain in the country.

Yet the material foundations of exchange and repair in daily life also show that urbanizing repair is in progress and incomplete: it operates without the full and final closure of state-orchestrated reconciliation, neoliberal apology, and the obligation to offer complete forgiveness. Instead material repair is a necessarily *limited* interpersonal endeavor that accepts both the need for relational conciliation and the irreparability of issues of lost life. It is by ac-knowledging that certain questions in postconflict environments are invari-ably irreparable that repair gains grounds for what is still possible to speak of and to rebuild.

Revisiting Kibuye

My engagement with the changing spatiality of Rwanda's towns and cities began when I visited Kibuye some eight years after the end of the 1994 Rwandan genocide, as a student studying the transitional justice process.[2] At the time, this seemingly serene town on the edge of Lake Kivu and not far from the border with the Congo was still recovering from the trauma of 1994, when it had been a center of the genocide in the western part of the country. Records show that at least 59,050 ethnic Tutsis were killed in Kibuye and the Gitesi commune in the early part of the genocide, from early April to mid-May 1994. Many of these victims were massacred in the Gatwaro football stadium, and others in the town center and the Catholic parish church (Verwimp 2004, using data from *Ibuka*). The condensed spatial landscape at Kibuye's center that I observed in 2002, and its specific texture, preoccupied me in the intervening years until I returned for research on urban change in 2018. Although much of this book focuses on urban transformation in Kigali, Rwanda's capital, the spatiality of Kibuye's center has been embedded in my mind as I have written this book, and its town center forms the setting of the complex scenes that I narrate below. These scenes connect national postconflict transition and urban transformation in a densely concentrated web of social and material relations. As observed over time, the reorganization of life in Kibuye forms a palimpsest of post-genocide erasure and spatial reinscription.

KIBUYE, 2002

In 2002 the center of Kibuye had four distinct areas: a bustling informal market area; the Kibuye central prison, which housed thousands of inmates, mostly genocide suspects awaiting trials in *gacaca* community courts and higher-level courts of justice; the Gatwaro stadium on the other side of the road; and a makeshift genocide memorial. The commemoration sign on the outside of the stadium compound read:

> Cimetery
> More than 10,000 people were inhumated here.
> Official ceremony was presided over by H. E. Pasteur Bizimungu,
> President of the Republic of Rwanda,
> April 26, 1995.

A low wooden fence separated the stadium as the site of massacre from the fourth space, the modest memorial next to it, constructed informally by survivors and residents of the area. Across the road, the central prison was a buzzing mass of industrial-like activity, with inmates dressed in pink shorts and shirts confined behind a main gate and a low fence and wall. In my field notes I recorded that I was struck by the cacophony of contested memory embodied in this concentrated space, and the unstable boundaries that separated the site of the massacre from the memorial site, the prison from external space—from the space of the market and the rhythms of daily life. It was this very permeability that characterized the spatial ordering of Kibuye's town center, and the difficulty of separating its multiple spatialized narratives, that struck me as a microcosm of a complex and ambivalent spatial ecology.

I found this spatial ecology expressed to varying degrees across the country itself, and writ large, in 2002. At that time, the state was nearing the end of the period of official governmental transition after the genocide of 1994. During the one hundred days of the genocide, between five to eight hundred thousand ethnic Tutsis and additional moderate Hutus were massacred in a wave of violence that ran from April to July 1994 (Des Forges 1999; Prunier 1997). Nested within a larger civil war from 1990 onward, as the Tutsi Rwandan Patriotic Army (RPA) guerrilla force invaded northern Rwanda from Uganda, the period of genocide was perhaps the starkest and most visible violence in a regional conflict that has been described as "Africa's World War" and which has continued to engulf areas of the eastern Congo (Prunier 2008; Stearns 2022).[3] Heralded by a new constitution in 2003 and the start of a new period of governance (often referred to as the "New Rwanda") under President Paul Kagame, the period of transition that followed was supplanted by a powerful developmentalist master narrative of national progress, and ambitious programs to rapidly modernize the country. Nevertheless, in 2002 social spaces in the town—spaces of quotidian memory, contested narratives, and vital post-genocide life—were still visible ruptures and open wounds in the official ordering of a new state and a new national society. I began to question: How does constructing a new national identity entail a reordering of space?[4]

Despite the wounds and ruptures spatially evident in the Kibuye of 2002, these condensed spaces in the town were open for circulation. Different groups of people shared common spaces, confronted each other on shared paths to the bus stop, and interacted in the bustling old market. These interactions were often uncomfortable and traumatic for survivors of the genocide who had to coinhabit urban areas. While meetings in shared space created moments of tension, the realm of the encounter was also a space of potential conciliation: living together as a process that might unfold incrementally. These spaces were hence places of everyday routine. Rather than seeing reconciliation as an event or as a singular meeting point, I found that relations with neighbors evolved over time, as trust was gradually rebuilt on faltering structures.

KARONGI, 2018

On my next visit to the area, in 2018, the town had changed. Not only did it have a new name, Karongi, but touristic enterprise had expanded, creating new areas of development. The town now had a centrally located methane gas generation plant, and strictly regulated fish farming was taking place where small-scale fishermen had once dominated. The prison had also been moved to a rural location in accordance with a national policy to deconcentrate prison development in urban areas, leaving in its stead empty spaces and disused buildings. Although Karongi was not one of the six secondary cities designed for master-planned rehabilitation according to the national governmental road map on green city development (Republic of Rwanda and GGGI 2015), the stark spatial juxtaposition I had seen in the Kibuye of 2002 was now absent. The heterotopic spatiality of the early post-genocide period was slowly being replaced in built environments around the country with a form of "blueprint utopia" (Holston 1989): ordered, planned spaces of green urbanism put into place by master-planning and its attendant large-scale dispossession.

The spatial ordering of the early post-genocide years that I recorded in Kibuye in 2002 was a condensed miniature of Rwanda's post-genocide society at the time: the town's spatial and normative boundaries transgressed through unspeakable violence, the debris of genocide still visible in its cities, and a multiplicity of narratives lodged in its informal settlements and old towns. In contrast, plans to remake Rwanda's urban spaces since the early 2000s have sought to reinvent space through order and concepts of the placeless model urban. If Kibuye's central areas in 2002 were a particular heterogeneity of place, then the "world-class" master-planning of the capital, Kigali, and its secondary city poles by international architectural consultants advances the idea of fungible policy, generic space, and spatial transfer: these redesigned cities subvert and ignore the specificity of local places and their particular architectures of space with designs and plans that could be located anywhere.

THE THREE MASTER PLANS

The foundations of violent spatiality in Central Africa today are durable and well entrenched. This book takes as its premise that three master plans operate in Rwanda in its current moment of post-genocide transition and urban transformation. I read "master plans" broadly here, as state forms of reordering and reorganization in mnemonic, social, and spatial terms. While I do not make explicit reference to these three modes of organizing space and memory throughout my chapters, their specters haunt all aspects of this text. The first plan of ordering is a *master plan of state aftermaths*, which takes the organized violence of the genocide of 1994 as its primary case but operates within wider contexts. This master plan considers the iterative programs of state-orchestrated violence that have affected the country since its independence in 1962—resulting in the generational exile of Rwandan Tutsis in the 1950s and 1970s—and speaks to themes of home, homeland, and belonging in Rwanda over time. This conception of the master plan extends into the borderlands of the eastern Congo, a region marked by its sheer complexity, its ethnic and geographic fissures, and the politicization of space and memory that operates within its traumatized terrain.

The second master plan, the *master plan of the colonial present*, extends and illuminates the first.[5] It exposes the entangled nature of colonial violence and programs of transformation over time. As I show in various chapters in this book, forms of top-down ordering and racialized planning were central to German and Belgian colonialism in Central Africa. Colonialism was itself a type of master plan, devised from its center and iteratively revised through the technologies of top-down planning and violent governance. Colonial governance fixed and racialized ethnicity, and segmented space and mobility for the colonized in both urban and rural areas. In doing so, colonial governance set the conditions for the post-colonial violence that has unfolded in Rwanda throughout successive decades. While this book does not explore the legacy of the colonial period in depth, its enduring imprints are present everywhere in social life and spatial organization in the extended life of "colonial presence" (Stoler 2016; Purdeková and Mwambari 2022).

The third master plan is the contemporary spatial *master plan of post-crisis fix*: transnationally orchestrated spatial master planning, with its own legacies of destruction and segmentation, moving into post-genocide terrain from regions of post–financial crisis fix in East Asia (chapter 1). Spatial master planning as a form of total spatial reordering also has a longer genealogy that dates back to the violence of colonial interventions in Africa and Asia (as analyzed in Rabinow 1992; Wright 1991; King 2012; Home 2013; and others), the functional zoning and monumental architecture of modernist cities such as Brasilia and Chandigarh (Holston 1989), and earlier experimentation with total spatial change in Europe (as is famously chronicled in Harvey 2004, on Baron Haussmann's modernization of Paris). This book takes the third form of master-planning as its ostensible theme and titular referent, but it is within the frame of the other two master plans that spatial erasure and transformation must be interpreted and understood in Rwanda today. The Kigali 2050 spatial master plan is a case of postcrisis planning, legible not just on its own terms but against the backdrop of other forms of master planning that have displaced populations and reorganized space over time in the Great Lakes region of Central Africa.

In this book I question the meanings and motives of large-scale planning in postconflict geographies. Forms of master planning in Rwanda depoliticize the built environment as a medium of ongoing spatial violence. Yet the space of the built environment is an inherently political milieu. Urbicide and more granular forms of violence against place show this when they efface lived connections that are embedded in social routines, embodied through homes, and kept alive through interpersonal relations (Coward 2008). Mass displacement effectively cuts off spatial genealogies, and excises modes of knowing that are physically embedded in the present. Accordingly, I look to *repoliticize* the built environment and the spatial renovation of towns and cities in a country where spatial change is intertwined with the experience of mass trauma and projects of transformation at various scales.[6] Identities remain splintered between and within regional, class, and ethnic lines here, and memory runs discontinuously between generations. Place instead gives mooring to different forms of social memory, and is hinged into modes of recollecting even as the project of spatial transformation proceeds apace.

As this book shows, master-planned spatial models are a type of transplantable spatial fantasy that seeks to dismantle the everyday conditions of post-genocide space and social relations through removing bricks and mortar and demolishing existing edifices of concrete. By reordering space, the state reinscribes a new national narrative of progress, and delimits those who can feasibly circulate in and access the renewed city. Such master planning effectively constricts the possibility of heterogeneous, lived encounters in shared space and an ethos of popular participation and coexistence in the city. Considering the spatial and the temporal together demands that we think beyond master plans of various forms, looking instead toward the topological space of the city as a material space for repair and coexistence in the present. I examine transformation in and around Rwanda's towns and cities as an "extended case" of social change in a country that has moved from trauma and rupture to erasure and renewal (Burawoy 2009). Trauma here is manifest spatially, and can be told or traced through the remaking of place. Such remaking constrains the encounter "face-to-face" and conditions the forms of interaction and reckoning that can be held in a society still coming to terms with its various pasts (Levinas 1979).

Research Methods

I conducted research on Rwanda in two phases, from 2002 to 2004 and from 2018 to 2020. During the first period I conducted research on the transitional justice process in the country, to understand the rifts and contradictions of the post-genocide period. I spent six months attending inaugural *inkiko-gacaca* community court sessions, visiting prisons and interviewing genocide prisoners, conducting interviews on national transition with officials struggling to address the judicial overload in the aftermath of the 1994 genocide, and interrogating the process of transition alongside local and international aid and civil society organizations, many of which were present in the country during this research period.[7] When I returned for thirteen months of research beginning in 2018, my understandings of the rapid development and ambitious urban plans for Kigali and secondary cities in Rwanda were broadly informed by the earlier time I had spent in the country, where I had found myself witness to a very different spatial and social order. This earlier spatial order was one still in formation: it was yet unchanged by the green urban aesthetics that would later come to characterize the capital. This previous social fabric was struggling with rifts visibly expressed through spaces of transition, such as the prison, and palpable through the discursive theater of the *gacaca* community court.

During the second period, my research focused on interviews with policy makers and planners in private practice, on studies of informal settlements and old neighborhoods in Kigali and in the urban periphery of Bugesera District—increasingly under threat by master-planned urbanism—and on interviews with residents and local leaders. I also attended participatory planning meetings in Bugesera District, held to oversee the master-planning and regularization of land in peri-urban areas bordering Kigali. I studied two integrated development program (IDP) model villages: in Bugesera District (Rweru Village) and in the north of Rwanda. Next, I conducted research on security and hygiene competitions in Kigali, under the ambit of the City of Kigali and focusing on Rwezamenyo and Gitega Sectors in Kigali. I also revisited Kibuye/Karongi and rural sectors where I had earlier conducted research. Outside Rwanda, I conducted several interviews with Rwandans in the diaspora, and with policy experts living in Nairobi, Kenya. Finally, I amassed an extensive collection of official policy documents related to the transitional state programs implemented from the late 1990s onward, and the plans and policies for urban transformation in the contemporary period.

I conducted semistructured and in-depth interviews with Rwandans in various spheres of my research—from policy offices to rural model villages—and used English, French, Kiswahili, and certain amounts of Kinyarwanda. I worked with a Kinyarwanda translator and research assistant in some of these settings, who accompanied me and helped when my language skills fumbled. Making newer friendships in the context of research and reviving older connections, I sought through my inquiries to understand how urban change connected personal histories and the built environment intertemporally. As a woman of South Asian ethnic background from East Africa and North America, who spent considerable time in Nairobi while growing up, my positionality during research has been inflected by the dynamics of being familiar with the cultural geography of East and Central Africa. Yet because of this background, I am simultaneously identified as an unfamiliar figure from elsewhere in the Rwandan research terrain. Ethnicity, class, race, gender, and citizenship have all had a large impact on how I was accepted and responded to in my various research sites. Much more can be written of this positionality: what it affords in terms of proximity to the East African social context, the forging of social theory by an African researcher, and also the challenges of conducting research in Rwanda's tightly surveilled environment as it changed across time periods. In this interdisciplinary work, I have chosen to ground my writing in the built environment as its primary texture, with the hope that my reflexivity emerges through the text. Relatedly, for reasons of the safety of my research interlocutors I have anonymized their identities—and at times their locations or identifiable surroundings—with the exception of interviewees whose views and stories appeared in Rwandan newspapers and were thus public knowledge due to their experiences or social positions.

My research methods have been largely qualitative, focused on in-depth and semistructured interviews, focus group discussions, and observation. I also draw on archival methods and textual analysis of primary and secondary sources, such as newspaper articles and policy documents. Throughout my second period of research, my concerns were grounded in the built environment and residents' interactions with its changing structures and milieus. The built environment textured my interactions, yet gave them a solid basis in practices of planning and changes in the environment and in the space of the home. While Rwandans of many walks of life are hesitant to trust and speak on the political situation in the country, the nature of commentary and complaint in relation to the scale of the home, the neighborhood, and questions of possession and dispossession have been constant concerns for both urban and rural residents. Thus, I found in my various spheres of research that individuals whom I interviewed—my interlocutors in the sense of engaged ethnographic research and exchange—were keen to share their perspectives on their changing environments and their concerns about the future in a sustained manner. The matrix of the city provided a milieu for research and interviewing of residents on their experiences of change at various scales, and for talking about this change over time in relation to personal histories of the postconflict city. The city after conflict is, after all, composed of both continuity and rupture: its built environment and the interactions of residents with their milieu, its present, its anticipated futures, and the texture of its pasts. It provides a generative space for discussion and interaction on topics that animate its inhabitants, who seek to "dwell" as best they can in changing space (Heidegger 1971; Sennett 2008).

Throughout my research, I grappled with the difficulty of conducting qualitative research in a tightly state-surveilled environment. I navigated layers of bureaucratic approval at the national level and at multiple subnational and sectoral levels. As an urban studies and planning scholar, I found it additionally challenging to justify qualitative research methods such as in-depth and semistructured interviewing and observation when officials expressed an expectation that I would use less personal and more "objectively" sound quantitative methods such as surveys, existing data sets, and geographic information system (GIS) methods. Nonetheless, I duly obtained numerous time-consuming approvals and permits from national, district, municipal, and sectoral offices and agencies in order to conduct my research work. In its focus over two periods of time, my research framework is informed by a longitudinal "extended case method" (Burawoy 2009). This focus is one that many studies of transitional justice and postconflict societies elide, since they concentrate instead on the moment of the sociojuridical inquest, and neglect to consider other spheres in which questions of rights, desert, and conciliation are mediated and decided.

Through this book, I demonstrate the complexity of loss, grievance, and anticipation in the post-genocide period as the city becomes the focal point for a political economy of reconstruction ("master plans") as well as a more localized politics of repair ("minor acts"). My hope is to convey the complexity of questions of rebuilding, reconciliation, and repair across scales in the country—where the urban question is as much an agrarian question of enduring divides in postconflict space as a question of globalized transformation. There is urgent need for a pedagogy of rupture and repair to better understand the delicate balance needed to rebuild the city and reimagine the polity after conflict. Such a deconstructive understanding would grapple with the grievances and forms of loss endured during the 1994 genocide in Rwanda, and the context of civil war and iterative violence in which they have been embedded. There is need as well for recognition of the potency of planning in postconflict

space, for attending carefully to spatial plans for order amid multiple mnemonic vernaculars and modes of dwelling, and for a vision of intervention that
treads lightly in contested space.

Chapter Outlines

This book is organized into two sections and seven chapters which analyze
the contours of urban change and rebuilding in Rwanda's post-genocide
landscape. In the first section (chapters 2–4), I look thematically at the post-
genocide period in relation to repair, injury, and transformation in Kigali.
I then move outward in the second section (chapters 5–7) from the capital
city of Kigali and its informal settlements to its urban periphery in Bugesera
District, and the model villages that organize rural spatial life. Amid urban
reconstruction, repair emerges as a spatial process embedded locally through
the contours of place. The two sections are separated by a set of poems I
wrote during my research visits to study the *gacaca* transitional justice courts
from 2002 to 2004, reflecting my concerns with memory and justice in post-
genocide space.

In chapter 1, "A Material Politics of Repair," I detail my main arguments
on the spatial nature of conciliation in Rwanda, and examine the histories
and conjunctures behind urban transformation in the current moment. My
ethnographic examination begins in the second chapter.

Chapter 2, "Repair in Old Kigali," analyzes two registers of rebuilding:
reconstruction through the master plan, and repair to homes and buildings
in old neighborhoods of Kigali. The work of repair—to social memory and
to the microspaces of the built environment—takes place in the midst of
the incursion of master-planned designs for the capital, which threaten old
neighborhoods and continuities in ways of life and social memory. I explore
the experiences of long-term residents who seek to remain through urban
renewal, and integrate the politics of memory and repair as they subsist in
the changing capital. Repair in this context is therefore theorized as a verb, a
process, rather than as a noun or a state-initiated goal. Repair to individual
and collective lives that continue through the relation to others engages an
ethic that seeks not to erase but come to terms with the past.

Chapter 3, "The Project of Reformation," focuses on the capital city as a
terrain of state authority through the securitization of space. I consider the
transitional dilemmas borne by the minoritarian Rwandan Patriotic Army
(RPA) as it entered the capital city and began its transition into a dominant
ruling party, the Rwandan Patriotic Front (RPF). Interpreting the sociopo-

litical metaphor of *isuku* (hygiene), I describe the transition from order to orderliness and from security to the securitization of everyday life, and demonstrate how the agendas of hygiene and security are inextricably linked. This chapter situates, and challenges, the aesthetics of global "green" development by contextualizing those aspirations within Rwandan history and local contexts, with their multiple points of rupture.

Chapter 4, "A Pedagogy of Wounds," visits four sites in Kigali—an informal settlement, a prison, the central market, and the Parliament building—to show more specifically how multiple narratives in the capital are being rebuilt and rewritten, as the master plan reconfigures social history through the reconfiguration of built space. The period of master-planning and urban renewal since the early 2000s has seen different kinds of sites erased and peripheralized through redevelopment and relocation. I suggest that a pedagogy of urban rebuilding based on "wounds" in the built fabric reveals the complexity of replanning sites of complex memory. This chapter visits some of these ambivalent sites in Kigali and describes palimpsests of a changing city; it also questions themes of home, homeland, and belonging that are embedded in spatial recomposition.

Chapter 5, "Political Abandonment," considers the effects of securitization on participation and the right to remain in the city for residents of "unplanned" settlements in Kigali. Following the case of the Bannyahe settlement that was expropriated with its residents evicted, I consider the landmark legal case of resident property owners in the settlement who contested for their right to appropriate monetary compensation rather than the alternative apartment purchases the city of Kigali offered them. In so doing, I examine the uncertainty and contention that exists in the interstices of the city master plan. I suggest that the local has become a space in which contestation is possible, if limited, given the control of the authoritarian state, and that it is a space of meaningful performance of the politics of place. Urban evictions and expropriations form the locus in which the abandonment of urban inclusion is most apparent. I demonstrate that convoluted questions of inclusion in the polity over time and the problematic of political abandonment are most evident through the symbolic space of the abandoned home.

Chapter 6, "Peripheral Conscription," analyzes the displacements that transnational finance and expertise produce in the lives and livelihoods of precarious residents on the peripheries of Kigali. I localize terrains of existential crisis that are experienced by individuals struggling to remain near the capital. At the same time I analyze the complexities of local political geography in Bugesera District as new investment peripheralizes complex pasts.

Finally, I examine participatory planning and laboring for the state in peri-urban Bugesera, and consider what possibilities for relative mobilities exist, as the significance of local place is unmade in the shadow of the city.

Chapter 7, "Rural Imagining," takes readers farther beyond the city to consider it as an imaginary and an imagined aspirational space for rural Rwandans, rather than solely a material space. The chapter focuses on two model villages that display a kind of staged or museumized modernity, as rural residents are relocated to "sustainable" showcase village settings that ultimately help attract global capital. Villagers' complaints and hopes for life in the capital city are starting points for questions about the enduring urban/rural divide and its links to repeated violence. What does it mean to remake cities as selective spaces, in the face of historic and contemporary spatial divides in the country that have indexed ethnicized space and fissures in regional power? I analyze questions of majoritarian rurality and minority-led urbanism that undergird the entrenched spatialized urban/rural division in the country and set up its core problem of genuine participatory democracy.

Finally, I revisit rural Nyarubaba to reflect on unfinished questions of repair that have animated this book's longitudinal study. I close with a coda that digs deeper into the contextual, relational, and existential meanings of reckoning with the city through its regional and global entanglements. What does it mean to reckon with cities as terrains of violence, accumulation, and debt in its multiple forms? And if the city is constructed through the reconfiguration of debt and violence, what might this mean for thinking of the city as a reparative terrain that sutures together contexts—in this case, Belgium and the colonial and postcolonial iterations of Congo-Ruanda-Urundi? On a larger scale, I suggest that repair requires reckoning with the multiple entanglements of violence and planetarity that Rwanda's case across time forces us to see.

A Material Politics of Repair

Rwanda's capital, Kigali, is a city under large-scale renovation: dusty land-scapes of the older city are rapidly erased and demolished, to be replaced by the green landscaping of the new. In this spatial reinscription of entire parts of the existing city, it is not uncommon for buildings to disappear suddenly; areas of the mnemonic landscape of the city change seemingly overnight. One relies more on one's own memory of the old city, and as time passes that too becomes more uncertain and less defined. For long-term residents of Rwanda's capital and smaller towns, the built topology of Rwanda's past is a disappearing artifact. For newer residents of Kigali—including some dia-sporic returnees, members of the state elite, international entrepreneurs, and members of the expertise class—the new facades of Rwanda's capital signal progress, modernity, and the chance to refashion the national image and be-gin again. This rapid renewal of the city may erase older buildings, but under the surface it sediments memories and displaces, rather than effaces, a sense of place and urban belonging.

"Pedagogies" of Postconflict Rebuilding

In the fast-transforming areas of Kabeza and Muhima—older neighbor-hoods overlapping one another with small shops and kiosks, buzzing *moto* (motorbike) taxis, and busy social life—there used to be a small cream and blue building on the side of the undulating hill that marked the area. Located uphill from the now-closed CHIC shopping mall and the still operational Chinese 2000 supermarket, the single-story building was unobtrusive. On its plain cream facade was painted a deceptively simple phrase in blue paint: "Peace Building Ltd" (figure 1.1). But during one of my visits I noticed that

FIGURE 1.1. "Peace Building Ltd" in Old Kigali

the building had been demolished. The small edifice was eventually rebuilt
in Kigali's reconstruction, with larger, multiple-story buildings on either
side. The building's design as part of an older Kigali, and its painted name—
"Peace Building"—which could be read doubly, was for me emblematic of
the multiple meanings of constructing peace through the built environment.
Through the enterprise-like ambitions of the state, urban reconstruction
aims to concretize new memory through Kigali's modernized facades, forming new spatial organization. For longer-term residents of the city, and for
those rendered precarious by evictions of lower-income areas of the capital,
remaining within the city is essential for continuing livelihoods, for building lives, and for the conciliatory labor of building peace in the city through
multiple small acts of repair.

My inquiry in this book ties social repair to repair in the milieu of the built
environment. I have been keen to capture how meanings of social relationality and place have materialized in Rwanda's post-genocide urban transforma-

tion. What are the stakes of access to urban space in this postconflict country where the city increasingly defines spatial, socioeconomic, and imaginative contours of belonging? And how might we think of postconflict transition as a multiplicity of material processes sutured through built environments and spatial relations around place, as an alternative to top-down forms of renewal, regeneration, and reconciliation?

Drawing on the name of the building I saw in old Kigali, I suggest that state-led "peace building" is a political arrangement solidified through reconstructing the built environment, interpreted through various state-directed "master plans" that seek to use the built environment as a portal for state transformation. Through "minor acts" of repair and continuity, building a complex and organic peace is alternatively a social process that contests state ordering through smaller-scale modes of reworking space, and alternative imaginaries of community. I attend here to the material stakes of building a durable peace through the built environment in the aftermath of Rwanda's civil war (1990 onward) and the genocide of the country's Tutsi minority (April–July 1994). Spatial planning is a core tool that gives form to this endeavor, with planning alternately emerging as a political and an expert-led intervention, and as a social process. I show that spatial relations of encounter and exchange are core templates for thinking through prospects for conciliation after mass violence. In turn, shared space in the city must be seen as a key determinant of thinking beyond transitional justice, toward continuous spatial processes rather than the singular juridical event.

The speed and scale of rebuilding the capital elicits disparate views on the part of urban residents. There are those who wish the rebuilding were more gradual—more "humane," as a market trader expressed to me. Others herald the reconstruction of Kigali and six secondary cities by transnational expertise and finance as a necessary step in moving Rwanda from the past toward a new "post" in this post-genocide state—signposted by the Kigali 2050 spatial master plan. Relationships to memory, trauma, and belonging have been convoluted, multiple, and unsettled in this city. For those who see changes to the capital in relation to experience over time, urban memory and the politics of place are intimately sutured into personal routines. Buildings, streets, and neighborhoods (*quartiers* in the francophone terminology) hold personal valence, tying moments of local history to daily practices in the built environment and reciprocal relations with neighbors over time. In contrast, the aesthetics of forgetting, materialized through the reconstructed world-class city, physically represent a moment of moving on. The ruptured memory of the old city was itself a problem, spatially and mnemonically challenging a national master narrative premised upon unity, development, and leaping forward. In this postcolonial and postconflict country, the city is hence a site of rupture and conflicted memory, as well as a crucible of contestation about popular imaginaries of the future.

"We need pedagogy to understand this city," said Marianne, one of my interlocutors, one evening in late 2018. As the city is rebuilt, rapid renewal creates a sedimented belonging for residents of the capital who have their own personal histories of place and memory, yet who confront displacement, and struggle for a new sense of place. Memory, even troubled memory, must be reckoned with and deconstructed, rather than written over through comprehensive spatial master planning as if the city were a postconflict tabula rasa. In this country which has gone through iterative conflict and genocide, the city is a body in its own right. As I journeyed through the streets of Kigali in the weeks after my conversation with Marianne, I reflected upon these insights. What forms of repair are materialized or foreclosed through rebuilding of the city?

Material Repair

In this book, I argue for a "material politics of repair." This first chapter expands on my central claim and details the contexts and conjunctures that underlie urban transformation at the current moment. I highlight the central role of the built environment and the city scale in grounding the materiality of repair, and in gradually planning and rebuilding life amid aftermaths. I also discuss the nature of "crisis capital" in structuring Rwanda's urban conjuncture, and detail histories of the urban/rural divide in the country.

In more granular terms, I grapple throughout this book with three lines of inquiry. What is a reparative politics in the aftermath of genocide and civil war, a politics that reckons with the complexity of repair and reconstruction after mass violence—and perhaps with their very *irreparability*? How is this process constituted *materially* through the built environment and the politics of possession and dispossession over place? Finally, what is the role of *planning* as social process involving local pedagogy and gradual change, as well as expert-led endeavor, in reconstituting postconflict social space in the city in the long aftermath of mass violence?

I demonstrate that in rebuilding life amid ongoing aftermaths, the city remains the core material scale for inclusive repair.[1] It is here that "disrepair," as a heuristic for incomplete and ongoing projects of gradual rebuilding, emerges in social life and in the built environment (chapter 2). I argue normatively for planning as a reparative process—one that is iterative in nature, confronts real differentials in power and voice, and operates incrementally in shared space. Reparative planning moves beyond precepts of participatory planning and community consent as processes for replanning the built environment. There are tangible remains of trauma and rupture in Rwanda that underlie planning endeavors to erase and recreate the city. Large-scale spatial planning must contend with the fragility of existing social life and the excess of lived memory embedded around place. Recent work on a reparative ethics in planning includes consideration of "trauma imaginaries" that are reactivated by planning intervention in a wide range of geographies (Knapp et al. 2022; Poe 2022). Such concerns follow upon earlier work on contested urban space in cities such as Belfast and Jerusalem (Bollens 2000 and 2012).

A material politics of repair focused on interpersonal conciliation through the built environment must also contend with the materialist stakes at play in a society riven by spatial and socioeconomic divides on larger scales over time. Planning in a postconflict environment is tightly bound up with materialist concerns of distribution and coexistence that attend spatial change. While my core focus here is on the possibilities of a material politics of repair, it is with awareness of forms of struggle surfaced through urban renewal that I proceed in considering the place of the city in Rwanda's conflict-affected trajectory.

Kigali's current expert-led spatial planning uses a vision for the form of a world-class city on sensitive postconflict terrain; this vision results in eviction and displacement as narrow forms of planning "in the public's interest" (Bhan 2016). I call attention to the tradeoffs and personal forms of conciliation required of a larger conception of the greater good in a postconflict context—for a vision of minor acts of conciliation in shared space—rather than the spatially enclaved master plans of order envisioned through spatial planning in the country today. What is at stake in a spatially just urban transformation is the right to shape inclusive national futures, to permit an open right to the city after conflict—as a key part of a durable and an inclusive peace.

From a space of refuge during overt conflict, the city can be seen as a normative space for resolution and incremental repair over time. In indexing the material politics of repair as focused on the tangible realm of acts of recuperation and restitution in the built and social environments, I point to the materiality of repair as a physical act of bridging space—whether between individuals and social groups or between worn wooden beams, riven asunder by rains and harsh weather, holding up the home. In a state grappling with a national project of transformation after mass violence, urban space has become a center for state projects of remaking. In this remaking, the old city of

Kigali is treated by state planners as a malleable space and a willing canvas. It is in this context that dispossession and repair become a tensely imbricated antinomy: one points to privation and exile, the other to organic attempts to hold together and continue with existing patterns of life.

I grapple with the different meanings of dispossession and repair as intertwined processes of life-making and unraveling amid urban transformation in Rwanda. The possibilities of repair amid large-scale dispossession in Kigali and on its peripheries at this moment of urban rupture are currently constrained. Yet various conceptions of dispossession—read doubly—might serve to unearth pathways toward repair in postconflict, post-genocide terrain, and might surface the limits of the project of repair in suturing the built and lived social environments. Rebuilding conciliation in an urbanizing Rwanda upon the idea of *irreparability* may also be a meaningful bridge between iteratively violent pasts and the ongoing disrepair of the traumatic present. The material here conditions both dispossession and repair, and colors attempts to reconcile, renew, and redeem the multiplicities of the nation. Through the material stakes of dispossession and repair, the potency of the politics of place are revealed to us in Kigali and on its peripheries.

Writing on an "ordinary ethics" in post-partition India, Veena Das elicits "the emergence of a moral life in the everyday" as a set of "threads woven into the weave of life rather than notions that stand out and call attention to themselves through dramatic enactments and heroic struggles of good versus evil" (Das 2012: 34). Das (2006) considers such "descent into the ordinary," rather than the flight therefrom, as a necessary ground for the interpersonal labor of connection and the hewing of moral subjectivities. In the fraught opposition of its subjective and temporal categories—victim and perpetrator, old Rwanda and the new "born again" nation—writing on Rwanda's genocide is often polarizing, struggling with moral categories in their absolute sense. Decoding the logics of atrocity leads to questions of *how to make sense*, and how to restore the ordinary in its barest forms. But what kind of an "ordinary" is this, and how is restoration possible, and for whom? Such questioning is particularly salient in a space where absolute categories of trauma and violence share space with quotidian landscapes. How then do we address issues of reestablishing a grounded sense of the everyday? Since Arendt's (1963) thesis on the "banality of evil," accounts of "the ordinary" have often been inflected by consideration of an underside to the everyday. In Rwanda, juxtaposition and paradox bring forth the presence of "ordinary" perpetrators, the routinization of violence, and the inversion of the quotidian. Das's (2006) conception of "ordinariness" instead shifts us toward *recuperating* this term, toward an understanding of the fragility of ongoing repair and the nuance required for such memory work.

In examining the material fabric of the built environment and everyday acts of sociality in this shared milieu, I draw on Das's pedagogy to show that built continuities in the city serve as a fabric through which a praxis of such "ordinary ethics" might be sustained. There is much in the process of Rwanda's urban transformation that can be generalized to other contexts where evictions, displacement, and demolition take place in favor of the smooth veneers of modernist master-planning. What distinguishes Rwanda's urban centers as specifically postconflict spaces saturated with communal trauma and social memory, however, lies *beneath* the surface in the lives and routines of long-term residents. Equally, the dispossession of informal settlements in areas of Kigali and on its peripheries engages with a form of repetitive rupture that takes on specific meanings in Rwanda's urban spaces. I suggest that while this morphology of urban displacement might seem akin to the harsh movements of urban change elsewhere—in other African cities—the *meanings* of dispossession here have particular resonance when one considers the built environment as a habitat and an anchor for an ethics of the ordinary. It is through such recuperative labor that an ethic of repair is enabled, and that multiple minor acts of sociality emerge through this fabric, however riven—operating beneath and beyond the directives of the state.

In moving from Kigali's old neighborhoods (figure 1.2), outward to its rural settlements and model villages, the arc of this book demonstrates that such a politics of place in urban Rwanda points to the specificity of sociohistorical depth that characterizes city making in this postconflict context. After genocide and protracted conflict, social trust and interpersonal bonds are reformulated on tangible material grounds, rather than singularly through the efforts of state-heralded justice and reconciliation efforts and schemes for enforced coexistence. I suggest that relations of gradual reciprocity tie together material environments and social relations after conflict, forming slow social bonds.[2] Recent work in political science also shows that frequent casual contact in shared urban environments can promote prosocial behavior and interethnic relations (Bollen 2022). In planning theory, shared space in the city further forms the foundation for the practice of communicative and collaborative planning (Healey 1997; Sandercock 2000). Furthermore, amid debates on liberal and postliberal paradigms of transitional justice, some scholarship has presented the need for socioeconomic justice as a lasting part of peacebuilding frameworks (Lai 2016).

At the core of material repair is the space of the home, which in its symbolic

FIGURE 1.2. Multistory construction work in an old part of Kigali

and social sense forms the hearth, the place of belonging and orientation, the root of stability, and the threshold of adulthood. The home exists both through and beyond theories of property, capitalization, and economic relations in urban and peri-urban space. As Hagar Kotef (2020) has suggested, the home is both a seat of self-composition and social ties, and a space of violence and exclusionary identities of possession and belonging. Such bivalent ties extend the home into the space of the nation-state as homeland. It is this juxtaposition between social recomposition and repair, and political exclusion and iterative violence that I engage through the study of material repair, national belonging, and spatial recomposition in Rwanda.

Building on the theme of the home, Marc Sommers (2012) considers the immobilized condition of incomplete adulthood faced by young men in Rwanda's rural areas. Here, an entire underclass of youth in the country faces a severe housing crisis as a result of post-genocide social policy and state control. Here too, the home stands in for social relations of possibility and their thwarted realization, as a generation of youth are stuck without the material possibilities to enable adulthood and personal progress. The sphere of the home and its dimensions of shelter, possession, and belonging thus hold out both privative and regenerative possibility for social repair in Rwanda's postconflict context.

For now, I consider one facet of this domestic materiality below: the incipient relations of social repair given form around the space of the home and relations of possession and recompense as bridge to tangible coexistence.

To engage with the material politics of such possibilities of repair, I turn first to Nyarubaba.[3]

Double Dispossession

Nyarubaba is a small rural sector outside a key secondary city in Rwanda. I first began research in Nyarubaba in 2002, observing the inception of the community justice courts around the country—called *inkiko-gacaca*. These courts pointed toward a form of community-based justice "in the grass," established to collect information on less onerous forms of violence that dated to the 1994 genocide, and to try cases involving them. With more than 100,000 prisoners awaiting hearings when the *gacaca* jurisdictions were formed in 2002, and with between 150,000 to 250,000 lay judges hearing lower-level cases in communities, the *gacaca* was seen as a bold and contentious experiment (Ingelaere 2016). At the time, the area of Nyarubaba was defined by a central local government office and a pole that flew the blue, green, and yellow flag of the "New Rwanda," a state "reborn" after the period of genocide. Small, immaculate houses with clay tile roofing dotted the steep and relatively dry terrain around the town.

As *gacaca* court sessions began in mid-2002, prisoners, local officials, residents of the area, and survivors of the genocide gave testimony on the events of 1994. During the genocide period in 1994, an estimated three to five thousand people were killed in genocidal massacres targeting ethnic minority Tutsis in Nyarubaba Sector. Collective testimony from area prisoners, survivors, and local leaders, collected by groups such as African Rights, provides evidence that mobilized youth militia (largely the *interahamwe*) using crude weapons targeted victims in the fields around Nyarubaba and in the Catholic parish and seminary nearby.

The testimony also shed light on processes of reconciliation—both state-sanctioned unity work and longer-term grassroots endeavors (for detailed critical analysis of this process, see Ingelaere 2016; Longman 2017; Pottier 2002;

and Purdeková 2015). Yet much of this engagement with the past aimed to follow state-sanctioned scripts, even as the *gacaca* sessions as living theater diverged from the state's controlled efforts. *Gacaca* proceedings were often unscripted and evolved spontaneously, including both official oversight and local rescripting. They involved "sensitization" and awareness by local officials of the importance of forgiveness and reconciliation; mass confessions by prisoners claiming to be "born again" in both religious and personal-juridical terms; and enforced reconciliation by community leaders, with disempowered survivors of the genocide often looking on. Tensions were palpable around the objectives of transitional justice; was its aim to serve the cause of gathering information, or to achieve reconciliation and social repair? These ostensibly oppositional aims of transitional justice at the local level have been discussed by scholars of Rwanda (Shaw et al. 2010; Straus and Waldorf 2011). However, little scholarship on postconflict aftermaths considers the effect on social repair of the built environment and projects of urban rebuilding that define space. As such, discussions of restorative justice need to consider more than the singular juridical event to think through repair as an ongoing spatial process.[4]

It became apparent from my research in Rwanda that as much as the criterion of "life"—meaning in this context the adjudication of responsibility over life lost—has been interpreted as a touchstone of reparative efforts and transitional justice, the built environment and its materiality, and questions of possession and dispossession related to the material politics of repair, are a more gradualist and tangible aspect of living together in shared yet contested space. Such a material politics might allow for more organic forms of community reintegration, broadening the purview of that which is *speakable* in a postconflict context, and allowing for the visibility of additional arenas of conciliation. Much testimony from *gacaca* courts focuses on lower-level crimes that these jurisdictional spaces were able to adjudicate. The loss of roofing materials and the destruction of buildings, including homes; the looting of domestic animals; the pillaging of firewood—these were some of the crimes that *gacaca* hearings confronted when they tried to make lists of loss, including lists of people who had died or had left the area and of those who had moved in. Addressing these incremental and material losses with a focus on the mundane—a roof tile, a pile of firewood—made it possible for neighbors and communities to envision sharing space once more, following norms for restitution and, often, physical repair. Consider this excerpt from a *gacaca* hearing in 2002:[5]

PRISONER: "I want you to forgive me (points toward local official, the sector head). I bought roof tiles for your house."

SECTOR HEAD: "Thank you. I can forgive you for that, but I want you to help me identify the person who gave orders to destroy down our house, and I want to tell you that I want to forgive you."

PRESIDENT OF THE LOCAL *GACACA* JURISDICTION: "I see you are all quiet, yet there are a lot of things to say. For example, some people collected firewood from houses destroyed by killers, and this firewood did not belong to you and others are people's animals, so please come forward and confess; otherwise this is also another crime which needs to be addressed. Some people collected tiles from roofs and have paid back (or not?), and they don't want to tell us. And we are asking for them to come forward."

WOMAN FROM THE ASSEMBLED GATHERING: "I remember two or three people have paid me back for the goats and my pig that they took from my home in '94, and these people are here in the meeting."

ANOTHER WOMAN IN THE GATHERING: "I lost my cows and goats and roofing tiles."

In urban areas, local tribunals, lower-level courts, and alternative dispute resolution mechanisms such as the *abunzi* adjudicated as core problems ongoing land and property claims after the genocide (Musahara and Huggins 2005; Payne 2011; Takeuchi and Marara 2014). Although these losses occurred in the context of larger acts of violence, including genocide, a focus on a material politics of repair makes it possible to envision the built environment and its connections to personal property, shared spaces, and cross-cutting paths as places of restitution and conciliation. Questions of material damage during *gacaca* also served at times as a proxy for more contentious disputes over larger forms of loss, including problems surrounding perpetration and guilt. Issues grounded in the tangible nonetheless formed a sphere of the everyday that was more readily accessible to contestation and discourse, and more amenable to repair and incremental rebuilding. The material created new dimensions of visibility and vocalization, going beyond what was unspeakable in the long aftermath of mass violence.

In the context of post-genocide Rwanda, these material conditions and politics of repair are essential to thinking through a tangible, reparative politics that holds out deeper and more radical possibilities for shared space after mass violence. The dislocation and "dispossession" that continues in the capital city of Kigali and on its peripheries has double meaning as something both privative and reconstructive (Butler and Athanasiou 2013).[6] A material politics of repair recognizes both the irretrievability of lost life and the possibility of reparation and restitution as alternative ways of thinking through restorative justice and sharing space across ethnic, communal, and interpersonal lines.

Drawing on Emmanuel Levinas (1979), Judith Butler and Athena Athanasiou theorize the interconnection between alterity and relationality, so that
"aporetic dispossession" is privative and forcible, as well as relational and ultimately liberating. There exists a "double valence" bound up with dispossession that threatens the sense of self and acts of possession, and also holds
grounds for profound human connection (2013: 4). Butler explains this double valence through a relational understanding of otherness:

> In the first sense, we are dispossessed of ourselves by virtue of some kind of
> contact with another, by virtue of being moved and even surprised or dis-
> concerted by that encounter with alterity. That experience itself is not simply
> episodic, but can and does reveal the basis of relationality—we do not simply
> move ourselves, but are ourselves moved by what is outside us, by others, but
> also by whatever "outside" resides in us (2013: 3).

This double meaning of dispossession carries with it salience for reconstruction and reconciliation in the contemporary urban moment in post-genocide
Rwanda. In a nation struggling with conciliation after genocide and civil
conflict, this double sense of "dispossession" hence offers pathways for living together once more: for reinterpreting mistrust, grievance, and loss over
lost life and destroyed property through a politics of unsettled inclusion over
space and place. Saliently, Levinas's (1979) theorization of the "face-to-face"
encounter does not account adequately for space. What engagement with
Rwanda's spatial transition offers is, therefore, a reworking of the terms of
such encounter, constrained by who is able to partake in humanizing recognition and exchange through the material strictures of urban renewal (for
example, those removed from informal settlements, as opposed to those included in the master-planned city). The politics of repair amid urban renewal
thus reveal post-genocide possibilities for seeing space as a core template of
the "dispossessive" encounter with the Other; but such reparative possibilities
also point to missed opportunity.

   Questions of possession and dispossession are hence embedded in the
moment of urban rebuilding as both threat and promise: the city can be the
grounds for connection and rights to space, but can also serve as an axis of exclusion. Butler points to the material foundation of social relations that sustain interconnection so that "the privative form of dispossession makes the
relational form of dispossession impossible" (2013: 9). Cohabitation is bound
up with a particular sufficiency of socioeconomic rights, material securities,
and political possibilities that serve to sustain social relationality. It is through
this double reading of the privation and possibility of dispossession that I
approach my interpretation of Rwanda's postconflict urban transformation.

Terrains of struggle in Rwanda lie between the spaces of home and homeland, and are intertwined with questions of hospitality and the ethics of hosting—sharing of space between host, guest, and Other (Derrida 2001). The home and homeland, writ large, demonstrate how Levinas's ethics of the "face-to-face" encounter extend to questions of spatial conciliation, and of citizenship in its most concrete and spatialized senses, localized materially and through social bonds around place.

If one traces the trajectory of Rwanda's national transition and urban transformation, then the materiality of the current reconstructive phase of city building and land reorganization stands forth as spatially salient. The current urban moment speaks to larger debates on redistribution and relationality, both within urban space and beyond it, in a society still healing from mass violence.

Postconflict Urbanism

In a 2014 piece for *the New Republic*, the photojournalist Tomaso Clavarino chronicles stories of amputees around Rwanda. Titled "Rwanda's Open Wounds," the piece brings together photographs and testimony of six Rwandans, survivors of the genocide, who suffered lasting trauma from the loss of limbs during the massacres from April to July 1994. Clavarino notes that despite the visibility of progress in Kigali, "Rwanda is still synonymous with the genocide—reminders of which are everywhere today, in the form of tens of thousands who survived the mass slaughter but were left permanently maimed. While few in Rwanda talk about its horrific past, amputees remain living records of it." One of Clavarino's photographic subjects, named Ngaboy, is an ex-soldier in the Rwandan Patriotic Army (RPA), the refugee movement that swept to power in July 1994 as a rebel army, ending the genocide of eight hundred thousand ethnic minority Tutsis and moderate Hutus (Prunier 1997). Formed in Ugandan towns and refugee camps during the 1970s, and instrumental in installing Yoweri Museveni's National Resistance Movement (NRM) in Kampala in the 1980s, the RPA had many members, including President Paul Kagame, who grew up in exile with little connection or attachment to Rwandan urban centers and the capital city in the pregenocide period. For his part, Ngaboy is circumspect about the prospects for reconciliation. He lost both arms during the RPA's "war of liberation," one chapter in a civil war that lasted from October 1990 to July 1994 and in which the Rwandan genocide was embedded. "The government is doing a lot to reconcile the country," he says, "but it'll be long, painful work, and it's by no means sure that it'll succeed. . . . They're forcing a process that has to be natural, spontaneous, with the risk of smothering latent tensions which, sooner or later, could flare up again. Rwanda is like a pressure cooker, just one spark too many can blow it up" (Clavarino 2014).[7]

This "pressure cooker," with its silent tensions in the entrenched space of the country's urban/rural divide—witnessed in segregated spaces such as the prison and at the genocide memorial, and etched into the body of the old *quartiers* of Kigali—has been simmering for thirty years. During this time, projects to reorder, reconcile, and recompose the narrative of post-genocide Rwandan national identity have preoccupied state elites eager to redefine Rwanda's image externally and to reshape society and space internally. Rwanda's post-genocide transition and its current state-led urban transformation can be seen as linked under large-scale processes of state building, through the reformation of population and the reorganization of space. There is continuity between large-scale projects of postconflict social engineering, chronicled extensively in scholarship on Rwanda since 1994, and the spatial re-engineering of cities, which this book excavates and extends.

Urbanization in Rwanda and urban planning in Kigali must be seen within a larger context of transitional post-genocide initiatives within the country, and they remain deeply informed by concerns about securitization and the preoccupation with symbolic and material order that emerged out of the transitional period. These programs and projects, spearheaded by state-party elites, have aimed to reorganize space and social organization among a population reeling from the aftermath of genocide, and still largely (albeit increasingly silently) socially and spatially divided. In a state with tenuous popular legitimacy, which has struggled to exert territorial control and popular domination in its early years through its military-party structure, developmentalism and modernization have become hegemonic national discourses and programs of state-led urban practice. Targeted urbanization thus constitutes the latest phase of this sociospatial reorganization, and the concretization of the transition from a nation characterized by a stark urban/rural divide and dependent on subsistence agriculture and cash crops, to one branded as a regional paragon of urban transformation. This dual logic of governmentality between an urban elite (propertied, with a speculative approach to land conversion) and a rural mass (governmentally ordered, with an emphasis on labor-based productivity), continues to define Rwanda's developmental trajectory as it aspires to large-scale urbanization; yet it remains one of its greatest challenges and apparent governmental contradictions.

The politics of spatial planning in the aftermath of genocide and civil conflict are contested and sensitive, particularly because the city in Rwanda has long indexed inequality and power-based cleavages in the country. Hence, planning must necessarily contend with the postconflict city as an axis of materialist struggle. Rwandan state elites have been planning for the modernization of the country through rapid urbanization, with the target of a 35-percent urbanized population by 2024, according to the National Strategy for Transformation policy blueprint. This is a rapid rate of urban growth in a country traditionally striated by a stark urban/rural divide. Rwanda was 5 to 8 percent urbanized when it gained independence from Belgium in 1962, and remained so until 1994.

The urban/rural divide in the country has featured prominently through various periods of rupture and unsettlement in the country. This spatial and social division was prominent during the "Genocide against the Tutsi," as it is officially named in Rwanda, or the "1994 Rwandan genocide," as it is interchangeably termed in this book—which was nested in the context of a protracted civil war that began in October 1990. The urban/rural division was central here, demarcating not just socioeconomic privilege but ethnic divides. In the postindependence period, Hutu elites governed from the core of the capital and from regional centers of power, first in the south-central point of Gitarama and later from the Gisenyi-Ruhengeri axis in the north, extracting productive gains from mostly Hutu peasant farmers across an urban/rural divide. As the order of the state imploded with the onset of the hundred days of genocide, it was again across this urban/rural divide that the organized violence of genocide took place. The genocide began in the capital, after the downing of former President Juvenal Habyarimana's plane, which led to the execution of prominent moderates and dissidents in Kigali. From this core space, a genocide that primarily targeted Tutsis engulfed various regions of the country in sequence, some with more virulence than others.

Survivors of the genocide swelled the capital's population during the postgenocide period, living alongside Tutsi returnees principally from Uganda but also from other parts of East Africa, and more affluent diasporic groups from Europe and North America. These groups formed the core of supporters and constituents of the RPA, which had emerged in previous decades principally from displaced Tutsis fleeing persecution in the aftermath of Rwanda's Hutu Social Revolution (1959–61) and its violent sequelae. Also in the city were suspected accomplices to genocide, and "ordinary" Hutus seeking anonymity in urban centers, as well as increasing numbers of foreign technocrats, aid workers, and young entrepreneurial investors. There were multiple fragments of the nation-state at this juncture: many versions of Rwanda interspersed between dusty, ochred fields and hills in rural areas, asphalted roads in Kigali, and secondary towns around the country.

When state elites turned their focus to planning in Kigali in the early

2000s, a considerable amount had already been accomplished in reordering society and space in the country. A conceptual master plan developed by the US firm Oz Architects in 2007–8 was later followed by a detailed master plan for the capital by the Singaporean firm Surbana. Whereas the Oz master plan had envisioned a more gradual change to the city and an entirely new central business district (CBD), the appeal of the branded promise of a Singaporean firm proved decisive in keeping the CBD in its original location in Nyarugenge District. The master plans were finalized, and they projected a green, futuristic "world-class" city (Roy and Ong 2011) based on a Singaporean township model. Published in 2013, the master plan initially did not adequately account for the granular demands of planning and building in the Rwandan context, so the plan was revised in 2019–20 by Surbana Jurong. The new master plan aims to harmonize district development plans, local building and planning regulations, and visions of a world-class city while allowing space for a variety of housing types. Despite these revisions, debates persist about how affordable these plans for affordable housing really are, and the widespread demolition of informal housing and vernacular dwelling continues apace. In 2015 the government of Rwanda published plans for six green-built, low-carbon cities at sites of existing secondary towns around the country (Huye, Nyagatare, Muhanga, Musanze, Rubavu, and Rusizi), advised by a South Korean multilateral, the Global Green Growth Institute (GGGI).

As the old capital of Kigali is reordered through spatial master planning and new cities are planned at sites of existing towns across the country, spatial palimpsests are cemented over. In effect, this constitutes a closure by brick and mortar. This is space in transition: new spatiality in the process of becoming, following massive rupture and orchestrated spatial reordering. The city is in various ways a seat of potential and rebirth, as well of one of rupture and undoing. Spatial planning by state elites and international experts acts to reinscribe a new spatial morality on traumatized and disordered landscapes. In so doing, it limits the potential of urban areas as spaces available for ongoing lived experiments in cohabitation and conciliation.

Crisis Capital

Urban reconstruction in Kigali involves a transregional and global network of capital and expertise that variously defines and delimits the city's future and who holds a right to the city. Kigali is targeted for master-planned rebuilding by 2050, and space is increasingly being divided into enclaves: unshared, regulated, and planned from above. Similar trajectories describe the planning of other postconflict capital cities. For example, the coterie of international financiers and experts that replans the capital in Rwanda also operates on conflicted Cambodian terrain, with old layers of urbanism being dismantled to accommodate the new. Surbana Jurong, GGGI, the World Bank, bilateral finance from the Middle East, loans and investment from China—these are the actors that purvey across postcrisis space, spurred as much by the logics of their own reinvention after the financial crisis of 2008 as by the national elites in Kigali and Phnom Penh who aspire for the teleology of modernization and national transformation through their cities. In these transnationally constituted spaces, the city remains central to restructuring a form of top-down order in the postconflict nation. A specific dynamic at play in Rwanda's urban transformation hence locates it in circuits of a type of postconflict accumulation by transformation.

Crisis capital, in this case, is that speculative capital that results from post-financial crisis capital mobility and seeks conflict-affected terrains to restructure, following the creation of new markets and state desires.[8] International markets for global master-planning and green urban design began to emerge soon after the 2008 crisis, this time from Singapore and South Korea. GGGI was formed in 2010 by South Korean President Lee Myung-bak, and later underwent changes in its governance structure as it was transformed into a treaty-based multilateral entity in 2012. Organizations such as GGGI promise stage-leaping green development, focusing on green cities, energy transitions, and ecologically sustainable fixes that align countries in the Global South with the green economy. Such solutions promise a so-called triple-bottom-line solution to the problem of linear brown development. Here, countries in the Global South such as Rwanda need not play catch-up to the stageist linear developmentalist trajectories of growth followed by the Global North. Instead, they might emulate some of the East Asian Tigers' own accelerated growth and speeded-up development trajectories. This type of neodevelopmentalist stage-leaping is appealing to a Rwandan state that seeks to reinvent and rebrand itself beyond the "post" of the post-genocide. In this way, Rwandan state institutions draw on the recent flood of green financing mechanisms to advance visions of spatial and social transformation with a green-branded signature. The designation "crisis capital" is here more than discursive: the climate crisis twins with the urban crisis to leverage funds for redevelopment on conflict-affected post-genocide terrain (Hudani 2020).

At the same time, design and planning solution providers such as Surbana Jurong (SJ for short) provide the urban architectural blueprints that work in tandem with the financing and designs for green economies. Founded in 2015 in Singapore, SJ works in more than 40 countries with more than 120 offices, and with its primary operations in Africa and Asia.[9] What must be kept in mind here is that while these solution providers harness neoliberal circuits of capital to transform spaces in cities in the Global South, many of them are state-founded organizations. SJ and GGGI were established by central states or in relation thereto, and only later became export-oriented and outward-facing solution industries, born from a web of national institutional politics. SJ openly describes itself as developing in tandem with Singapore's economic growth through the Singaporean state Housing and Development Board (HDB) in the 1960s. In this way it embodies and transports aspects of Singapore's national economic success to new geographies.[10] From 2001 onward, various Singaporean government organs began to form outward-facing exportable consultancy and investment vehicles with ties to China and its investments in Africa. In May 2003 the HDB's building and design division formed itself into a corporation "in a bid to export Singapore's decades of urbanization expertise and experience to other countries."[11] In 2005, part of the HDB was rebranded as the Surbana Corporation, and soon merged with Temasek Holdings, which serves as the Singaporean government's investment vehicle.

Particular tropes of state-capitalist developmentalism are hence at work setting up urban remaking as an industry that operates across contexts. Accumulation by transformation here references a specific dynamic of "accumulation by dispossession" (Harvey 2005), which targets postconflict contexts for capitalist fix through urban transformation. State ambitions accordingly seek to reinvent their brand and transform urban space. Seeing the postconflict environment as a constellation of terrains for urban accumulation by transformation provides a different mode of visioning urban change, and an alternative way of understanding cities in the Global South over long time periods.

The 2021 edition of *Surbana Jurong Sparklers*, a catalog of contributions made by the planning, engineering, and architectural firm, states that the firm "has developed master plans for more than 60 countries and over 100 industrial parks globally, including Lagos Free Zone in Nigeria. . . . The US$2.1 billion Lagos Free Zone is Nigeria's largest privately owned special economic zone, designed by Surbana Jurong in partnership with China Harbor Engineering Company."[12] The octopuslike firm also extends its reach to operating SJ Defence, "a homeland, civil and military defence infrastructure and training solutions provider [that] employs cutting-edge drone technologies to meet critical safety and security needs," and which operates drones in and beyond urban areas. SJ Defence has also actively trained military personnel, "has designed, built and managed facilities for the training of more than 800,000 soldiers, policemen and firemen over the last eight years in Singapore," and "manages a fully integrated live firing range," the first of its kind in the Southeast Asian region.[13]

That this multisectoral urban architectural and spatial planning firm has expanded to security and defense should come as little surprise. The regimes to which it caters often have questionable human rights records, operating off transnational forms of crisis capital. This focus on the architecture of defense also speaks to the genealogies of Singapore's heavily regulated green urban model, and to trajectories of covert securitization that mark the visible aesthetics of the world-class city in multiple landscapes, Kigali among them. Seen in this light, keenly designed and enforced urban regulation and the material effects of the aesthetic order of the city have tangible outcomes in the construction of a securitized city and, in many ways, the reconstruction of the security state.

Writing on Abu Dhabi's Masdar City as a demonstration project for eco-city development elsewhere, Federico Cugurullo comments, "Capital does not bother to fix crises, Harvey (2010) observes; it moves past them following new geographical trajectories in search for more profitable areas" (2013: 34).[14] Unlike the mobile trajectories of the residents of Masdar City, of whom Cugurullo surmises that "80 percent of the population is comprised of what we can define in essence as capitalists," questions of home, homeland, and stable imaginaries upon which to build a national future are central to Rwanda's conflict-affected urban problematic (2013: 34). Rwanda's more rooted dilemma is that most citizens are bound to the physical futures of their homeland, and are tied in some way to the stakes of material security and imagined solidarities there. Unlike Masdar's mobile residents, therefore, Rwandans have core emotional attachments to the futures of the postconflict polity; and for some, notions of perceived security are bound up with its reconstruction.

That urban solutions industries landed in postconflict terrain draws attention to the dynamics of capitalist transformation and local repair. It is clear in Rwanda's case that global master plans and transnational finance are repurposed in local ways to respond to the political intentionality of the state. As Kigali's politics of displacement and its configuration of accumulation by transformation exile marginalized residents from the city, sending them across the river and into rural settlements, one considers—given the genealogies of its expert planners and financiers—what crisis capital does in postconflict terrain, where questions of memory, reconciliation, and reckoning with the past are still living issues. Dispossession in this postconflict context has specific logics that build on the totality of genocide-period erasure and destruction. Urban space is fertile terrain for the implantation of crisis capital—flowing in from other ruptures, other forms of global-local restructuring and spatial fix.

Again, Levinas's (1979) conception of the "face-to-face" encounter is particularly salient in Rwanda's postconflict terrain, calling forth the uncomfortable nature of this encounter, which is at once unsettling, larger than life, and constitutive of mutuality—of what it means to repair and live side by side—hence *spatializing* the relationship to "the Other." In turn, we might use the conditions of this moment to think through both "dispossession" and "possession" as doubly valent: as both capitalist encounter and potential relational exchange, premised upon rethinking questions of distribution and their entanglement with spatial proximity in urban space.

Contextualizing Urbanization in Rwanda

An intertemporal genealogy of urban space is critical to contextualizing questions of the spatial nature of repair and the local meanings of the urban within Rwanda over time. I provide historical context and throw critical light onto how the urban question is constituted in the country today, at this moment of large-scale urban sociospatial restructuring. I also emphasize the intersectional nature of geography, ethnicity, and class over time in conditioning various dimensions of the urban question in Rwanda. Examining this Rwandan urban question connects the possibility of a material politics of repair to the materialist realities of spatial and social division over the course of the country's past. Targeted urbanization in contemporary Rwanda must be calibrated against these varied histories, which have selectively cast populations as reformable for and amenable to urban futures.

There is considerable literature in the corpus of Rwanda studies that emphasizes the rural as a heavily governed space, and urban/rural relations as central to calculi of power and logics of rule in the country.[15] The urban/rural divide has been a pivotal axis that has shaped political governance over time. I extend this focus to look at the urban intertemporally, in relation to the current period of urban renewal. Rather than providing an overview of the 1994 genocide as constitutive of Rwanda's history, I instead frame the politics of urbanization and the urban/rural divide over time as central to the way in which concerns over national reproduction and development form the backdrop to questions of violence, regional geography, population, and territory. These concerns also condition questions of repair and cohabitation in shared space, which are the core concerns of this book's intervention: to consider a politics of repair in relation to the space of the city.

Since the colonial period, the "urban question" in Rwanda has been one of managing a majoritarian rural population through urban power, where the country's capital has constituted a node of centralized control. Through its various periods of dominion—colonial, postindependence and post-genocide—Kigali's changing elite base has rendered it an urbanized node, separate from rural areas. Contextualizing the reemphasis on the urban in post-genocide Rwanda in the face of the rampant antiurbanism of earlier periods remains important. Refocusing on the urban helps us understand how urban/rural relations in Rwanda are material and are conditioned around a largely agrarian economy. In some ways, models of the global urban in Rwanda perform an inversion from earlier pre-genocide nationalism centered on the ethnic Hutu rural base. Instead, the country's urban-centered model of development emphasizes elite enclaves, transnational urban forms, and foreign investment, which are in favor with transnational experts and investors alike. Idioms of urbanization in contemporary Rwanda purposively serve to rescale the city as a driving force for a new type of urban nationalism. Such newer models of development move away from the focus on solidarity among the majoritarian Hutu rural base that has traditionally underpinned postindependence politics in the country.

Yet in other ways, governing the rural as a productive frontier and a space of controlled mobility remains as central to contemporary Rwanda as it has been in previous decades. The "urban question" in a post-genocide context like Rwanda's is thus a "biopolitical" one (Foucault 2008; Mbembe 2003). The contemporary urban question in Rwanda is biopolitical not simply because of its genocide-period embodiment, with the landscape as an extended necro-environment, but because the calculus of life and death and the calculus of population and development stayed central to postindependence modalities of politics and policy in the country. This biopolitical rationality *exploded* at the time of the 1994 genocide, driven by the onset of the civil war against the Rwandan Patriotic Army (RPA) from 1990 onward. In the next sections I move from the precolonial period to the post-genocide period to underscore key themes relevant to thinking about urbanization and urban transformation today. The repeated biopolitical management of the urban/rural divide is a central obstacle to the emergence of an ethic of sociomaterial repair in shared spaces.

PRECOLONIAL URBAN MOBILITIES

Rwandan precolonial rulership has traditionally been associated with a core peripatetic character. During a meeting to discuss urban change with an elderly cultural historian in Bugesera District, my interlocutor announced that he would not discuss urbanization with me, and thought it significant instead to recount the mobile nature of the precolonial *mwami,* or traditional Tutsi king: "While you today want to talk about one city, it is important to remember that this is a new concept in our country. The *mwami* used to go about the entire country with a mobile court, covering the entirety of his land."[16] Indeed, Jan Vansina's (2005) examination of the centralization of power around the Nyiginya state from the eighteenth century onward focuses a great deal on the "hub" of the mobile royal court and its elaboration over time. Vansina notes that "*ubuhake* contracts and armies were the tools used to accomplish the erection of this Nyiginya state, but the court was its hub, the workshop in which it was fashioned."[17] Thus Vansina analyzes the role of elites, chiefs, and ritualists who accompanied the mobile court and contributed to the role of the king "as a pole of attraction" (80) and "the only living and permanent receptacle" of *imaana* or fecund divine essence (83).

With the increased centralizing function of the mobile court, the mirroring of this court by the city stands in central significance during the Nyiginya period, and continues to remain resonant in contemporary times. Vansina elaborates on this pairing of the court and city and its symbolic valence, noting, "The king and the Karinga drum resided at the center of the capital. Together they were the concrete manifestation of the very existence of the kingdom and its unity. For the king was a person of a special kind" (82). Vansina's description of the court is important in the details of its structure and ambulant character:

> The court reminds one of a city: a large agglomeration with specialized functions, not just a political and spiritual center, but also a manufacturing hub where objects in metal, wood, bark, cloth and plaited stuffs were produced, where one found feathered arrows, game from hunts or from trappings, ceramics, tanned leather, blocks of vegetable salt and construction teams. It was also an economic center where wealth flowed in the form of cattle that collected and redistributed in the name of the king. But the court was not a city in that it was ambulant. During the eighteenth century it moved at least three times under Gisanura, nine times under Mazimpaka, seven under Rujigira, and five under Ndabarasa. By itself, a shifting court was an important means of centralization, since it exercised direct control of a radius of about a day's walk from around the palace where it was located and so a change in locality also led to a change in that direct control. Moreover, each locality where the court had resided became a sacred spot (2005: 81).

The significance of urban space as a historically courtly space of the minority king and his entourage is replicated in contemporary Kigali. The court ritualists and diviners who were present during precolonial times and were ordained by the king to enable "flow" and fertility through the region (Taylor

1999; Vansina 2005) can be positioned in relation to the mobile capital and transnational urban expertise now summoned to the country to remake its urban spaces and reconstructed cityscapes. Standing opposite the solid Parliament building, the colorful exterior of the Kigali Convention Center (built 2009–16) points to such a renewed register of state ambitions. Designed by German architect Roland Dieterle and constructed at a cost of $300 million,[18] the five-thousand-capacity green-built Convention Center has positioned Kigali as the second largest conference destination on the continent after Cape Town.[19] The building's rounded dome facade sits atop this redesigned enclave of the new Kigali, inviting interpretation as a monumental reminder of the King's Palace Museum in Nyanza, once home to the *mwami*, now symbolically relocated to the country's capital.[20]

Yet while the Convention Center revives the symbolism of the precolonial past, and relocates tradition and charismatic authority from the old center of the kingdom to the new center of the nation-state, it does so with repetition. The City of Dreams complex in Manila, the Philippines, subverts the iconography of the new Kigali with its architecturally similar structures and facades.[21] On the surface, such "world-class city" facades run the risk of dreaming through simulacra, seeming everywhere alike in their reconstruction, and questioning their ambitions of being both world-class and inimitable (Roy and Ong 2011).

ETHNICITY AND URBANISM IN COLONIAL RWANDA

Rwanda saw both German (1885–1916) and Belgian (1916–62) colonial rule of "Ruanda-Urundi" as a single territory. For part of this period, the colonial territory was unified under the administrative mandate of the Belgian Congo (1926–60) with a governor in Bujumbura and lead colonial "resident" administrators each in present-day Rwanda and Burundi. A complex system of "indirect rule" structured colonial administration: it set up local authorities to divide and rule over populations and to act as intermediaries for the colonial administration (Mamdani 2018). Mamdani demonstrates that this colonial system's administrative and legal dualism created enduring differences between colonial administrators and settlers as urban denizens and colonized rural subjects under local control, and paved the way for solidifying complex legacies of ethnic identity in the postcolonial state: "Just as civil society in the colonial context came to be racialized, so the Native authority came to be tribalized," Mamdani writes (2018: 110). Prior to the incursions of contemporary master planning and certainly in the colonial period, the geography of

Kigali played out on this spatial-juridical nexus of administrative segmenta-tion and spatial segregation, which limited access to the capital for all but a limited number of laborers and a few local administrators.

Although Kigali was established as a colonial outpost in 1907 by the Ger-man administrator Richard Kandt—to whom a museum is still dedicated in the city—its population growth was limited to colonial settlers, many of whom built in the area of Kiyovu, on Nyarugenge Hill. As the counterpoint to the "formal city," the *bidonville* or informal areas known as *Kiyovu cy'abakene* (poor people's Kiyovu), which housed laborers who worked in colonial house-holds and for the colonial state, emerged thereafter. When independence from Belgium was declared in 1962, Kigali's population of approximately six thousand was soon affected by urban migration and demographic growth (Manirakiza 2014, 2015; Sirven 1984). According the last pre-genocide census, the capital's population stood at just over two hundred thousand in 1991, hav-ing grown from sixty thousand during president Gregoire Kayibanda's First Rwandan Republic (1962–73) to more than one hundred thousand under the Second Republic of Juvenal Habyarimana (1973–94), who overthrew Kay-ibanda in a 1973 coup.

The Hutu majority in the country comprised about 85 percent of the pop-ulation in 1994, residing primarily in rural areas—with various geographic differences and class divisions compounding ethnic divides. During the pre-colonial and early colonial period, ethnic Hutus were subject to more flexible forms of labor and taxation under Tutsi chiefs and subchiefs (including *ubu-hake* patronage contracts and *ubureetwa* labor required of Hutu men; New-bury 1988). As the colonial period progressed, however, ethnicity became less fluidly structured and relational, and Hutus became the primary conscripts of the rigidified *corvée* labor demanded by the colonial administration (see chapter 6). The infamous ethnic identity card was established through Bel-gian colonial decree in 1933, and proved central to materially marking dif-ferences between Hutu, Tutsi, and Twa until its abolition in 1996. The ad-ministrative classification of ethnicity was salient to unfolding biopolitical violence, as well to limits placed on social and spatial mobility over time. This rationality of ethnic demarcation exploded at the time of the 1994 genocide, when identity cards were searched by *interahamwe* militia to target Tutsis for massacre, resulting in a decimated ethnic Tutsi populace within the country and social landscapes scarred by trauma and mistrust.

Fixed and hierarchized forms of ethnicity came to function as the primary categories around which ethnically demarcated rural collectivities were struc-tured, hence entrenching social divisions between groups in society. Griev-ances over the oppression of the Hutu population combined with increasing popular political consciousness to culminate in the Catholic Church–backed Hutu Social Revolution (1959–61), which abolished the Tutsi-led monarchy and propelled the state into the independence period under a majoritarian Hutu government: Rwanda's First Republic. The Rwandan nation-state's moment of independence in 1962 was thus one of liberation for ethnically inscribed Hutus, and one of dispossession and violence against the Tutsi minority, as waves of Tutsis were forced into exile.

Kigali had been central to the organization of violence during previous periods of rupture, and was the primary site of massacre during the first days of the 1994 genocide. On April 7, the murder of Prime Minister Agathe Uwilingiyimana by hardline Hutu factions signaled the death of moderates in government. The spark that ignited the hundred days of genocide was ostensibly the downing of the plane carrying Habyarimana and Burundian President Cyprien Ntaryamira the day before. This event now sits amid a cyclone of controversy as different accounts of the 1994 genocide's origins circulate (authoritative histories of the genocide include Prunier 1997; Des Forges 1999; and Lemarchand, 2009, 2021). It is not my aim to parse these accounts, focusing as I do on the city, the built environment, and conciliation within the post-genocide period. Such ongoing questions, however, mark perspectival divisions both within and outside Rwanda, and condition how the politics of repair in the post-genocide period are apprehended in public arenas and private life-worlds, informed by oppositional histories and personal experiences of grievance, exile, and loss.

What is clear is that from early April 1994 onward, the violence of genocide was often targeted against urban centers around the country, where large numbers of ethnic Tutsi lived or had sought refuge. Stadia, churches, and schools became sites of some of the worst massacres, as urban spaces were transformed from spaces of refuge into arenas of death. As the exiled Tutsi Rwandan Patriotic Army (RPA) moved into the capital in July 1994, these signs of disorder marked urban space as the army advanced. Sources recount that when the RPA succeeded in capturing Kigali on July 4 and thereafter established a new transitional government led by the Rwandan Patriotic Front (RPF) party, there were just fifty thousand people left in the city (Manirakiza 2014). The capital's demography was remade, as the return of Tutsi refugees from the diaspora ("old caseload" returnees) increased, along with the movement of displaced residents seeking refuge in the capital, and the eventual movement of "new caseload" Hutu returnees primarily from the eastern Congo. The city became a space where returning refugees lived in tents, with rudimentary equipment provided by the government's Tent-Temporary-Permanent (TTP) program to encourage incremental building (Michelon

2008, 2016), and where suspected genocide perpetrators later sought anonymity even as victims of the violence sought safety.

As I will present in later chapters, to secure the city and sanitize disordered space came to be an enduring governmental mission in urban areas. Through this period the city continued to be a locus symbolic of the state's control, and its reordering was a statement of enforcing authority.

POSTINDEPENDENCE ANTIURBANISM

The symbolism of the city and the management of the urban/rural divide are two concerns of enduring relevance in analyzing ruptures in postindependence Rwanda. From the early 1960s onward, sentiments of antiurbanism were rife. The capital city was seen as a space for the postindependence Hutu elite and well-off Tutsi groups. In contrast to this, the Rwandan peasant was characterized by Hutu state elites as the figure embodying postindependence values of productivity, loyalty and obedience to state authority. The significance of the urban/rural divide in shoring up this rural productivity and political support, and delimiting the capital as an elite space was hence reinforced.

The conjuncture of ethnicity, class, and geography at work in postindependence Rwanda drew certain parallels in countries across East and Central Africa. Antiurbanism was present across contexts during the period of postindependence nation building, which saw countries such as Tanzania, under *Mwalimu* Julius Nyerere, work toward compulsory villagization (*ujamaa*) by segmenting off urban space. The move to deemphasize the city as a popular base was further emphasized by scholars and policy elites in the 1970s and 1980s, many of whom propounded theories of "overurbanization" on the continent as responsible for the underdevelopment of the rural base (Bradshaw 1987). This was followed by interventionist programs of structural adjustment that sought to transform national economic crisis by defunding cities, scaling back social services, and enhancing rurally driven commodity economies (Mkandawire and Soludo 2003).

The Second Rwandan Republic of Juvenal Habyarimana and his National Revolutionary Movement for Development party (MRND, 1973–94) demonstrated the state's continued preoccupation with this division between urban and rural space and ongoing antiurbanism. This biopolitical spatial governance was manifest through its preoccupation with managing reproduction and development across the urban/rural divide. The governance of the "population question" in Rwanda as a concern and calculus of managing population, resources, and space has over time been one of controlling rural population and urban migrants, as well as of instigating individual behavior change aimed at reforming certain sections of the populace (see chapter 7). The triune of "population, environment, and development" was central to the publications and concerns of the postindependence National Office of Population (ONAPO). This vision remains important because it reveals concerns with population policy in the period before 1994, when urbanization and elite life in the capital city were seen as antithetical to the Habyarimana government's aspiration for a strong rural peasant base. The rural and the urban were thus clearly demarcated through the political geography of policies on population and development.

The Rwanda scholar Philip Verwimp (2000) analyzes the population policies of the Habyarimana government through political speeches from the period. Verwimp posits the former president as a pronatalist who galvanized his peasant support base to encourage an orientation of self-sufficiency and an antiurban bias. The traditional Rwandan was a peasant farmer who drew upon his cultural and material need for a large family to advance rural development in his region. ONAPO itself was preoccupied with questions of population control in relation to the developmental problems of the Rwandan state, as evinced in the multivolume policy monograph *Le problème démographique au Rwanda et le cadre de sa solution*, published in 1990, the year in which family planning and national population policies were introduced on a large scale. Questions of population control and of managing the urban/rural divide were intimately tied to those of urbanization and the city. The population question was thus a specific kind of urban question for the country: an enduring, convoluted problematic that projected questions of the governance of the urban/rural divide into the future.

Rwanda's capital hosts more than one million people today, in relation to a national population of more than 13 million (WDI 2022). Given its central role in visioning for the rebuilding and modernization of the Rwandan nation-state, I suggest that master planning for urban space renders the city a *pharmakon*—a substance that offers both "remedy and poison"—(Bauman 1990: 55) and therefore remains ambiguous and "undecidable" (Derrida 1982: 79). The city here is in its various ways a seat of potential and rebirth as well as a locus of rupture and undoing. Planning acts to reinscribe a new spatial morality on space deemed traumatized and disordered. The meanings and modes of intervention and spatial planning in postconflict space are hence multivalent and complex. It is this dualism between master planning for an aesthetic of order and the slow repair necessary for continuous sociospatial reproduction at the local level that I ask the reader to keep in mind as both a material politics of postconflict rebuilding and a metaphor for an ethics of cohabitation.

"The Greater Good"

In February 2020, the popular Rwandan gospel singer Kizito Mihigo was found dead in a police cell in Kigali. His death was characterized as a suicide by local police, but questions over the nature of his demise continued to proliferate at home and online among Rwanda's diasporic population—many of whom changed their social media profile photographs to Mihigo's in the aftermath of the event. Mihigo's image was thus regenerated in death as an icon of personal reconciliation and popular peacebuilding on Rwanda's contentious terrain, where formal reconciliation is spoken of according to state-defined lines. A survivor of the 1994 genocide himself, Mihigo overcame personal trauma to sing for the nation, performing his signature gospel songs at state commemoration events and speaking across the country's divides (Grant 2021; Mwambari 2020). From being looked upon as a beloved performer by the regime, he fell out of favor in Kigali by March 2014 when he released his controversial song "Igisobanuro Cy'urupfu" (The meaning of death), which spoke of the gravity of Rwanda's struggles and the need for reconciliation between the country's main ethnic groups, which were affected by the genocide-era violence in different ways. Soon afterward, Mihigo was imprisoned and sentenced to ten years for conspiracy against the state, and was pardoned and released only in 2018. Just before his death he was accused of attempting an escape to Burundi, which landed him in a police cell in Kigali.[22]

In his now famous song, Mihigo calls for attention to "the greater good" as essential to the meaning and purpose of a just transition and a lasting peace. In the music video, dressed in a suit, he sings in front of churches in Rwanda and then is seen playing an organ in a church, while surrounded by empty pews. The lyrics of the first stanza of his song read:

> *Urupfu nicyo cyibi kiruta ibindi,*
> *ariko rutubera inzira,*
> *inzira igana icyiza cyiruta ibindi*

> There is no worse thing than death
> But there is a way forward,
> A path to good
> A virtuous path to the greater good.[23]

Rather than an urban fabric built upon state directives for the narrowly defined "public's interest," Mihigo's articulation of the idea of "the greater good" (or the "best of all") as the foundation of a reconciled social order speaks aptly to the questions of material repair and spatially just urban transformation in the aftermath of mass violence, which are examined in this book.

The Vietnamese-American author Viet Thanh Nguyen (2016) similarly writes on the urgent need to recognize all forms of grievance that war generates as it fractures societal bonds.[24] From a philosophical and an ethical standpoint, Nguyen points to the need to think through the "inhumanities" as a form of repair bound up with an "ethics of recognition" (2016: 97). He asserts that it is by thinking through violence and agency on both sides of conflict that we might better comprehend Levinas's (1979) concepts. Like the "greater good," it is this sum of all grievance, the multiplicity of different forms of agency, and the impossibility of knowing what one would have done *as* the "Other," in their temporal and spatial positioning—in their shoes—that renders the question of an ethics of recognition complex and potentially redemptive. Rather than resorting to humanistic fantasies of a benign "otherness," it is this larger concept of a disquieting "Otherness" that takes into account the collective grievances, grief, and forms of agency that prevents an escape to utopian formulations of closure. The encounter Levinas prefigures is hence larger than life; it is unsettling and incomplete, and is also a form of unknowing. Yet, precisely because of this unknowing, such an encounter also gives way to the potential regrounding of relationality, and of the ethical itself.

I read idioms of repair, continuity, and a praxis of slow rebuilding in relation to "the greater good" as such a larger form of recognition—recognizing that spatial rights are embedded in social and communal ties, in histories of continuity and connection, and in more complex stories and multiplex narratives. Such multiple narratives of Rwanda's urban transition belie binaries between modernity and backwardness, order and disorder; and they recognize that the personal rights to shape space and dwelling are reflective of larger potentials.

PART 1

Master Plans

2

Repair in Old Kigali

Jeanne is fixing parts of her house.[1] It is the second time in two weeks that the joint between the metal sheet that covers her ceiling and the corner of two walls has gotten dislodged, exposing gaps. She tells me that the crack between the roof and the walls lets in cold air that keeps her up at night. Her neighbor's son is assisting her with the repair work. Both Jeanne, who lives alone, and her neighbor, a widow who lives with a son and nephew, are survivors of the 1994 genocide. They live in Rwezamenyo Sector, close to the Nyamirambo area of old Kigali. Typical of Kigali's topography, Rwezamenyo is hilly, and its sector and cell office (a "cell" is the lowest administrative division in Rwanda) overlook the valley below. To get to Jeanne's house, I walk behind the sector office through a few side lanes, which are wet and muddy from recent rains. Near Jeanne's area is the sector of Gitega, which has recently been declared a high-risk zone (HRZ) due to the gradient of the land. Regulation forbids residents of HRZs like those in Gitega from upgrading or rehabilitating their houses while they wait for their notices to evacuate the area. Unlike those residents, Jeanne lives on less steeply graded terrain.

Long-term residents of the area and survivors like Jeanne, seeking to remain in their homes in the center of the city, labor over the built environment, and the politics of intervening in this built milieu are fraught with ambivalences of meaning and intention. A different form of intervention—incursion into the built city—is being exercised by various appendages of the state through expropriations, demolitions, and dispossession.

Urban Trauma and the "Embodied Home"

During several of our visits Jeanne walked me around the corners of her home, describing the changes she has gradually and painstakingly managed

to make, each repair wrought with difficulty, as she has overseen the rehabilitation herself: "I have changed mostly the walls of my house. If you understand well, before, houses were built in a hurry from simple little pieces
of wood. I gradually replaced that with dried mud bricks, and in other places
with terracotta bricks. In short, it is a mixture of terracotta bricks, mud bricks,
and even pieces of wood."

The story of Jeanne's house is also the story of her life before, during, and
after the genocide. "I have reached this place in 1986," she recounted one early
evening in old Kigali. "I was coming to my own home, married to a man. We
lived together until 1994, that it is when he was killed during the genocide."
Her voice conveyed both pride and sadness as she told of complex relations
with neighbors before the civil war and genocide began:

> Before the Nineties, it was easy to say that this wasn't a problem, knowing that
> you are Tutsi and the other Hutu but each one living their life. We seem to
> have been better financially, and we had to give something if we wanted peace.
> But we lived together, despite this situation. . . . If there was a wedding, you
> might well join them, and even during hard times, comfort them. . . .
>
> You could work well and business was good, taxes weren't exaggerated and
> that made good profits for any business. Another thing was, when you started
> any selling, no one would come out and compete against you, to sell identical
> items. We had a potato and bean warehouse, and there was no one else who
> had the same warehouse there.

Jeanne turned again to the walls and roof of her house, taking a pause. The act
of remembering, for a moment, became tangible and solid. "Before, we used
to build by means of wood. Fixed wood today, and added some tomorrow,
and on the third day . . . you put a ceiling and you settled in and could sleep
in it. Because you build without an authorization document. At that time, if
it happened that they checked [the house] and found you inside, they would
not destroy it!"

During another visit, Jeanne continued to recount her life after the genocide: the solitary struggle to rebuild her home economy with the help of
neighbors, friends, and groups of fellow survivors.

> Before the genocide, my husband and I helped each other. But after the geno-
> cide, I no longer had him by my side. I had to be strong, in order to find what
> to support my children. I started by opening a small shop here. I was selling
> alcoholic drinks; this is thanks to the money that was given to me by a person
> so that I could buy something for the children. Then I bought a crate of beers
> to start.

She spoke of the growing burden of operating her business alone:

> I sold that way, but when it happened that someone spoke about a subject that
> I didn't want to hear, I chased him away. It was because we were still under the
> weight of trauma and injuries. It caused my customers to no more frequent
> my shop, and that upset me! There were other women in my neighborhood;
> they seemed much stronger. One of them had been lucky to not have had her
> relatives killed, another also had her husband killed but she was strong, she
> always had her children with her.

After the genocide, Jeanne navigated survival and the city alone; and as she
detailed the trauma of post-genocide life, her voice and facial expressions
became muted, as if she was looking for something more solid, a semblance
of stability and permanence:

> Losing your loved ones is a difficult thing, but losing your children is much
> worse. My eldest child was killed, I couldn't admit it to myself at that moment.
> But these women supported me by their presence near me. They were doing
> selling in *agakinjiro* [the furniture market]. Every time when they returned
> from their shops, they used to come to see how I had spent the day, looked to
> the little I had in my shop, and then went to their homes. We lived like this.
> One morning I told them I couldn't take it anymore, that I was going to close
> my sales. I didn't want to see my customers anymore because they used to
> bring back my memories of the past.

Before I departed on that visit, Jeanne commented on the urban changes in
Kigali. She had not seen the city's master plan, but she hoped that she would
be able to stay in her house and that roads would be built so that sick people
could be transported to the hospital. Interpolating between past and present,
Jeanne draws out trauma, memory, and survival once again, and they are
rendered tangible and solid in the very walls of her house and in the labor of
rebuilding—a home, a personal economy, and a mode of navigating the old
city, even if she now does so alone.

Stories of continuity, such as that of Jeanne's house, and long-term residents' struggles to endure trauma give texture to questions of displacement
and the personal and social disorientation that it produces. Labor to maintain
residence in the old city through keeping up a home economy and repairing
the walls of the house, gradually and with incremental improvement, is an
ethical praxis of care and continuity that contrasts with the ordered aesthetic
of the master plan, an ideology of erasure that has besieged the capital. In
this context of continuity, repair, and belonging, I conceptualize the home
in old Kigali as an "embodied home," coexisting with the bodies of survivors and their practices of care. The traumas and social memories etched

into survivors' very homes and the *quartiers* marked by years of repetitive quotidian routines and ordinary acts of rebuilding resist the encroachment of the aesthetic order of the master plan and urban spatial reconstruction. Wars of attrition of memory against forgetting unfold piece by piece in the material rehabilitation and repair of homes in the old city. Struggles to remain in informal settlements such as Bannyahe (chapter 5) may clamor loudly in the political discourse of place-based resistance to displacement. Meanwhile, in older parts of the city, attachment to *quartiers*, homes, and routines in Nyamirambo and Muhima is deeply etched over time. Here, long-term residents are metonymic keepers of the place-based social memory that is now under duress.

As the central state attempts to reconstruct legitimacy through official memory and national narrative, urban space and the built environment become a terrain of confrontation between the old and the new: between continuous social memories and ways of life and the rupture of rebirth, erasure, and reinvention. The politics of survivorship are key in the reconfiguration of the city: for one thing, the old city of Kigali is home to large numbers of genocide survivors, many of whom are women. The 2007 census of genocide survivors, the last on record, counts a total of 58,416 survivors of the 1994 genocide in Kigali out of a total of 309,368 in Rwanda as a whole.[2] The old city also remains at the core of the struggle to spatially maintain social memory in the capital. The fantasy embodied in the new city master plan is disconnected from the embedded social memory in old Kigali's quartiers and buildings, and thus the city is a body in crisis. State projects of erasure through spatial master planning operate as master narratives that state appendages seek to inscribe on post-genocide terrain. The "big planning" of the city master plan—its synoptic view and projects of erasure and remaking—reveals transformation as a project of state-making through the city in fragile postconflict space. It replans the city from above, from a God's-eye view, and occludes histories of quotidian life in the city's older neighborhoods. State-sponsored spatial planning remakes postconflict social worlds by remaking the very texture of the built environment.

In contrast, survivorship as a praxis of care manifests in old routines and built environments, operating on the scales of the home, the building, or the neighborhood, as opposed to the city scale of the master plan. Scale is itself reconfigured here, as the city becomes a ground for coproduction and contestation between that which is familiar and represents continuity (the environments of the home or the neighborhood), and the overarching incursions of globalist spatial master planning that rupture that continuity and seek to defamiliarize the city and render it anew. The genocide survivor similarly gestures at continuities of memory that subsist in and beyond the public sphere; the body of the survivor points to an embodied politics of remembrance, to the continuities between trauma and memory. In other words, the survivor is a bridge between the legitimizing trauma of the genocide and the post-genocide rebirth of the New Rwanda.

In the first part of this chapter I analyze the politics of urban reconstruction and the loss of social memory as they implicate the survivor and the body of the nation. In the new capital, set with comprehensive master planning to be remade into a world city by 2050, the ambivalent figure of the genocide survivor and the space of the old city itself are both used in the service of state narratives of national trauma and regeneration. In the built environment, anachronous old quarters and neighborhoods are construed in the Kigali city master plan as elements of heritage and tradition that add authenticity to the new city being built. By the same token, the participation of genocide survivors in authenticating rituals of state commemoration and the construction of national memory renders particular kinds of trauma narratives useful in the public sphere. The survivor's participation is required for the state to legitimize its agenda of development, and therefore must be involved in the aesthetics of commemoration—but then will be erased and hidden from view behind the veneer of progress and development.

The master plan's aesthetic of order envisions a future that materializes the act of forgetting, as recollections are lost through destroyed houses and attrition to the built environment. But social memories persist. The second half of this chapter describes an ordinary temporality of rebuilding: the repair of homes and lives, and struggle to preserve memories of neighborhoods in older parts of Kigali. The grand designs of state-led planning and the large-scale reconstruction of the built environment are disjointed from the politics of preserving lived memory in the capital. The embodied politics of memory here are kept alive in and through the body of the built environment of the old city. While the master plan is a built narrative of progress, central to the construction of post-genocide truth, I draw attention instead to the politics of *surviving urban renewal* in the capital's old neighborhoods. I focus on the stories of two sets of "survivors": the old city of Kigali, itself an organic memorial milieu, and the memories of long-term residents who live in this old city. These "survivors"—both human and built—persist as increasingly ambivalent figures and anachronous spaces as the city changes through urban master planning and the national master narrative of "speeded up" progress. They stand as heterogeneous infrastructures of social memory—as "counterpublic" spheres (Warner 2002) to the future posited by the state, and as reminders of painful temporal and spatial continuities between the periods of pre-genocide, genocide, and the present.

Through a mode of inquiry that interpolates state narratives with personal memories of individuals, I suggest that quotidian life in the post-genocide city is a form of knowledge production metaphorically born from wounds. Rather than being interested in a form of official knowledge production by the state, where commemoration and memorialization prevail as state-sanctioned discourse, I pay attention to the private sphere of memory and its social routines. This quotidian sphere of remembrance is a form of vernacular and embodied knowledge within the realm of personal memory and the private ways in which survivors inhabit the city.

I demonstrate that through "minor acts" of repair and maintenance, residents of older neighborhoods in Kigali are able to enact continuity in their modes of engaging with the city. These acts between neighbors living near one another over the *durée* of time after mass violence are also the basis for different relationships that individuals form with one another—in the milieu of their proximate built environment (their home, the neighbor's home, the streets in their quartier)—and with the city more generally. These are gritty relationships marked by personal memory and histories of repetitive interaction between individuals, and between individuals and the markings of what constitute place. Rather than the homogenizing reconstruction underway in the city master plan, these acts of repair give residents temporally differentiated senses of place and belonging. It is this localized, repetitive constitution of place that resists the future of Kigali as one of forgetting. I suggest that it is the deep memory and spatialized social recollection, lodged in personal routines in old Kigali, that renders the older quartiers of the city polysemous. These old urban sites are multivalent and impenetrable spaces that the city master plan targets for remaking (figure 2.1).

Survivors and the Politics of Memory

The annual anniversary of the 1994 genocide is commemorated during two periods of the year in Rwanda. The first period, commemorating the hundred days of the genocide itself, begins on April 7. The second is the period of liberation, when the capital fell to the incoming Rwandan Patriotic Army in July 1994. During the week of commemoration of the "Genocide against the Tutsi," as it is officially named,[3] a collective silence overtakes many people in Kigali. Offices and shops close early or remain shut, official commemoration events take place in the national stadiums in Kigali and outside the capital, and expats living in the city often temporarily leave. For many survivors of the

FIGURE 2.1. Motorbikes speed past pedestrians in an old *quartier* of Kigali.

genocide, a large number of whom are afflicted by posttraumatic symptoms because they witnessed or experienced extreme violence, the commemoration week is an ambivalent time space of remembrance. A survivor recounted to me that many people she knows wish to go to sleep at the beginning of the week and not wake up until it is over.[4]

The first day of the genocide commemoration week runs close to Easter, a remembrance of suffering and crucifixion in the life of Jesus, and his resurrection as the Christ. Since the period's mythological structure in many ways parallels the narrative of the Rwandan state, I expected Easter to be commemorated widely in Rwanda as it had been before 1994, when the Catholic church drew in multitudes of faithful. Yet as early April arrived, many churches in the capital lay silent, their pews deserted. Easter is no longer marked with symbolic fervor in Rwanda's capital today,[5] and several survivors I spoke to commented wistfully on lost faith and feelings of abandonment. "I can't believe in God since it all happened," genocide survivor Evelyn, told me one weekend as we met in old Kigali.[6] "I don't even think he cares. There's no going back to faith for me." Her older brother survived, but she had lost her parents and younger siblings in the genocide, and had been forced to take up work and consider marriage early, to achieve some level of financial stability. Other female survivors with whom I spoke in older parts of Kigali echoed Evelyn's story. As revivalist, Protestant, and Pentecostalist churches proliferated after the end of the genocide, drawing followers away from the traditional strictures of the troubled Catholic church, survivors' faith has been often tortured, ambivalent, and without fixed venue.

State-led commemoration ceremonies marking the anniversary of the genocide against the Tutsi in early April each year are new rites of faith for a state that has built its governing power on a particular public version of legitimate ways to narrate and commemorate trauma. Although many may prefer to experience this time as a quiet period of remembrance, through its ceremonies and official narrative on the genocide the RPF-led state deploys specific discourses of trauma in the public realm. In particular, it operationalizes a version of state memory that uses the trauma of survivorhood in public arenas: ceremonies that take place in venues such as stadiums, and at official genocide memorials. The figure of the genocide survivor is thus central to the construction of the RPF-led state as heir to the trauma of genocide, and it is from this figure that the developmental state fashions its own legitimacy.

And yet, while the state instrumentalizes public trauma narratives on a national level to generate legitimacy, official narrative operates on two registers. As a state seeking middle-income status by 2030, ideas of development as progress and developmental state ideology permeate numerous facets of Rwandan government policy, coalescing in particular on urbanization as modernization. The urban transformation of the capital by 2050 and the development of six secondary cities at the sites of smaller towns around the country are designed to be centerpieces of this developmental state strategy, performing modernization and a clean break from violent and cataclysmic pasts. Accelerated development is thus a state ideology that on one register stands on the back of legitimating national trauma narratives, yet on the other register seeks distance from a traumatic past in order to leap into a vastly different, modernized yet orderly future.

The relationship between national trauma narratives and developmental ideology is thus uneasy and complex. And in this relationship the figure of the genocide survivor is fraught: she is at once necessary for state legitimation and hidden from view in terms of development and veneers of modern urbanism. Scholars of the post-genocide period have claimed that survivors are neglected by a Rwandan state apparatus that still holds them at the center of state commemoration and legitimation ritual. Many continue to languish in poverty, their lives and livelihoods disordered and their memories ruptured and contested (Burnet 2012). Prunier (2009) observes that survivors were termed the "walking dead" (*bapfuye bahagaze*) by diasporic Tutsi returnees who came back to Rwanda after the genocide (3). Dauge-Roth (2010) insists that survivors unsettle the fiction of the nation's progressive improvement, and draws attention to the "excess of memory" (3) that underlies daily life in Rwanda. Literature by survivors in recent years has shed further light on this ambivalent relationship with contemporary state-led efforts at national rebuilding. For instance, the survivor Yolande Mukagasana terms official efforts at peacebuilding through unity "amnesiac reconciliation," as opposed to the more open "truth telling" that survivors need in order to heal (Mukagasana 2001: 9–10). The testimony of sixteen-year-old Fabien H, an orphan and genocide survivor, speaks candidly of survivors' invisible wounds as Rwandan society moves rapidly toward development: *"Personne ne nous aime. Nous sommes devenus un probleme de la societe rwandaise"* ("Nobody likes us. We have become a problem for Rwandan society") (2001: 110).

As progress is implemented from the top down, with great speed and with intentions to expedite the road to national modernization, the lived trauma of survivors is sidelined. For instance, *"Kwihutisha amajyambere"* (Speed up progress) and *"Birashoboka"* (It is possible) are two phrases heard frequently regarding to state developmental visions such as the "Vision 2020" national policy blueprint.[7] Williamson Sinalo writes, "There is pressure for survivors to hide their challenges and sing to the government's song of 'progress'" (2018: 41). It is not unusual for supporters of the current regime to describe Rwanda's strides under the current government by noting that social and economic rights have been promoted through development programs, and arguing that a particular version of "freedom of speech" is a modest price to pay for such progress. A 2017 *Financial Times* article demonstrates this protective nationalist vision as expressed in an interview with a key governmental strategist and academic:

> A central part of the strategy to eradicate ethnic divisions is nation building. . . .
> A presidential adviser . . . says the idea is underpinned by a strong sense of
> Rwandan nationalism. That explains, he says, the pull felt by exiles in refugee
> camps to return home and the willingness to make personal sacrifices in the in-
> terests of national progress. 'If you don't understand that, you can't understand
> Rwanda, why people are giving up some freedoms for a greater goal.'[8]

Progress is thus seen as the distance traveled from the cataclysm of the 1994 genocide. It is defined as a forgetting and erasure, and the reconstituted national community is expected to make personal and collective sacrifices toward that goal.

Narratives of progress are interleaved with practices of commemoration and memorialization of the 1994 genocide, having evolved over time as the RPF-led government has further entrenched its centralized state control. Burnet (2012) and Vidal (2001) note that in the early years of the post-genocide period, commemoration events drew on more inclusive discourses. Burnet describes how the first commemoration ceremony, in April 1995 under the Government of National Unity (1994–2003), recognized that both Tutsi and Hutu were profoundly affected by the genocide. The politics of victimhood had not yet solidified around the body of the Tutsi victim and a singular "Genocide against the Tutsi," which elides the numerous Hutu directly and indirectly affected by the massacres.

After 1995, discourses and practices around the Tutsi as the sole legitimate victims of the genocide began to coalesce. The massacres of Hutus at internally displaced persons camps—such as the one in Kibeho in southwest Rwanda on April 22, 1995, where RPF-led government forces killed several hundred to several thousand—led to mass resignations of moderate dissenters in government.[9] Although a few key power brokers were Hutu, there was a decisive move toward homogenization within the government. This concentration of power created an environment for the consolidation of the official narrative on the genocide, and for its promulgation through commemoration ceremonies, national memorials, and the dissemination of an official version of Rwandan history.

As the priorities of national unity and lasting peacebuilding in official messages were superseded by a discourse that demarcated victims and perpetrators, these ceremonies became vehicles to inculcate acceptable narratives and discourse on the genocide. In effect, the body of the genocide victim, the fragility of the genocide survivor, and curated display of genocide remains in official memorials around the country were placed at the center of state commemoration. Particularly in the post-transitional period after 2003, when a new constitution was created and the first post-genocide elections held, a new consolidated power base began to solidify under the RPF government. The central state began to strengthen its internal control and external moral legitimacy through these commemorations, and the power to reconstruct the state out of the chaos of genocide became its legitimating discourse. Burnet writes of the symbolic power of dead bodies in these state rituals thus: "The ceremonies mobilized the dead as powerful, polyvalent symbols that divided those in attendance into two categories: victim and perpetrator" (96).

Master Narratives

During my first visit to Rwanda, in 2002 near the end of the transitional period, the government was promoting a new official history, following the
formation of the National Unity and Reconciliation Commission (NURC).
Titled "The Unity of Rwandans" (Republic of Rwanda 1999), the document
proclaimed that "all Rwandans" were born of the same ancestors. Pointing to
the colonial period as the major source of popular division, leading to the formation of the ethnic narrative of Rwandan identity that formalized divisions
between majority Hutu, minority Tutsi, and tributary Twa, the new official
history alluded to the birth of a "new Rwanda," where ethnicity was now itself
a fraud. "We are all Rwandans," it proclaimed. The post-transitional governmental narrative pointed to a uniform precolonial Rwanda that the new post-
genocide government would resurrect.

Since the end of the post-genocide transitional period in 2003, the master
narrative for the nation-state has been premised on this de-ethnicized unity.
The official narrative casts the colonial period as a rupturing event that produced division and misinformation and led directly to genocide. In recent
years, however, a significant new change in the direction of national narrative
for the country has emerged. It tells Rwanda's story as one of progress—a
move forward linearly and, more recently, a leaping ahead over developmental stages. As regards the nation-state and its infrastructures, the progress is
characterized as technological. The developmental narrative is also evident
discursively in the abandonment of the "divisive" rhetoric of identity politics.
"Progress" is further conceived of as spatial, with regard to informal settlements that are seen as physical antitheses of spatial order—at once impenetrable, disorderly, and unmodern. Finally, this progress and forward movement
is personal and subjective: it includes a "mindset change" and an attitude of
progress at the level of the community and the individual.

Within this state narrative of technological progress and forward momentum arguably lies a deeper orientation and monopoly on the way trauma is
identified, legitimated, and defined in relation to the nation's future. On collective and individual levels, and in opposition to the techno-optimism of
national progress, trauma is a binding despair. In contrast to the speed of national progress, this trauma persists as endured survival. As the nation surges
forward on its course of punctuated equilibrium, evolving overnight into an
urbanized global portal and green hub, a model for other regional nations
and a paragon of postconflict recovery, an authoritarian techno-politics of
national trauma is manifested in the master planning of urban space. For the
Rwandan government, trauma as state narrative is curated and made useful,

and through its increased legibility it is made the subject not only of personal anguish but of a national rationality of progress. A particular state-sanctioned display of "trauma" thus becomes a yardstick by which to measure the technological and developmental visions and progress of the nation. In this context, the city master plan is a national developmental master narrative. State-led national reconstruction after genocide implicates the built environment. And the old city is a space where routines of quotidian life struggle to survive against the erasure of the global urban aesthetic that threatens established modes of circulation and social memory.

Older facets of genocide-era memory nonetheless endure in bodily forms, from the physical body to the built environment, from the necropolitics of death and the preservation of dead bodies to the living memory of survivors repairing lives and homes in older quarters of Kigali like Nyamirambo and Muhima. In her essay "Illness as Metaphor" (1978), Susan Sontag writes: "Illness as a metaphor for political disorder is one of the oldest notions of political philosophy. If it is plausible to compare the polis to an organism, then it is plausible to compare civil disorder to an illness. . . . Illness comes from imbalance. Treatment is aimed at restoring the right balance—in political terms, the right hierarchy." Sontag further writes about the evolving modern sense of disease as a "master illness" in the body politic; as opposed to its earlier positioning as a discrete point of infection that could be amputated and removed, modern illness points toward "a total contagion of society." I analogize these bodily politics to the Rwandan state's evolving approach to addressing urban change in the contemporary post-genocide period. The "master illness" of the post-genocide polity, an embodied existential crisis that endures in sociospatial memory, is metaphorically seen by state elites to be treated through uprooting the built environment—through the comprehensive "master plan" and its erasure and reinscription of built space, social memory, and ways of life.

Applying Sontag's sociopolitical metaphor of illness, this phenomenology of trauma can be extended to the body politic of the city, suffering from a crisis of social memory. As planning attacks continuities expressed through the built environment, constituting another point of rupture—a rapid discontinuity of time and space, following upon the first rupture of the genocide—the polity of the old city is similarly an extension of the body in crisis. Reconfigurations of national memory, and ruptures in the built environment and in individual lives, can be conceptualized as being layered and interconnected. Trauma in the context of the reconstruction of this post-genocide society is both a conceptual and a material space. This space is represented at one pole by the politics of national memory and the use of trauma for state legitimation; at the other, by the figure of the survivor and the complex embodied performances that survivor makes in and beyond state commemoration ritual. Finally, the space of trauma as defined here is anchored by the transformation of the body of the urban built environment and the practices of changing urban social memory.[10]

The City as a Memorial Milieu

The remainder of this chapter draws on interviews with long-term residents of old quartiers of the city to describe how the affective geography of master planning in Kigali is traumatic. The renovation of the built environment in Kigali is replacing the city as a living milieu of memory (Nora 1989). It is socially and spatially remapping the city, its legibility and navigability, and the encoding of its memories, and this remapping especially affects many long-term urban residents. Writing on Rwanda's post-genocide transition has examined the texture of official memorials as staged and selective, and as its main markers in the built environment (e.g., Meierhenrich and Lagace 2013). Here, I extend that writing by exploring the changing spatial and social configuration of the capital city as a contested memorial milieu through narratives of its quartiers, which serve as residents' living maps of memory. Trauma, memory, and the urban renewal of Kigali are thus revealed to be interwoven. It is precisely because trauma—an inherently ambivalent discursive field—persists into the present that renewal is deemed necessary as a state project of disambiguation and erasure. Urban renewal, as a symbolic restructuring of the built body politic of the city, seeks to close materially the circle of genocide-era trauma and post-genocide remembering.

NYAMIRAMBO

John's mother, Florence, lives in Rwezamenyo Sector, near the sector administrative office and the cell headquarters in the Nyarugenge District of Kigali.[11] As a survivor of the genocide, she reveals that she is keen to live near these administrative centers as they give her a sense of safety. Soon after the genocide ended, people of all kinds lived around her in her neighborhood. "We were living near people who could have killed us!" she warily exclaims. "Many perpetrators moved to our neighborhood in the city to gain anonymity and avoid returning to their home villages."[12] For weeks during the hundred days of genocide from April to July 1994, Florence and her family hid in the attic of a nearby school. They would come down only at night, and then go back to hiding in the attic.

Located in Nyamirambo not far from the new Rwezamenyo Sector head-quarters, the Chez Gisimba school (formerly Centre Memorial de Gisimba) and orphanage stands as built testimony to these ordeals. The late Damas Gisimba is well known in Kigali for having saved just over four hundred Tutsis, many of them young children, during the worst of the genocide.[13] Having moved to the Nyamirambo area in the 1980s, he lost his parents a few years before the onset of the war between the Uganda-based RPA and the Rwandan government's Rwandan Armed Forces (FAR). "After seeing the increase of tension and hostilities between different groups in Kigali," he says, "I began my personal fight against the militia *interahamwe* and the extremist militaries that took part in the genocide."[14] Ultimately, with the help of an American aid worker who refused to leave the country during the genocide, Gisimba managed to evacuate the survivors just as the Kacyiru area of Kigali began to fall to RPA troops, bringing the genocide to a close in July 1994. In a newspaper report, he recounts the horror of those days and his meeting with the aid worker:

> When he got here, he found us in serious and immediate danger. He saw it with his own eyes. I also explained to him the whole dire situation. There was no electricity, no water, no hygiene, no nothing! I took him to where the babies were. They were our biggest cause for worry. I told him they were about to die in my hands. I had little milk, that wouldn't last a week. No water. Nothing! He told me he was going to do his best to supply me with water. If he was lucky to find milk too, he would bring. So, he left and after about two days he returned with a truck full of water. Our numbers had grown over-night and water was the main problem then. I had a container of food but how can you cook without water? And people were thirsty and congested in a small house.[15]

It is well reported that Nyamirambo was one of the safer areas in the city. The Biryogo quartier's Muslims were mainly not of Rwandan extraction, and their area—the heart and soul of the old Islamic neighborhood in Nyamirambo—came to be a relatively safe space amid the horror of other areas in Kigali. "I wouldn't say Nyamirambo was necessarily any safer than other parts of Kigali," Gisimba interjects during our interview, before reflecting:

> On the other hand, it was an area where everybody came to take refuge. Kicukiro and Gikondo were both attacked, people kept on fleeing from there to here. In such worst moments, people simply run without knowing where they are running to, and people thought that Nyamirambo was calmer than elsewhere. Beyond all that, there are some people who hid Tutsi. Many of

FIGURE 2.2. Restaurant in Biryogo, Kigali

them were Muslims because in their beliefs, charity is their priority. Let's also remind that there were many people who were not originally Rwandans, but they had married Tutsi women, so they were not involved in killings as such. That's why we say Nyamirambo saved many people.

Today, the Biryogo quartier of the Nyamirambo area—home to 24/7 food shops, mosques, smaller houses, and narrow streets, as well as an old and now relocated market —is set for rebuilding as a touristic and cultural hub as part of the master planning of Kigali (figure 2.2). Yet if, as I claim, trauma and renewal are not separate but deeply enmeshed affective processes of claiming continuity and enacting rupture, the effective "museumization" of areas of Biryogo amounts to an erasure of continuities—a replacement of the ethics of care with the aesthetics of order. A living milieu of memory (Nora 1989) is hence replaced not just building by building, but in one sweep. The master-planned edifices of preservation and cultural showcase have been designed far away from those who actually lived through the genocide and survived within the enduring contours of Nyamirambo's areas: Biryogo, Mumena, Cyivugiza, and Gitega.

The zoning reports for the earlier Surbana–City of Kigali master plan show areas in and around Nyamirambo vastly redrawn and conceptualized anew. Thus, Kimisagara, a vibrant area termed "high risk" (HRZ) by local authorities, housing a large youth center heavily used by the area's young people, has been rezoned as a "prime residential area along the slopes of mount Kigali." Gitega, also designated as an HRZ, is conjured in a proposed vision as an area for "compact urban living at the CBD [central business district] fringe." Nyamirambo Sector is envisioned for touristic development, and is seen to "offer new attractive lifestyle choices" with a "vibrant regional center and new growth areas." Rwezamenyo Sector, where I conducted a considerable amount of my fieldwork, has a "proposed vision" as "quality housing at the urban fringe." "Rwezamenyo is envisioned to become an important urban node in Nyarugenge District offering a range of commercial and civic facilities as well as quality housing options for the locals and the expats," reads the text of the detailed master plan report for Nyarugenge District (2010: section 7-5).[16]

Locals from this area are keen to see its contours preserved, rather than being incorporated into fringe development for the CBD, or zoned for partial preservation as part of a touristic "heritage village." For Salim, a local shopkeeper, Biryogo's local places of circulation need to be preserved for traditional life to continue:

> Apart from the mosque, for me the important places in Nyamirambo are from Biryogo when you go up from Majengu to [an area called] Mirongine (40), and all along the Majengu road that used to be called Dialogue. It is the place where you find people sitting down and talking, drinking green tea, coffee . . . in the evening.[17]

Claudette, another long-term resident of the changing quartier, reminisces:

> Nyamirambo is an area with plenty of life where you can walk till night; where you can find people mingling without any conflict; where you can find something to eat for five hundred Rwandan francs, five thousand Rwandan francs, even for fifty Rwandan francs. It an area which progressively changed. You can see where the hospital of Kigali is located. On another side you get to Gitega; you reach the Muslim area not far from the first mosque of Kigali, and then you go up to Rafiki club, TRAFIPRO [Cooperative], Seventh-Day Adventists' church, then Mumena, Cyivugiza. And when going up on right side, this is the Nyamirambo, which was built later, where there were houses for officials and some nice houses, as they used to say, for rich people. Slowly as we approached

the nineties, the highest building was Baobab restaurant, and some house on
the same line only . . .

Claudette continues, reflecting on the genocide and the damage done to
Nyamirambo: "The areas that grew from nowhere, like Mumena and Cyivugiza, are areas which were first destroyed by the genocide. Later on, life came
back with great difficulty."[18]

MUHIMA

During a series of interviews in late 2018, Marianne, an elderly Rwandan who
lives near Kigali, comments on the effective destruction of the older ways of
life in the city, and how the master plan has changed quartier life in Muhima,
a textured neighborhood of migrants to the capital, with bustling business
areas on sloping terrain, cozy restaurants for gathering, winding streets, and
small houses nestled in the shadow of the old Kigali central prison.

> This master plan has been made as if they had to build in a new country where
> there is almost nothing. People who saw Kigali in 1994 here in the center of
> the town—those people today don't recognize the districts anymore. It may
> seem good to hide the old memories, maybe . . . but I'm not so sure Kigali
> has all changed for the better. There are new areas that raised up very quickly,
> and there are others which are going to suffer and are already suffering from
> changes that had not been given time to apprehend and integrate. I'm not say-
> ing that changes are bad, but every change destabilizes, every change which
> comes after the heavy collapse of '94 requires support, requires pedagogy, to
> integrate it and live it.

The idea of repetitive rupture, as Marianne terms it, is central to understanding Kigali's predicament in the space between genocide and urban renewal.
Layered on top of the rupture of colonialism is the rupture of the postindependence period, the Hutu Revolution of 1959, the 1973 coup by General
Habyarimana, and the anti-Tutsi sentiments of populist nationalism—all of
which deepens rifts that are etched as much into the built environment as
into memory. We must see the 1994 genocide, then, as having been built upon
these successive ruptures: a genocide against the body of the Tutsi, against the
body politic of the city where many Tutsi lived, and against what Christopher
Taylor (1999) might describe as the continuity of flow, sanctity, and purity in
the body politic of the Rwandan nation itself.

   During our interviews, Marianne continues to speak of successive rupture
and the loss of social memory in specific areas of Kigali, which she terms
"disappeared life":

There are repetitive breaks in Rwandan history, and the master plan comes as if to fix it. We cannot ask amid these breaks and we cannot go back saying, "How did we get here?" . . . I remember the former Kiyovu area. It has been destroyed less than ten years ago right now. It was destroyed, and finally there is nothing at all today. The buildings that have been built there, nobody considers them as a sort of life, and we no longer talk about the disappeared life, not during the genocide period but during that period of deconstruction of the city.

In the early 2000s, in its pre–master planning period, Kigali still had ochre dirt roads and layered informal settlements on large tracts of land located centrally in the city. The old colonial part of the city, upper Kiyovu, settled by colonial administrators, was shadowed by its foil: lower Kiyovu, known as "Kiyovu cy'abakene" or "Poor People's Kiyovu," where the labor force for the colonial capital lived. When this area was expropriated in 2007 and 2008 to make way for the "higher and better uses" of a planned capital city, the area next in line for planned renovation became Muhima.

Muhima is a difficult quartier to generalize because it is so engrained in popular memory, into the rhythms of daily life for ordinary Rwandans—from migrants moving to the city for the first time to those working in the city and settling into its distinctive regional subareas, looking for work. Muhima makes its appearances in Rwandan literature as well: it is home to Jean Mahoro, the office clerk protagonist of Aimable Twagilimana's (1996) *Manifold Annihilation*, a prophetic novel set in the early 1990s that eerily foreshadows the impending tension of the genocidal period itself. Located just beneath the old Kigali central prison built in the 1930s (the prison is now vacant and slated to become a museum or a church), the area runs downward into the city's valleys, near the bustling Nyabugogo bus terminus.

Continuing her depiction of the changing city, Marianne vividly describes Muhima:

> The quartier of Muhima nearby is a popular area for people coming from the outskirts of the city. For people who come from the north, those who come from the south, and also the southwest, it is the gate of entry to the city of Kigali and it is located between two high mountains: Mount Kigali here and Mount Shyrongi, and Mount Jali. The road is like a river which snakes through these mountains. In general, people who come to the city used to stay around this area.

From the late 2000s, when city-scale planning began in earnest, the expropriation and demolition of settlements began apace. Kimicanga and Ubumwe (Kiyovu cy'abakene) were among the first to go, but Muhima was also affected. Jean, a male interlocutor who lives in Nyamirambo, describes the city authorities' changing demands on dwelling in Muhima and other areas set for expropriation and demolition:

> Fifteen years ago, in several parts of Muhima, the city of Kigali announced that it had to change, that people were no longer allowed to renovate their houses. They were not very strong, durable houses as such; they were small houses, but with extraordinary lives inside.

Jean pauses to consider the many lives and the layered built environment that supported them, however fragilely:

> I know many people who stayed there. They [city authorities] told them: As your houses are going to be destroyed . . . we will give you compensation, but you no longer have any right to make changes or renovate your houses. Some people, having learnt that their parcels were going to be rebought in expropriation, began to cheat, trying to renovate in order to further gain more money as they will be leaving. The rule forbids any kind of renovation. It's now several years ago. The houses which were already of bad quality got time to collapse and to decay. Either you live in that situation of disrepair or you leave hoping the expropriation will take effect. But till now, nothing has been paid.
>
> I know many people who were in Muhima, who were genocide survivors, others who had survived time in prison, who had to leave because the place had become unlivable—whereas before, it was a poor zone but with a minimum amount to make life decent.

For Jean, building and dwelling are incremental ways of life, such that life operates through "day-by-day" improvement:

> We improve gradually; it is also constructing. Building is not only raising new buildings. It's a kind of trying to improve day by day the space where we live. A Rwandan doesn't have a huge house, but the sort of care he manages to give to his house regardless of its size, that's important; sweeping, filling small holes. . . .

"Repair" as a praxis of building and dwelling illuminates the connections between the built environment and the ethics of city dwelling, as well as questions of homemaking and placemaking. Bhan (2019) has recently articulated "repair" as an idiom of a "Southern urban practice," in contradistinction to more formal building practices and, in turn, intentionally distinct from the "modern infrastructural ideal" (Graham and Marvin 2002), with its bundling of services, a homogenous singular edifice, and a network of connections. Bhan writes of this "Southern urban practice," invoking "*squat* as a practice not just of subaltern urbanization but of the state; *repair* in contradistinction to construct, build and even upgrade; and *consolidate* rather than focus on the building of a singular, universal network within services and infrastructure" (Bhan 2019: 639).

In the context of a post-genocide society where rifts and cracks from trauma of different kinds requiring "repair" are both materially etched into the buildings of the old city and socially inscribed on the bodies of survivors and the body politic of the nation, idioms of rebuilding have dual meanings. Vernacular dwelling in quartiers of old Kigali is here analogized as treated wisely through slower forms of repair, rather than through enforced reconstruction or through interventions about rapid schemes for national progress.

An Ethic of Repair

State reconstruction is a material act that implicates the built environment. Like the evolving politics of memorialization from 1995 onward, where raw post-genocide space was covered over by curated memorial space and a totalizing narrative history, homologous politics of reconstruction can be seen in the current renovation of the built environment in Kigali. After the genocide was over, ruins, ruination, and disorder characterized the built environment. During research in 2002 I saw partially destroyed houses, and shells of abandoned cars on the sides of arterial rural roads. These visible markers are now all but covered and erased. I elicit space in transition as a heuristic for paying attention to the way in which built fabrics lie open, being simultaneously made and unmade. Rather than maintaining the old city—houses of multiple scales and sizes, mostly older and in need of repair—city and central state officials have found new ways of erasing spatial ambivalence: the apartment building, the high-rise office tower, the green park, the tourist hub, the space of cultural excellence, the special economic zone, and the multilane highway.

"To stay in an old house is to know all its old corners," jokes Emil, a long-term resident of Nyamirambo, when I meet him near his home to discuss the changes he sees in his area. Emil is worried most of all about practical issues: with the new building regulations, people will find ways to move into his neighborhood, building multistory edifices (*étages*) and driving up prices. "Then we will have to renovate our house and apply to the sector for permission," he admits. "Maybe the price will be too high and we will have to leave the city." Drawing from Emil's comments, to build anew rather than repair is not only to erase the past but to avoid familiarity with it. Emil's practical concerns about the state of his house in relation to the building regulations mandated by the attempt to modernize Kigali's built landscape can be read in the larger context of reconstruction, of which it is a part. Emil's concern speaks to a "politics of disrepair"—one that entails greater governmental intrusion into private space and memorial landscapes of old Kigali through inspections, renewed building permits, forced sales, and urban relocation.

At his office in Rwezamenyo Sector, overseeing parts of Nyamirambo, Mr. Eric, who is in charge of planning and building, reports that 150 applications for repair and rehabilitation of old buildings were recorded in his area in 2018. Whereas permits for new construction are handled at the district level in Kigali's municipal offices, repair and rehabilitation are the responsibility of the sector administration. Many of these old buildings and aging structures are made of timber, in contrast to new structures composed largely of glass and concrete. For residents applying for rehabilitation permits at the sector office, the extent of areas for repair must not exceed 50 percent of the entire building. Residents are often referred to the district rather than the sector, as new construction becomes prioritized, in part to accord with the stipulations of the stringent building code.

As Mr. Eric notes, many newcomers to the area are buying up old buildings and applying to the district for permits. Rents have increased as Nyamirambo's central location and twenty-four-hour economy make it attractive to upwardly mobile officials and members of the urban middle class. Mr. Eric states that older residents resist moving out due to increased costs of rent, rehabilitation, and new construction: "Not many people want to move from this area; they instead subdivide their houses and their existing land. Individuals then sell the subdivision and live in or improve the other parts of the building." Still, many residents who fall into lower income brackets and *ubudehe* categories are unable to afford to repair and rehabilitate, let alone subdivide or construct anew.[19] For them, the disrepair of buildings that do not conform to the new building code (2015) and the master plan's designs for the area as a cultural and touristic preserve translates into dislocation and the search for new dwellings.

The politics of disrepair on the scale of the neighborhood and the repair of buildings that do not conform to the city's new aesthetic and material requirements for construction also point to a larger politics of repair at the national level. Rather than dwelling within its complex national trauma as if it were a well-worn house, with multiple narratives of memory as its various inhabitants, master planning is a metaphorical, materializing project of defamiliarization set in concrete, built into the project of creating an urban landscape with a certain aesthetics of legibility and foreignness. It is a spatial and narrative project that refuses to engage with the complexity of geographies of trauma. As an older single-storied adobe-concrete home sits near an apartment building under construction, the palimpsests of space in transition remain apparent. Traumatic memory and multiple narratives are inherently ambivalent, and in space in transition the reconstruction of the built environment speaks to the desire to forcefully enact definite spatial and narrative closure. If trauma is a metric to measure national progress, then rather than dwelling within the complexity of trauma and its fissures, the Rwandan state apparatus is leaping over it. Through official commemoration, a certain narrative of trauma is held up as a starting point from which progress and technological development ensue. The city and its built environment hold a central place in this national narrative.

The politics of memorialization around bodies in the aftermath of genocide and the body of the old city as it is experienced and remembered by long-term residents constitute the two poles of post-genocide reconstruction. State-led national reconstruction after genocide is a material act that implicates the built environment. In contrast to this official version of master-planned space, old Kigali city is a milieu replete with memories of its own, forged by the memory maps and routines of those who traverse its spaces and serve as witnesses to the changes wrought by master-planned reconstruction.

THINKING THROUGH MINOR ACTS

In contrast to large-scale spatial erasure and reconstruction, "repair" emerges as an alternative praxis of rebuilding. Repair here is a politics of minor acts: it speaks to the connection between the ethical and the political that seeks to repossess the ordinary. As an ethic, repair is a *temporality* of gradualism, connecting past, present, and future. Repair stands in opposition to the rapidity of erasure from wholesale master-planning. It is a "situated knowledge" (Haraway 1988) of placemaking and endurance. Repair is also a spatial practice of care, of tinkering with and regularly maintaining (Corwin and Gidwani 2022; Mattern 2018; Millington 2019); it asserts continuities, and an inevitable heterogeneity and ambivalence that defies the master plan's erasure of social memory. In theorizing life made peripheral to the city, AbdouMaliq Simone (2022) calls for an ethic that infuses value into the temporality of the present. Rather than waiting for many deferred futures elsewhere, this is a call for engaging with the present as a portal for theorizing and repairing from within the existing peripheralized parts of the city, however derelict. This temporal engagement with the present also recognizes that which is beyond repair: it is "an approach to urban life that concedes its brokenness," one which focuses on "the infrastructural and social endurance of specific neighborhoods" as reconnection and relationality emerge as reparative practices, and as a "quilting of the fragments" in what remains of locality in the city (Simone 2022: 31).

The city is hence a material, affective, and experiential site of knowledge production about postconflict aftermaths. The afterlives of conflict are traces that linger and can never said to be fully expired or expunged. They reside in personal memory, in social routines, and in the built environment. I point here to "minor acts" as a form of localized repair, and also as a heuristic that demonstrates the heterogeneity of conciliation and cohabitation to highlight the very real claims, desires, and longings that Rwandans of all walks of life have in relation to the city. Many Rwandans enact quotidian repair in relation to and beyond the meta-narratives of reconciliation and enforced closure of the state. Amid inflows of capital and expertise that bring together state projects of profit and transformation through "global cities" capitalism, daily life unfolds in relation to built space and local projects of maintenance and making do. This then is the paradox of repair in Rwanda's new global age: the elite state-capitalist project inhabits space with contiguous realities of daily coping and the aftereffects of ruptures in local terrain.

Here, where the intimate and the scale of the state are not necessarily opposed but *intertwined* in daily life after mass violence, I use the term "minor acts" also to refer to the practice of enduring and living *with* traumas and memories of the past while motivating for local change. By theorizing forms of knowledge production through this landscape of trauma, I bring into view alternative narratives of social inhabitation and ways of engaging the state through the tangible: by way of a material politics of repair. Through encountering the state's spatial practice of master planning in ways that recapitulate Asef Bayat's (2013) "quiet encroachment of the ordinary" (as we will see in chapter 5, on contestation in Bannyahe), it is possible to think of conciliation and cohabitation as necessarily incomplete and ongoing. Material repair also points cumulatively toward larger debates on reconciliation and the redistribution of power and resources, in the process of reimagining more inclusive futures.

Amid layered master plans of various orders that dictate master narratives of memory and trajectories for action in physical space, repair is an antistructural form of agency. By forging pathways through the built environment through personal routines and everyday forms of exchange, relationships are rebuilt. Just as master plans as forms of social engineering and spatial transformation are "durable" (see chapter 3), minor acts of repair as counterhegemonic incursions of their own leave imprints through social memory and the co-constitution of place. "Minor acts" are hence small but potent declarations on the necessary durability of place, and on alternative meanings and enactments of "transformation" amid state reordering.

An alternative form of healing is a spatiality of the continuous: the body of the old city, left legible to the lives of its inhabitants and visible to the gaze of onlookers—a tangible, public "pedagogy" of successive ruptures, with all their historicizing wounds.

3

The Project of Reformation

If one image could capture the spatiality of urban Rwanda in the 2020s, it would be the green, terraced streets and orderly spaces in the central thoroughfares of Kigali and other major urban areas that have come to define the iconography of the modernized Rwandan city. In 2008 Rwanda's capital was named the cleanest city in Sub-Saharan Africa by UN-Habitat, and it is not unusual for visitors from other parts of the continent to admire Kigali's rapid developmental transformation from the disorder of the post-genocide period. From the old urban facades and dirt roads covering large swathes of the city, the Kigali of the early 2000s has quickly metamorphosed into a futuristic green urban terrain. Spaces of order have become more visible through these green urban facades, which serve to signal and securitize. I ask what this ordered aesthetic reveals about the disciplinary ethos centered on hygiene and environmental labor, and what it obscures. In appealing to images and ideals of the world-class green city (Roy and Ong 2011), much of the labor-based infrastructure of local compliance that operates in the country remains hidden behind a green veneer. On a more symbolic level, I ask what Kigali's green streets disclose about the genealogies of ordering urban space through hygiene and environmental labor in the capital as a specific post-genocide project of ordering and securitization.

How is the project of hygiene—in this case, spatially cleaning and reordering urban areas—linked to the experience of injured memory in the city, to the ruptures of a complex and painful history? This is the deeper inquiry that guides this chapter; I tie together worlds of municipal cleaning, regulation of public and private space, and transformations of various sizes that have guided the project to reorder the city and reform urban Rwandan residents in the post-genocide period. As an aesthetic of order unites the reconstruction

of Kigali and secondary urban areas, the idea of cleaning out and covering up
a traumatized national memory is everywhere present beneath the surface.
As I will recount later, my interlocutor, Michel, reflected upon my urban research on the meanings of cleaning and reformation thus:

> The questions you ask when we talk about change, how a city evolves—through
> them we also talk about life, and in life there is everything. . . . In my opinion,
> the work that you do, the questioning that you pose, is not a questioning that
> can leave aside the question of memory, and unfortunately the memory here is
> *an injured memory—I would even say memories*. . . . So it's a central question,
> and not a question one can push to the side [emphasis added].

Looking first at the surface as Kigali engages in greening and urban cleaning, and moving beyond this to the larger project of national transformation
through the aesthetic, I probe how this injured memory is visible and is also
relocated in the city over time. In this way, the aesthetic serves as an index of
the larger normative project of material repair.

Isuku as Sociopolitical Metaphor

The word "*isuku*," which literally means "cleanliness," has come to denote
"hygiene" in state practice in the contemporary period, particularly in local
government. "Isuku" expresses a state of cleanliness, an absence of contami-
nation. Emmanuelle, an interlocutor in Rwanda, described the term this way
after I asked about the conceptual dimensions of the term: "It is a cultural
value that does not stop at the material sense alone; it also has meaning in
a moral dimension." The verb from which "isuku" derives is "*gusukura*," defined as "to clean," but also, relative to isuku, a desired material and cultural
state—one of "putting isuku back, removing what was preventing isuku," as
Emmanuelle explained. In the Rwandan household, concepts of cleaning and
removing dirt have specific contextual meanings: for instance, "taking away
the dirt in the household after sweeping, which is done every day very early
in the morning."[1] The clearing of wild grass around the home also draws on
gusukura as an action of cleaning social space: "Rwandans don't accept the
idea of having wilderness or uncleared, nonsocial space [*igihuru*] around
him, such as a field with wild grass," says Emanuelle. The action of clearing
wild brush and bush around the home compound in the community took on
particular import after the genocide, when individuals called on one another
for help to be together (*dufatanye*) in clearing social space such as paths and
spaces of erstwhile sociality. "Help each other, '*Dusukure bugufi bw'aho dutu-
nye duteme ibihuru n'ibindi*,' we called. This means, let's clean up near where

we live, let's stay and live and cut wild bushes in our areas,'" Emmanuelle recounted. In the cultural religious sense of gusukura as purification, churches often use the phrase "*gusukura imitima yacu*" (to clean our hearts), calling on the faithful to purify themselves and be healed through Christ.

"People don't ask these days, what does *isuku* mean, how is it being used, why has it become a concept of government in the city?" Emmanuelle surmised. "But we have to be alert and pay attention. What you are asking about is raw data." In the post-genocide period, isuku represents a complex sociolinguistic reality and sedimented data, revealing much about state practice and social life. The fact that various agents and interests use the term and its linguistic variants in different ways to various ends, with degrees of self-consciousness about its itineraries, arguably attests to the depth of this metaphor and its meanings in post-genocide society, where national renewal after the pollution and stain of genocide is both a material and a symbolic task.

Hygiene as an ethos of transformation through work, symbolized by the conversion of unruly nature and disorderly pollution into spaces of order and regularity, is central to this project of national conversion after the disorder and pollution of genocide. This conversion from raw to cooked, from tradition to modernity, and from rural to urban has been examined in scholarship on the nature/culture relationship (Williams 1975; also Watts 2005, and in the context of Senegal, Fredericks 2018). In the specific context of a postcolonial state, where the colonial administration of violence segmented existing divisions between ethnic groups and left enduring wounds, hygiene has represented varying logics of differentiation, discipline, and distance. The post-genocide project of spatial planning is also one of ordering the disorderly and remaking normative boundaries through the city. Christopher Taylor's (1999) influential scholarship on the binary logic of flow and blockage, order and disorder, and fertility and barrenness inherent to Rwandan cosmology is key here: processes of transformation are central to hygiene as an operation of ordering the Rwandan polity both symbolically and materially. There is an intersectionality between genocide, urban planning, and the larger project of hygiene as sanitization that acquires unique significance in this postconflict context. As Ruth Rogaski (2004) examines in her study of the resignification and mutations of *weisheng* as "hygienic modernity" in Tianjin, China, isuku is similarly reconfigured and redeployed through state practice, through the multiplicity of its meanings and uses: in the context of genocidal violence, as a metaphor for reordering and cleaning, and as a configuration of urban greening that is a key aesthetic signifier of Rwanda's urban transformation.

In this chapter, I examine three areas of the resignification of greening and hygiene in the work of remaking the city, centered around isuku: the

FIGURE 3.1. The Parliament and Kigali Convention Center, as seen from the roof of the Parliament building

role of green aesthetics in re-creating the city as clean and secure (figure 3.1), the work of local government in municipalizing campaigns of hygiene, and the work of state transformation through environmental labor. During our conversations, several of my key interlocutors discussed with me the role of hygiene in the historic transformational project in Rwanda. In demonstrating the links between hygiene and security, isuku emerges as a larger sociopolitical metaphor, or deep concept, that makes tangible ideas of transformation as a state project. In this chapter's final section I consider how putatively novel green concepts replicate various earlier, troubling forms of conscripted labor. I hence describe how isuku resonates with earlier colonial and postindependence forms of environmental labor, including the very material and macabre project of "transforming" society through sanitization during the genocide. For now, I begin with the form of the city and follow the green aesthetic inward through its history in urban space.

The Ordering Aesthetics of Greening

The greening of the city is an ordering aesthetic, one that signals change and reorders space. Studies of green cities have proliferated in multiple locales, with greening often taken to be a hallmark of the "good city" (Angelo 2019 on the "greening imaginary"), the ecologically advanced city, and the realization of modernizing aspirations of the world-class city. I contend, however, that green is ambivalent, and not simply a "good" element. Greening functions in ways specific to locality, and generates deep meaning in these local urban environments. Specifically, it operates in Rwanda's post-genocide context, where idioms of cleaning and environmental work have convoluted meanings, as an ordering "chronotope" (Bakhtin 2010) of the changing postconflict city. Greening as considered conjunct to isuku compresses sociolinguistic time-spaces and referents that date back to the late Belgian colonial era and extend through the 1994 genocide period. The facade of the city therefore invites excavation, and raises the question of how greening works to signal and to securitize in relation to the sediment of these past experiences.

The concept of regulating and securitizing through an *aesthetic of order* powerfully helps to explain the confluence today in Kigali of securitization and sanitization aims. Both goals are partially achieved through governmental techniques of ordering via hygiene and urban greening. The hygiene-security nexus in post-genocide urban space in Rwanda is composed not of discrete urban phenomena (sanitization, greening, renewal of urban spaces, hygiene, and securitization), but of a constellation of governmental elements working in concert to respond to the crisis of disorder and disorderliness that the RPA confronted in the aftermath of the genocide, as it transitioned from being an incoming army to being a governing force. Although greening is characteristically analyzed solely in the context of "world-class city" aesthetics (Ghertner 2015; Roy and Ong 2011), there is a deeper need to focus on the context-specific meanings of securitization through spatial ordering and the green aesthetic, particularly in contested and postconflict urban space.

During my time in Kigali, I met with officials who had been present during the early post-genocide years when the RPF government was consolidating its authority. My interviews reveal the evolution over time from *order to orderliness*, and toward urban aesthetics and hygiene as forms of securitization and regulation. The greening of Kigali's streets began soon after the transitional period (1994–2000), after the RPF had secured the countryside and the capital from Hutu rebel "infiltrators" and had imposed order in Kigali. With central parts of infrastructure in better repair (with the exception of large unplanned areas, many of which remained off the ambit of colonial and postindependence master-planning), and under the governance of a series of authoritarian mayors in Kigali—most notably Theoneste Mutsindashy-aka (2001–5), who served as mayor of Kigali soon after Colonel Rose Ka-buye (1994–98)—attention in the capital turned from order to orderliness and from territorial security to the securitization of daily life.[2] Hygiene and sanitation became more than idioms of greater security and transitional or-der, and were transposed into the aesthetics of the built environment and the landscape through programs of greening, landscaping, and reform of older areas of the city.

In the years since its municipal hygiene and greening programs began (first under Mutsindashyaka, but in earnest from 2005 to 2007), the aesthet-ics of the street in Kigali and on its peripheries have been amplified and can be read as a visible index of order. Green terraced streets in the center of the city encode citizen compliance. The terraced streets index the area's modern-ization and its growing importance, signaling the importance of the people likely to pass through these areas. The ordered, terraced thoroughfare signals to local and foreign elites that Kigali has become a vanguard of urban green-ing; the street has become a state-controlled space and it powerfully sets the direction for further urban development. The green street and its aesthetics can hence be seen as markers of the state's territorialization: its physical and symbolic control over space. The farther one travels inward, into peri-urban and informal areas yet to come under the force of city master-planning, the more the street becomes a quotidian and unregulated space. Roads in in-ner areas are often unpaved and irregular, security forces are not visible, and social interaction is more fluid and less regulated. There is a clear difference between the typology of these streets (the first ordered, urban, green, and terraced, and the other inward, meandering, and unpaved) and the aesthetics of order and securitization that the spaces display. One could almost read the street as a measure of the degree of official state performance, but its function goes beyond signaling order or visions of prosperity and modernization.

For pedestrian traffic, urban ordering of the street in central areas has meant that paved sidewalks now line these routes, along with police officers and palm trees at set intervals on main roads (figure 3.2). Conforming at once to the world city's green aesthetic and the postconflict city's paranoia about security, the aesthetic of greening in Kigali configures the unique idiom of securitized green in unique ways. The urban aesthetics I have described com-bine with securitization in many areas of the capital: one has the feeling both of being safe walking alone at night and of being watched, regulated, and overseen by a type of developmental policing that pervades the reformed city.

FIGURE 3.2. Cars drive down a newly terraced arterial road in Bugesera District near Karumuna.

Officially unwelcome in Rwanda, Human Rights Watch (HRW) continues nevertheless to produce research reports on the country's spatial transformation. One of its most recent reports (01/2020) focuses on the abusive
treatment of street children in the capital as part of state efforts to sanitize
the streets. The report documents "arbitrary detention" of street children at
Gikondo Transit Center (also called *Kwa Kabuga*) for up to six months and
builds upon earlier work on detentions of adult informal workers in the same
center.[3] Earlier scholarship has also chronicled detention of street children,
orphans, and "delinquent" young men at Iwawa Island (Lovgren and Turner
2019). The ordering of the street through the intertwined projects of aesthetics and security has hence created along with it the category of the "delinquent," criminalizing informal trading on and occupation of the streets in
favor of a formalized, ordered, and securitized idiom of work. The targeting
of informal street vendors (*abazunguzayi*; literally, the itinerant movement of
those traders) and the issuing of public health directives against trading food

informally on the road make the street a regulated space, with sidewalks and securitizing aesthetics militating against less regulated use of public space for livelihood and circulation.

In an analysis of modernist state planning in Brasilia, the capital of Brazil, James Holston (1989) describes the disorientation produced by the new city's modernist cityscape, with the evisceration of the street as a public space, and its replacement by car-centric design, *superquadra* monolith housing blocks, and zoned spaces of commerce and residential life. Holston argues that the sociality of the street corner has been erased to make way for a "utopia without intersections" (101), and that the modernist planning characteristic of Brasilia's streetscapes reorganized public and private space and resignified the space of the street: from public sociality to locomotion and zoned functionality.

A similar resignification has been taking place in Kigali. When in 2000 Mutsindashyaka's mayoral government began to target street traders, the city was emerging from a post-genocide phase to reestablish basic infrastructure under Colonel Rose Kabuye. I was visiting the capital when in 2002 and 2003 I heard that local merchants were talking about pedestrians being arrested for not wearing shoes. Businesses were required to clean and paint their facades—a regulation I attributed to the fact that a film was being shot on location at the time. Regulation as a mode of governance in the city only increased after 2004, when the central Nyarugenge market was closed and demolished along with the central bus station, which was closed in 2005. The Gikondo detention center was established during the same period. As master-planning began to proceed under Oz Architects and then Surbana, demolitions proceeded apace, and any apparent dirt or lapse of hygiene in the city was treated with heightened vigor. The new spatial physicians of the city were planners, using their expertise in the service of the central state to cut through settlements and then suture those spaces back together to create a normative aesthetics of order.

The remaking of Kigali by planners, however, perhaps worked too well. The president reportedly complained about the lack of street life in new areas of the CBD in Nyarugenge district, with its hotels, shopping plazas, and office buildings that replaced older single or double-storied establishments. The large footprint of urban high-rises was reportedly "dehumanizing," and it minimized life on Kigali's new streets by reducing pedestrian traffic. So the president appointed Peter Rich Architects to design a new vernacular for areas under renewal through the Surbana master plan (according to an interview, the architect's recommendations were released in 2013). This production of a new built environment with "traditional Rwandan cultural characteristics," even as the existing vernacular of the actual old city was getting erased, recalls the work of urban planning to produce a new local vernacular in colonized Morocco (Rabinow 1989; Wright 1987). According to my inter-locutor, the resulting architectural report recommended the incorporation of elements of "traditional" Rwandan building. These included the court-yard (*igikari*), which was an example of "good" building practice, as were the arched colonnade, the veranda, and contact with the street from the ground level up. The aim was to integrate these traditional elements within the exist-ing urban design proposed under the master plan.

In the context of master-planning writ large it was ironic that the more traditional structures of existing architecture in old Kigali would have to be erased to make the revived new vernacular "come to life." Like Timothy Mitch-ell's (2002) reconstruction of old and new Gurna in Egypt, the isolation or erasure and then reinvention of the old vernacular was the precondition for its reintegration into the new, with the affluent Kigali dweller replacing those un-able to afford to remain within the city. Select spaces in the new Kigali hence perform an "authentic" version of traditional Rwandan urban design even as the master plan's larger vision looks toward large-scale modernist inscription and urban greening. A particular type of reinvention of urban vernacular form is thus acceptable in the new "spatial hygiene" of the master-planned city, even as the uncontrolled and impenetrable disorder of the original vernacular is deemed "out of place" (Douglas 2003), polluting, and unwelcome.

Urban order and its expression through a green aesthetic is nowhere more visible than on central roads in Kigali. Since the early 2000s the ochred roads in the capital have been transformed into spaces lined with green facades, such as those along the main arterial routes through Kigali. There are well maintained sidewalks and street lighting on main thoroughfares, with abun-dant motorbike taxis (*motos*) as the only semblance of buzzing disorder as traffic increases in the city.[4] An intense infrastructure of labor underpins this work of urban greening, with district governments hiring twenty-four-hour cleaning services and garbage removal companies to order the city. The city of Kigali maintains interdistrict roads and those leading out of the capital—eleven roads total, at a cost of 720 million Rwandan francs annually.[5] District budgets augment the work of road greening and maintenance.[6] A newspaper article reports that Kicukiro District in Kigali spends approximately 30 mil-lion Rwandan francs a month on the cleanliness of its central roads, so

this means that if the remaining two districts spend the same amount, this is equivalent to Rwf 60 million a month or similar Rwf 720 million annual

spending on cleanliness. . . . If you add up to the same figure spent by City of
Kigali on cleaning its designated roads, the bill could go up to Rwf 1.4 billion
annually on cleaning the entire City streets.[7]

Hired on three-year contracts by city and district administrations, companies
like Royal Cleaning, Limited, are on call twenty-four hours a day: "These
trucks sweep every dust on [the] road," the head of the cleaning company told
the local news source, the *KT Press*. "Wherever we meet mud, especially in the
rain season, they mop the mud." Other reports note the low salaries earned
by the employees of these cleaning companies, many of whom are women:
individuals earn approximately thirty to forty thousand Rwandan francs a
month, and some reports note that cleaning companies deduct health insurance funds from wages.

With approximately 135 registered cleaning and garbage companies and
more than 13,000 workers hired to clean the city, the cleaning and garbage
collection industries have been booming since the sector was liberalized
about ten years ago.[8] Despite long working hours (6 a.m. to 5 p.m.) and low
wages that barely keep pace with the minimum cost of living in Kigali, this
army of workers stands behind the collective fantasy of Kigali's clean, green
facade. "Kigali City has won global acclaim for cleanliness. Every visitor finds
meticulously neat roads, streets and neighborhoods. The clean Kigali comes
courtesy of a combination of monthly *"umuganda"* [monthly communal la-
bor], garbage collection trucks and an army of cleaners working for private
companies," states the Rwandan newspaper *The Chronicles* on the green army
that stands behind Kigali's world-class fantasy.[9] Although the green terracing
of main roads may also help mitigate soil erosion and landslides, the aesthetics of the street have taken on a life of their own. They have become branding
staples of the clean capital and Rwanda's secondary cities.

Hygiene in Contemporary State Practice:
In Pursuit of "Small *Isuku*"

Beyond the main roads of the capital, local administrators are left to implement the material ordering of green terracing and clean drainage. Area sector
offices oversee community hygiene work, and the participation of residents
in this collective labor exceeds mandatory monthly communal work (*umuganda*). The purview of daily "hygiene" work in the Rwandan capital blurs
the separation of public and private spheres as it infiltrates the home, the
rhythms of daily life, the crafting of "green" orderly citizens, and the "performances" they must make to one another and to local officials who have been

co-opted into the centralized state organism. These performances include contributing to greening and communal hygiene by performing the roles of transformed subjects, as green urban citizens appreciative of the benefits of hygiene, modernization, and national duty. Landscaped roads are merely one visible facet of a deep governmental interior that supports a green apparatus of governmentalized order at the local level. Here, to extend planning in its various forms into impenetrable areas of the city—old neighborhoods, informal settlements, markets, and prisons—and to change their spatial ordering is also to change their sociality. Through the imaginary of greening and its implementation in daily practice, particular ideas of hygiene and the reform of the self are imparted and imposed. In this sense, urban planning is more than a technology of orderly, rationalized urbanization. In this post-genocide state specifically, planning is a key signifier of state power and a representation of political order. It reorganizes sociality, relocates place, and repossesses space—and in so doing, it exerts territorial authority. Planning as an idiom of order territorializes state space and perceptibly diffuses central authority throughout the city.

As part of my research, I was drawn into understanding how the veneer of the master-planned green city—where the term "green" codes for both "world-class" and "secure"—stands in as a particular form of "small isuku," but is consistently underpinned by a larger and less visible infrastructure of community compliance and citizen reformation through the work of hygiene and cleaning. My work began in the sector administrative offices in Kigali's Nyarugenge District, and it continued through research on hygiene that I undertook with local government officials at Rwezamenyo sector and cell offices. I also conducted interviews with Kigali municipal officials and at national government offices, held conversations with residents in Rwezamenyo and Gitega Sectors, attended Community Hygiene Club (CHC) meetings in the sectors, and interviewed NGOs and local health officials on regimes of hygiene in the capital and in peri-urban areas. Through this maze of encounters and repeated observation, it became clearer that the work of hygiene was both symbolic and material, and that it blurred boundaries between public and private space, even as it established a relationship between the "spaces of the state" (e.g., the street) and those of the home and the workplace. Through the disciplining work of hygiene and the penetration of local administration into the community, Rwandans in Kigali are rendered "public citizens." Individuals' levels of performance for the state and compliance with local directives together define orderly subjects who remain visible to various levels of local administration through their performances of order.

The neighborhood known as Kwa Reuben is a good place to begin, with its local shops and small kiosk bars indicative of a semiprivate space of sociality. The road to Kwa Reuben is asphalted, but changes to unpaved closer to the neighborhood entrance. A few shops sell drinks, food, and basic rations at the entrance to the area. It is 7 a.m. in late March 2019, and the patrol is already on duty, cleaning the well-ordered dirt roads and the concrete drains off the main neighborhood road. Talking to residents over the past few days, I have been introduced to Mr. Yves, the ex-army member who heads the area's patrol. "You can't have security with reduced hygiene," Yves tells me as I arrive and join the *isuku irondo* (hygiene patrol) team on their duties. "Hygiene and security, they are linked. Physical security encompasses all these aspects: the body, illness, human security, they are all linked to life." As I ponder this expanded definition of security and its links to concepts of health and hygiene, we begin walking around the neighborhood roads. Four members of the team—two men and two women—dressed in blue overalls and coats, with the words "isuku irondo" printed in bold letters across their backs, clean nearby ditches and drains and rake grass. Yves tells me that here the *irondo* was initiated eight years ago and has fifteen members, drawn from households in the area and from individuals appointed to the task in the sector. The daily work of cleaning the street has become part of the rhythm of administrative life.

Yves has a prominent injury to his arm, and reports that this disability is linked to his current role in the community:

> I am a former soldier with RDF [Rwanda Defense Forces, the national army], so after I left RDF because of an injury, they transferred me to do activities in the community. They pay me a salary, just like the cooperatives of soldiers who collect parking fees in the city. All former soldiers are recognized by the government, and jobs are created for them in the community.

This does not surprise me, as I am well aware, through visits to the municipal landfill and cleaning companies, that the national defense forces occupy privileged positions in the cleaning and hygiene business sector. RDF-operated subsidiaries and cooperatives take part in jointly managing the landfill at Nduba as well as running various food production, construction management, and municipal service companies in the city. This is a testament to the complexity of demobilization in a militarized state, but also to the lucrative business by which defense companies serve as adjuncts to the central state.

Yves continues that he is not part of the local environment committee on the cell administrative level, but that his duties are linked to theirs in his capacity as head of the isuku irondo. On another day Emil, Yves's deputy, details his conceptualization of local hygiene:

> There are two paths to hygiene in the community. The first is hygiene in the house and bodily security, and freedom from illness. The other is security in general, which is still linked to hygiene but extends to one's way in the city: limiting informal selling and markets, and *akajagari*.

The concept of hygiene and its links to "security in general" is hence capacious as well as penetrating, touching on everything from the body to the physical built environment. The relation of planning to disorder and disordered space is also notably linked to security. *Akajagari* means not only "disordered conduct" but also disordered space and ways of living that defy and subvert official, ordered forms of life. The term has become something of an idiom of planning and ordering in the post-genocide period, and is applied to the specter of the "unplanned" in urban areas, whether it be informal settlements with their vernacular architecture and forms of dwelling or modes of informal trading and unregulated markets across the old capital. To this extent, forms of oppositional living embodied in spaces termed *akajagari* undercut idioms of order and discipline in the planned spaces of new Kigali.

Through discussions with hygiene officials in Rwezamenyo and residents in Kwa Reuben, the conception of "spaces of the state"—principal among them being the street—referenced by both residents and officials stands out in my field notes and my memory of this research. "Isuku irondo cleans roads and spaces that don't belong to people, but which belong to the state [*état*]," Emil in the irondo patrol tells me during a morning visit. "We have to deal with community hygiene challenges, like illegal wastewater connections and people resisting compliance with sanitation charges, and also people who dump wastewater into public drains." Individuals comply because of the threat of punishment and the "strength of community compliance," irondo patrol worker Jean confirms. In contrast to *akajagari* as unplanned space and disordered social practice, the space of the state is planned and orderly. It forms an arguably ever-expanding frontier of the public domain, as the regulation of hygiene blurs boundaries between private and public life and breaches the former.

Rwezamenyo Sector has been keen to keep its first-place ranking in the isuku sectoral competition run by the city of Kigali. Last year, the sector placed first in the city, bringing it much prestige and recognition. A four-wheel-drive land cruiser was awarded to the sector for the hygiene patrol to use on its inspection rounds. The car is worth thirty million Rwandan francs (US$25,872 in July 2023) and has greatly increased the sector's prestige among fellow administrative teams. The vehicle now accompanies the village and cell irondo teams as they patrol the neighborhood streets, checking in on households that are reported not to be in compliance with standards. Started in 2006, the *isuku* competition runs for six months, from January to June, and is judged by the city of Kigali. Awards are based on the sector's hygiene performance contract (*imihigo*) with the district government, and on municipal site visits to inspect the fifteen villages located in Rwezamenyo Sector's purview. Sector officials report that residents also actively contributed to defraying the costs of participation in the competition, using their own funds to improve drainage and clean spaces in their neighborhoods.[10] Inserting a competitive governmental ethos into isuku through sectoral competitions is one facet of the *imihigo* performance contracts (chapter 6) in the context of peri-urban development in Bugesera District. This competition encourages and motivates sector officials in Kigali, but it is important not to lose focus on the longer genealogies of ordering space and securitizing the capital in the transitional period in which these competitions were born, from 2006 onward. Government regulation slowly incorporated hygiene and cleanliness work as a municipal duty, but also as something overseen by the national police in the city.

Laws and regulations on hygiene and security are central "sites" of government by transformation. They operationalize isuku as regulatory practice by local government. Regulations regarding greening and hygiene in the capital have been formalized through official gazettement. Thus, the regulatory instrument, "Instructions no. 01/09 of 15/09/2016 of the City of Kigali Council relating to Hygiene in the City of Kigali,"[11] establishes the parameters of responsibility for residents and visitors to the capital. The regulatory framework extends beyond hygiene in general and penetrates other spaces of informal communal gatherings. Section 3 relates to hygiene in bars, and section 4 to hygiene in marketplaces. Other sections relate to hair salons, schools, bus stations, prisons, public lavatories, saunas, health facilities, places of worship, petrol stations, bakeries, factories, milk sales centers, food processing plants, car washes, garages, residential houses, roads, public gardens, protected areas, unconstructed plots including "marshlands," and so on.[12] These regulations are operationalized through a set of laws, foremost of which is the 2005 law on the environment,[13] combined with laws on urban planning, domestic animal safety, and a host of other legislation. It is salient that hygiene and greening have been combined through law and regulation, rendered matters of public concern, and cited as being among the key duties of citizens, particularly *urban* citizens and visitors. The urban denizen is the epitome of the environmental subject (Agrawal 2005, on "environmentality" and the making of environmental subjects in India, is relevant here)—not just a model citizen but a green subject of environmental regulation and discipline. Thus, Article 3, clause a in chapter 1 of the regulatory document delineates the responsibilities assigned to urban residents of Kigali, who remain "'primarily responsible" for hygiene in the city:

> a) The responsibility for hygiene of the City primarily lies with any City of Kigali resident, who is also the foundation for the image of the City; every City of Kigali resident shall maintain hygiene for his/her body, household, path and workplace. . . .

Significantly, the law sets as its object the resident's body, incorporating it into the law, and extends this responsibility for hygiene into areas normally seen as spaces of domestic life: "the household" as well as areas of public life and state purview, such as the "path and workplace." As the resident is made subject to the law and their body is incorporated as a subject of the law through the operative construct of hygiene, their household is also rendered open to state directive, oversight, and surveillance.

Clauses b and c of Article 3 are relevant in this light: whereas clause c states that the private sector and nongovernmental organizations share the responsibility with urban residents for promoting hygiene, clause b sets up local government and administrative teams to oversee the provisions of the regulation, on residents' "bodies, households, paths, and workplaces" (clause a) through the work of locally administered community hygiene clubs (CHC).

> 3b) The responsibility for hygiene also lies with administrative authorities from the Village to the City of Kigali level, the Sector shall set up a hygiene club in every Village chaired by the in charge of social affairs in the Village and the club has the responsibility of sensitising and following up on all activities related to hygiene in the Village.

In the course of my research on community hygiene in Kigali, central government officials preferred to center their models of hygiene on best practices and international models. They did not mention that hygiene as a field of governmental action in and of itself had been codified through specific regulations and tied to the securitization of space.

The ultimate effect of municipalization and the localization of hygiene is a system that effectively blurs public and private boundaries and the infiltration of the state's hygiene-security nexus into the home. The intrusion of the duties of hygiene into the private sphere, the household, and the body intentionally blurs public and private space; I interpret this as an authoritarian mode of governing social space emerging from the state anxieties of the post-genocide period. The "space of the state" as one of my interlocutors put it, "is now in the home and behind the curtain."[14] State space (Lefebvre 2009) in Kigali has become corporeal, and intrudes into practices and "technologies of the self" (Foucault 2019; Purdeková 2012 and 2015 are also useful here). It includes efforts to reform police citizens with "suspect" hygiene practices through incursions into interpersonal relations and "mindset change." This focus has become a ubiquitous mode of operation in contemporary state developmental practice in Rwanda. In a population seen to need subjective reformation after the genocide—named as a "criminal population," by Mamdani's interlocutor in describing his return to Kigali (Mamdani 2020)—the years after 1994 have seen the practices of hygiene and security transform otherwise impenetrable populations through the subjective reform of "mindset" through hygiene, and through policing of the community, the household, and the body itself.

I make the case that the state's trespass into private spaces discloses the underside of Kigali's state fantasies of greening, hygiene, and cleanliness. The state is itself produced through a paradoxical condition of governmental absence and intrusion into the private realm: the unburdening of public duties onto private citizens. In other words, an exhaustive and intricate infrastructure of labor and an edifice of regulation buttress Kigali's urban fantasy, which reveals not the state's presence but its practical absence in the duties of public life. The state has shifted the burden of productivity and labor extraction onto the bodies and into the personal time of ordinary residents, who then form the state's extended body, expanding it uneasily into private space.

Hygiene as an operative concept in quotidian life in the capital is at once both intimate and governmental. In this context, it is no coincidence that hygiene was a regulating trope during the colonial period in many African cities (Corburn 2013). Hygiene and sanitary regimes served as rationales by which colonial officials were able to enact legislation, enter the home on inspections, subject the colonized body to regulation and searches, prescribe improvement, and proscribe certain activities and conduct (Myers 2017; Njoh 2009). Hygiene enabled colonial officials to dislocate, relocate, disorient, and reorient colonial subjects and their spaces according to dictates of law and policy. That space and urban planning continue to be animated by this form of intimate governmentality can be seen in the design of many African cities with native quarters—*cordonnes sanitaires, la ville,* and *le bidonville* separated spatially, through architectural tropes and vernacular forms of building and design (Rabinow 1989, 1992)—and in permissible mobilities and activities that remained possible despite omnipresent regulation. That this colonial precedent persists in Rwanda is significant, as it is a country where regulation of the person and the body was formally codified through the colonial ethnic identity card (instituted in 1933 by the Belgians), which also served to monitor and regulate dwelling places and the relative social and physical mobilities of individuals and groups. Today, to regulate hygiene is not just to enter into the realm of community sanitation and neoliberal visions of behavior change;[15] it is to go beyond this into the realm of individual and social transformation, and into new forms of space in which these transformed "new men" might live.[16] And it is also to go backward, reviving older, sedimented practices of control over bodies and persons.

As the most intimate dwelling environment and the ostensibly impenetrable hearth of domesticity, the home serves as both the obstacle to the state's vision and the primary space of transformation for its projects of behavior and mindset change. Programs of hygiene breach the threshold of the home environment in ways that governmental programs to transform space cannot do. While recent attempts to order the "disordered" space of informal settlements in Kigali tend toward spatiality and sociality (spaces are seen as unhealthy, and their occupants are deemed to be ill-accustomed to hygiene and ill-informed of new norms), many of the larger homes in informal settlements I visited in Kigali nonetheless sought to maintain the basic domestic spatiality of the traditional Rwandan homestead. The single-level home (*urugo*), with its brush fence, entrance threshold, courtyards, separate living and sleeping quarters, and separate spaces for washing forms the core of the family's private space in relation to the social space beyond the home's fence. In this context, space is also a vehicle through which to address orderly norms of hygiene, militating against the "disorderly" low-income space of the informal settlement.

National Transformation and "Big Isuku"

In the context of post-genocide governance, "big isuku" connotes a deep concept, or sociopolitical metaphor, for the problematic of national transformation and the question of citizen reformation after the traumatic genocide. With modernization and urbanization programs in Rwanda today seen not only as projects of transformation but of national salvation, the redemptive language of transformation and renewal has double relevance.

State elites arguably aim to extend the project of reforming the nation through transforming its urban spaces, seeking a clean break with the past and spatially realizing the project of renewal. The role of environmental labor in disciplining the Rwandan peasant from the colonial period to the immediate post-genocide period, including its role during the genocide, foregrounds the current local preoccupation with regimes of hygiene. Here I focus on the agrarian roots of the environmental discipline extracted as labor in urban areas, and ask fundamental questions about the nature of urban change in the country. To what extent can "green" be seen as a novel "good,"—a "clean break" from the past—and to what extent does it simply repurpose older forms of state-directed production and labor that point us beyond the city?

Forced labor centered around rigidly defined ethnic patron-client relations were foundational modes of rule during the Belgian colonial period in Rwanda (1916–62). Catherine Newbury (1988) documents the formalization of ethnic relations involving the majority Hutu population—over 80 percent of the population, prior to the genocide. She terms arrangements of privilege offered to Tutsi subjects over Hutus in schools and administrative posts as a "collective subordination of this [Hutu] ethnically defined group" (Newbury 1988: 116). In collaboration with the Catholic Church, labor governance of the rural Hutu masses became increasingly rigid as Belgian rule continued, so that the earlier flexible patron-client relations between Hutus and ruling-class Tutsis became formalized and more coercive. There were two forms of labor demanded of the Hutu peasantry: *ubureetwa* (customary labor without pay, demanded of Hutu men) and state-led *corvée*, which was demanded of all adult males but administered more rigidly on the poorer Hutu population through an increasingly centralized system of chieftainship, including the later introduction of hill chiefs, who exerted local authority with central legitimation (Chakravarty 2015; Newbury 1988: 140–1).

Such extractive labor-based relations, which were designed to control the masses and partly intended to increase revenue extraction for the Belgian colonists, featured prominently in the grievances that led to the Hutu Social Revolution of 1959–61. The revolution eventually led to the emergence of an independent Hutu-dominated state, under the Parmehutu party of Gregoire Kayibanda (president of Rwanda 1962–73). These revolutionary ideals, which focused on the emancipation of Hutu masses from forced labor, eventually became the core of a more militant form of Hutu nationalism seen in both the first (1962–73) and second (1973–94) Rwandan republics.

Nonetheless, the Hutu-dominated state continued to require unpaid community work, or *umuganda*, from all Rwandans for one day every week. This form of labor continued to focus on environmental duties, largely tied to agrarian conditions: stopping soil erosion, clearing brush near houses, cleaning streets. During the genocide of 1994, the idiom of "work" was used by hate media such as the RTLM radio station (Radio television libre les milles collines) and the propaganda publication *Kangura* to urge Hutu peasants to go about their "duties" of killing (Li 2004). The same metaphors of hygiene and public order, as in "clearing the weeds and brush," were used as coded messages to encourage and enable the daily "work" of genocidal massacre.

In 1992, when a coalition against the ruling MRND party came together and demanded an end to umuganda, the move was seen as revealing the need to reorder the state-citizenry relationship and the weight of its history. During the RPA invasion, similar promises to drop the umuganda requirement were also issued. Despite these early efforts, umuganda continues—one day a month, with fines imposed on those who seek to avoid participation by leaving the city.[17] It serves to communicate state power and draw on idioms of "participation" and "community" to galvanize citizenry and co-opt their labor. The work to combat erosion and clean roads and drains now operates not in the service of the colonial state, but to reinforce the need for hygiene and compliance at the community level. Through interviews with citizens present during umuganda Saturdays, I became aware that the language of environmental protection and urban greening is invoked during regular meetings after umuganda work. Such meetings are used to disseminate messages from the state and ensure community participation. The continuous repurposing of umuganda through successive periods of rule is significant as the capital modernizes. As the veneer of world-city urbanism is resituated in local contexts with their own local histories and sociopolitical conceptual genealogies, it remains vital to consider Kigali's clean-and-green aesthetic in the context of its history and the use of a durable, repurposed ethos of hygiene for local discipline since the colonial period.

The Hygiene-Security Nexus

I was fortunate to meet an unusual group of long-term Rwandan residents in the capital, in Bugesera District, and outside the country in Nairobi who inspired me with regular meetings and reflections on my evolving research. The three individuals, pseudonymously named Valerie, Michel, and Paul, helped me to understand and interpret the state's fear of disorder and the genealogy of planning as transformation of the city. Our interviews and discussions took place between January to May 2019. I have transcribed our exchanges as they took place, but have amalgamated several points made on different occasions to represent a type of conversation that evolved on trauma, transformation, and regulation. Through this connection, the links between isuku and umutekano, trauma and renewal, began to crystallize for me as genealogies of ordering space and social life as the city transitioned from post-genocide debris and disorder to modernization as a transformative fantasy (Watson 2014, on "Africa's urban fantasies"). I use the word "fantasy" not because the effects of this concept are immaterial or unreal; in fact, they are steadily materializing in concrete, glass, asphalt, palm trees, paved sidewalks, green buildings, and reconditioned wetland parks. Rather, the idea of "fantasy" refers here to the power to transform one thing into the image of something else, to reorganize space and reshape society according to will and image. I use fantasies in the context of modernization and governance through transformation to indicate a very real, if subterranean, bond between renewal and trauma.

As recounted earlier in this chapter, having met Michel one afternoon for tea and soda after researching isuku in Bugesera District, I was surprised to hear him bring up the links between traumatic experience during the genocide and other moments in the country's history, and the changes in the city, including stringent urban regulation:

> The questions you ask when we talk about change, how a city evolves—through them we also talk about life, and in life there is everything. . . . In my opinion the work that you do, the questioning that you pose, is not a questioning that can leave aside the question of memory, and unfortunately the memory here is an injured memory—I would even say memories. These are memories that are cut and reduced, memories that add up. And they are also are memories mostly about being torn apart, as well as about *attempts to relocate these memories* and the terrain upon which they are fixed. . . . So it's a central question, and not a question one can push to the side [italics added].

I was particularly struck by Michel's articulation of the accumulation of social memory over time, such that recollections multiplied and were cumulatively traumatic to the social fabric. In his expression of the attempted reconfiguration and the "attempts to relocate these memories," I understood isuku as working in tandem with the master-planning project to literally remove and figuratively relocate "injured memory" spatially. Michel continued, tying urban regulation to questions of memory and trauma:

> And so, in part, when you talk about isuku and umutekano, you already have here two big concepts that can be traversed by the issue of memory and trauma. For example—it is a phrase that I often say while laughing but at the same time being very serious—when people say, "Oh wow, Rwanda is clean,"—"It's clean," I answer with a disenchanted laugh, saying "Yes!" . . . We're already carrying enough things that are not clean on the inside. This is a way for me to evoke a kind of collective trauma. We know that our face, our image is not something clean, so we need clean, clean! . . . Clean to redeem a certain image of the past, clean to remove this dirt that we have! It can be physical dirt; it can also be like demolishing things, like removing a house whose memory is

sinister, trying to put something else in it. So it's more a question of level than of difference.

When we talk about security . . . we have to choose the concepts used, to be clear on them and their complexity. . . . When you say umutekano, what does it mean? Is it peace? Is it security? Is it securitization? Is it pacification? Is it stabilization? What is it, exactly? . . . We also need to know where we are positioned [when we speak of umutekano].

Valerie, later present as we drank cold sodas and talked about my research, drew again on this theme, discussing hygiene and its enforcement by the police, as well as its interpretation:

In people's lives, nobody has asked the question about the fundamental meaning of [isuku]. Umutekano, yes. This is the very foundation of the police, but isuku has nothing to do with the police. . . . Hygiene, cleanliness, sanitation . . . it has nothing to do with the police. Somehow, it's nonsense. But in fact, why do the police want to be the leader of the isuku? I would like you to ask the question; is it isuku in the sanitation sense? For example, the services that clean the dirty water, treat the waste that comes out of hospitals, or treat areas that have been infected . . . that's sanitation. Beyond sterilization, we are looking for ways to establish cleanliness and order. For example, the redistribution of water and wastewater management . . . that can be sanitation. . . . I think the very idea of isuku is one that is not much questioned, but it covers a lot of things.

Like Michel, Valerie explained isuku as operating on different levels of depth, like a fossilized sociopolitical metaphor running through the core of social space in the city. As I reflected upon these comments and our ongoing discussion, Michel's observation resonated in my mind: the larger project of managing trauma, repetitively and through different formations of isuku, has become sedimented as a problem of governance. As we see below, Michel reflected on trauma as a type of baggage or condition "that this country is dragging and doesn't know how to get rid of" as cycles of violence unfold, belying ideas of aftermaths:

We have lost everything and we need to reassure ourselves, a front of a "clean" concept that we put on the front of our houses, and we avoid thinking. It's the same as " 'Isuku n'umutekano' is just a new slogan." We say isuku and repeat isuku, but do not ask to define what isuku is. It's isuku on my body? Isuku where I sleep? *Isuku hehe* [Where is isuku]? And then, how is "isuku" connected to people's lives?

I believe that [these questions are important] when it comes trauma and governance. We must remember [that] the citizen is not a cardboard; [he/she] is a human being in [his/her] own right. I think it's a kind of trauma in governance that this country is dragging [along with it], and that it does not know how to get rid of.

On a different occasion, Paul told me that isuku draws on legacies of communal labor (umuganda) that the incumbent government had committed to transforming or eliminating when it came to power, but which now undergird hygiene efforts in the community, so that citizens are fined heavily if they do not attend:

> And when people remember—you know, the RPF, when they were in the liberation fight, said, "We're going to abolish umuganda," because it was a kind of forced labor. And finally, umuganda started small [and became] big isuku. . . . The language of genocide used terms of isuku too. After the genocide, then we say, we could reconstruct the houses that were destroyed; [we used terms of] umuganda, isuku . . .

Paul paused before concluding:

> When someone says I'm going to transform, what do you want to transform? Who are you to transform? What is a durable transformation? . . . The genocidal project [was] a transformation project in a bad way. . . . So was the colonial project. So, when we talk about a transformation, we must be careful. We need to understand and deconstruct it properly.

As Paul states, there is something intrinsic to isuku as a mode of transformation that has been reiterated on Rwandan soil through its successive ruptures. The transformational project as an ongoing and "durable transformation," as Paul terms it, reflects on successive periods of governance in the country. Isuku as a concept that focuses on transforming the city and reforming the population has metaphorical depth ("as big isuku," as Paul qualifies it) that betrays continuity between the work of hygiene as a disciplining practice in contemporary Kigali and the role of labor extraction and enforced compliance in colonial and postindependence regimes which, far from disappearing, are still palpably present.

Insecure Memory and Urban Space

The idea of "security" (umutekano) is connected to the theme of isuku, and to how urban order has evolved from a general military logic to a policing logic—in other words, from a focus on security to the securitization of everyday life. Like isuku, umutekano has been influenced by plans for urban transformation. As a means of operationalizing governmental control, security has both contemporary and genealogical resonance, and feeds on the fear of infiltrators and "disorder." The work of transformation in Rwanda's urban spaces is enabled by the hygiene-security nexus, such that concerns about securitizing the city and sanitizing its polluted, genocide-era spaces are annealed. The capital city has moved from the material and symbolic pollution of genocide debris to the more symbolic and ineffable remains of genocide-era pollution: social memory, spatial practice, and built environments that need to be securitized through the technologies of the modernized smart city and the reinscriptive tools of world-class city master-planning. In the early post-genocide period, practices of hygiene and security were invoked to weed out infiltrators who hid near or in people's houses in the community; but now the same idioms are repurposed through programs to securitize the city. This suggests that there is an intimate connection between securitization and sanitization, security and hygiene, that lies behind the overt impulse to order and renew the facade of the built environment in Rwanda's capital.

Security (*umutekano*) and hygiene (*isuku*) are a governmental nexus to restore order in the city in the aftermath of genocide and civil conflict. Rather than simply "seeing" the city as a space for ordering (Scott 1998), I suggest that there is interpretive depth in the local meanings of "legibility" and order in a given society—particularly in a *post*-traumatic one. During one of our discussions, Valerie tied together hygiene and security in their local genealogical contexts:

> You have to look at the history of isuku [hygiene] in Rwanda in the postindependence period as intertwined with umutekano, which developed in an insecure environment after the genocide and the period of uncertainty after the genocide, from 1994 to 2000.

As I visited the Parliament building and its museum (chapter 4), the interdependency of the processes I had been studying over the past few months began to crystallize for me as part of a unified and multilayered formation. The *isuku na umutekano* (hygiene and security) banners and signs I saw around the city, which that advertised municipal hygiene campaigns and local competitions that I took to be emblematic of a neoliberal ethos to clean and green the city, blended into my vision of the RPF's experiences and challenges as they entered a disordered Kigali—urban space not metaphorically but *literally* strewn with the debris of genocide.

Speaking of the period of insecurity and infiltrations at the end of the genocide, Valerie went on to explain the context of umutekano and its links to the securitization and sanitization of spaces in the capital:

A big part of this isuku and hygiene drive in the immediate post-genocide
period was knowing where the population is, and surveillance. The period of
"loss of security" from 1994 to 2000 and the presence or fear of infiltrators in
the community led to the use of local authorities and community mobilization to go into the community and increase the security of the population in
the name of hygiene and security. Let us call this "the period of infiltrations,"
and it is important to think through in understanding where to place isuku
and umutekano in Kigali today. . . .

This sensibility of the "'period of 'loss of security'" that Valerie references
continues in varying forms today: isuku and umutekano speak to ordinary
aspects of the governance of everyday life in Kigali today, which are institu-
tionalized as standard functions of city administration. Insecurity is thus an
enduring state affect in Rwanda. Urban unease helps to explain some of the
rationale behind citizen duties, which include ubiquitous community surveillance and required participation in local government at the grassroots level.

Valerie continued, describing the history of post-genocide insecurity, and
tying it to the drive to clean and secure spaces around the home and in the
community:

> As people returned to the city [after the genocide], many were afraid of aban-
> doned houses because of animals or criminals hiding there, so this was a way
> to mobilize people to act on these abandoned spaces.

Instead of being little more than contemporary terms about disparate issues
such as cleaning roads and conducting night patrols of neighborhoods in
the capital, *isuku na umutekano*—hygiene and security—became foundational for my understanding of how the RPF came to comprehend the city,
indicative of the worldview operationalized in post-genocide Kigali. The
ethos encapsulated by these thematically contiguous terms explained how
the development of a militarized approach to disorder gradually evolved into
practices of urban sanitization and the preoccupation with security and everyday securitization. Rather than being about a "thin" form of hygiene (Scott
1990; Gramsci 2005)—if hygiene is ever "thin" or solely visible, discursively or
materially—isuku is very much a concept tied to umutekano as a metaphor
for securitizing the everyday. To paraphrase an interlocutor Mamdani (2020:
6–7) interviewed after the genocide ended, there were two essential problems faced by the new forces in power: transforming a rebel army into an
entrenched governing force, and reforming a population seen to be complicit
in the violence of the genocide into orderly and compliant Rwandan citizens
(a "criminal population").

Isuku na umutekano as sociopolitical metaphors are foundational to how the new Rwandan state approaches the transformation of the city and its citizens: performing spatial surgery through urban master-planning of its old quarters, and deploying securitized approaches to surveillance and local administration. These two concepts are foundational pillars for the new order, through which one can discern connections between accounts of rebel nationalism and state accounts of the material and symbolic purification of the national core.

Writing on spaces of possibility in the wake of apartheid in South Africa, Carol Long (2013) describes the complexity of these "transitioning racialized spaces," where distinctions between the past and the present had begun to open up to negotiation and questions of difference, to the possibilities of transitional "third space" and to creativity not possible under the apartheid regime. Analyzing the all-or-nothing tension of apartheid spatial separation, she surmises,

> Apartheid institutions can be understood as the opposite of transitional spaces. Rather than opening up potential spaces to play, apartheid structured space, creating rigid rules about where and where not to play, who could play with whom and what was serious and thereby unavailable for creativity. . . . A shared space was against the rules [Long 2013: 63].

Long's work brings out the incompleteness of transitions from violence: the "after" of aftermaths that are ongoing. "After" apartheid, South Africa has been an ongoing space of "in-betweenness" with a "dual orientation towards the past and the future," Long writes (61). She suggests that spaces of openness are central to social healing and creativity, so that "the metaphor of a society in transition could be said to be one that hopes to be in the process of coming alive, of apprehending difference, and a certain in-between space not wholly defined by what it 'transitions' from, or to" (62).

As we have seen in this chapter, spatial hygiene and the sociopolitical metaphors of isuku and umutekano structure and divide space. Through the aesthetics of greening that underpin the spatial master plan, isuku and umutekano speak both to the fantasy of the world-class city and to the ordering of subterranean trauma and injury that underlie the city above ground, materializing a bulwark that makes manifest the fear of insecurity. Yet social healing occurs through alternative, spontaneous forms of belonging such as Long's openly rendered "transitional spaces," rather than through a sanitized and partitioned city. Space here is an undertheorized component of *repair*—an ongoing and incomplete process of opening up and creating spontaneous possibility, of "third space" in the making (Soja 1998).

Instead of dwelling amid transition, the legacies of isuku as governmentalized transformation and of isuku as subjective reformation haunt the green spaces of master-planned order in Kigali today. At this particular conjuncture of world-city master-planning and post-genocide national change, idioms of "green as secure" and "green as clean" must be excavated for their deeper local meanings and resonance. The sedimented meanings of isuku demonstrate that "aesthetic governmentality" (Ghertner 2010, 2015) has specific, locally resonant meanings in traumatic space. In this postcrisis context, global iconography is localized and specified in ways that demand attention and understanding equally from scholars of planning theory and from area studies interpreters of Rwanda's post-genocide transition.

4

A Pedagogy of Wounds

Located on the side of the main Gikondo road, under contract for reconstruction by a Chinese firm, the white building housing the digitized National Archives, boldly named Le Prestige, emerges from a cloud of dust as I drive up. As Mr. Egide, one of the enthusiastic archivists, tells me, the repository of the National Archives in Kigali will soon move to Kacyiru, the governmental office area of the capital. Mr. Egide beams as he reveals this information, taking me to the back of his office area and pointing to the paint peeling off old concrete walls. He is entranced by the newness of the proposed office tower, set in Kacyiru, a reorganized and modern area of the newly planned city which is being realized block by block, one streetscape at a time, according to the venerated Kigali spatial master plan.

As I am logged into the archives' digital repository on one of three desktop computers, Mr. Egide returns with what he claims are some new finds. He pores over articles and pictorial representations of the conceptual master plan on his computer, jumping between images of the projected new city and newspaper articles of the old city center and its residential district of Kiyovu. He is particularly focused on the area that houses urban workers near the city's old European quarter, and which has been known as "Kiyovu cy'abakene" (Poor People's Kiyovu)—most recently home to large informal settlements that have been subject to multiple demolitions and evictions as the new city evolves. "*Ca, c'est un bidonville!*" he exclaims, pointing to images of old settlements in the capital's core, before jumping enthusiastically to representations of the new Kigali with its glass-veneered buildings and green streetscapes. The irony of an archivist performing temporal jumps between the old *centre-ville* and its new facades strikes me for a while. Here as well, the keepers of Rwanda's selectively digitized past dream of the new city in master-planned technicolor. Forms of longing and loss in the old-new city intertwine and are woven together in this period of transitional reconstruction.

Reflecting on the nature of archives in relation to the Rwandan post-independence period, Marie-Eve Desrosiers comments on the structural power behind the articulations as well as the silences or elisions of the archive: "Archives are always a reflection of the power relations of their time, and of what and who they take to matter. What becomes an archive always comes down to what a state and society deemed worthy to preserve and what was not. Archives are therefore a space of selective, privileged, powerful, or 'stately' voices, simultaneously overshadowing others, sometimes in the form of a violent act of rejection or neglect" (Desrosiers 2023: 49).[1] In its post-genocide incarnation, Rwanda's capital has been an archive in its own right, displaying through its sedimented layers different periods of time in the country's history—concretized through built space and testament to the spatialization of changing power relations. Various forms of spatial planning are used for its desired political constituents: Belgian colonial town planning, postindependence popular spaces such as the central market and the stadium, and most recently the spatial master-planning of the post-genocide period. Here the remaking of the old city operates on temporally graded terrain, with built markers representing various types of identity and belonging, suturing together a space characterized by complex and injured memory. Looking at the "woundedness" produced by differing ideas of home, homeland and belonging in contemporary Rwanda, and at the "wounds" in the built environment that encapsulate such complex memory in urban space, I characterize the city as an enduring archive of remembrance and loss. In their built forms, such "wounds" in urban Rwanda call for a deeper reading of forms of identity and injury that endure in social memory and built space, and also for what they offer to a pedagogy of postconflict rupture and rebuilding, for which the city serves as a living repository.[2]

At the official termination of the genocide in July 1994, Rwanda was what Achille Mbembe would call a necro-environment: the genocide's bleak logics of death were inscribed onto the landscape, rendering it an inverted space, a national heterotopia. Post-genocide remains were present in disordered environments: genocide sites strewn with corpses, destroyed buildings that lined roads, towns with broken-down infrastructure, rivers clogged with the dead, and refugees and a returning diaspora living in transitional tents and make-shift housing. Fear and suspicion, material disorder, and a palpable lack of security in urban environments characterized this period. The transition from this landscape of disorder to an aesthetic of order embodied in the spatial master plan has had complex effects on memory, meaning, and circulation in the capital.

As a form of administrative and spatial reorganization, master-planning has left enduring imprints in many postcolonial cities. In places like Nairobi and Zanzibar, these remains have lingered long after colonial town planning entrenched the master plan as the core spatial tool for segmenting, racializing, and fixing the city (Corburn 2013; Home 2015; Myers 2020). In the contemporary period, master-planning has reemerged as a prevalent spatial trope of ordering in African cities, with governments seeking to assert authority through reorganizing space in the capitals and in secondary cities, and enabling circuits of financing in the service of national and elite-class ambition (Hudani 2020; Harrison and Croese 2022). In this chapter I consider the master plan as more than a comprehensive plan. Rather, in a postconflict context with complex sedimented memory, the master plan is a narrative and spatial tableau written over multiple webs of history and convoluted narratives of the nation. It is a modernist spatial narrative, but also an experiential framework that conditions which stories are told and what is remembered and rendered visible through the milieu of the built environment and beyond it. Through its monumental homogenization of time and space, the master plan works to erase the heterogeneity of the postconflict "everyday" (as long-term residents recounted in chapter 2).

In contrast to the single spatial story of the master plan, there have been multiple postconflict narratives operating in urban Rwanda until the present. As complex sites of social memory, these spaces proliferate multiple narratives of spatial history and social rupture in postconflict Kigali. Looking at postconflict aftermaths that have unfolded in the built environment during the immediate post-genocide period and until the beginning of urban master-planning, I demonstrate how these multiple spatialized narratives are gradually being rebuilt and rewritten. The spatial master plan reconfigures social history through the reconfiguration of built space. The period of master-planning and urban renewal since the early 2000s has seen different kinds of sites erased and peripheralized through redevelopment and relocation. I visit some of these complex sites in Kigali and describe palimpsests of a changing city: the informal settlement, the prison, the popular market, and the Parliament building.

As the historic city is reordered and renewed, the visibility of these older sites of complex social memory—its "brown" spatial configuration, evocative for me of streets in the older part of the city—is recalibrated. These contradictory sites and sedimented layers of the older city are removed and replaced by a renewed "green" spatial aesthetic and the contemporary spatial order of master-planning. While the removal or decommissioning of central prisons and popular markets in town centers was a response to the need to "modernize" spatial planning and reformulate spaces characterized by overcrowding and lack of security, this recalibration also erases more ambivalent spatial markers. In this way, spatial reorganization occludes places of historical and social significance along with the narratives that go with them (Trouillot 2015). The aesthetic contours of visibility in the city are hence reworked, even as emotional and psychic wounds and attachments to place endure in personal memory and private space, reproducing long-term problematics that layer and sediment in urban space. Such enduring attachments recenter questions of spatial recomposition and access to the polity after conflict, pointing to the need for deconstructive reckoning that unpeels layers and unwinds questions.

Fanon and the Tabula Rasa

I was discussing my research on the effects of master-planning and building in old Kigali one evening with Jacques, a long-term resident of Muhima who recently had been compelled to move to a less central part of Kigali. Perplexed, Jacques interjected: "Why is it that in countries in Africa, we are always reconstructing the city after there is a new government? Why can't our leaders leave it as it used to be? Why must they always change it every time a new leader comes in?" His questioning led me to reflect on the many demolished old buildings that marked my routines in areas of old Kigali. How does the built environment reflect changes to the political project of the nation in its various incarnations? How might we understand master-planning in this spatial epoch in relation to these successive ruptures?

Writing on violence and the project of decolonization, Frantz Fanon commented suggestively on the iterative process of violence on the eve of decolonization as native and colonizer changed places and the world of the former was remade in the image of the latter: "Decolonization is always a violent phenomenon. . . . Without any period of transition, there is a total, complete, and absolute substitution . . . that kind of *tabula rasa* which characterizes at the outset all decolonization" (Fanon 2007: 35). Much like the spatial tabula rasa Jacques and I talked about that evening, this decolonization has been not a singular, one-time project but a repetitive one. In the political experience of the Rwandan nation, successive ruptures and an extended temporal period of disorder and unsettlement have been constitutive of national and personal experience. Each rupture has been a convulsion of the central state, an attempt to purge variant meanings of the nation and reinscribe space with new symbolism.

The political project of building the newly independent nation can in many ways be analogized to renovating a house, one that has already been lived in, endured harsh storms, and been subject to rounds of rebuilding and repair. The political project of building the Rwandan nation began before the moment of independence in 1962, carrying with it divisive legacies of the colonial period even as it sought to find new foundations as a postcolony. In many ways, the project of founding the nation was never one of a singular nationhood, but of multiple incarnations and politicized visions of citizenship and belonging. The Belgian colonial period created segmented spatiality between the city and the countryside (Mamdani 2020; Newbury 1988), with an axis of exclusion generating iterative division over forms of access, habitation, and belonging. What Fanon would term "compartmentalization" (Fanon 2007: 37), the separation between the colonial city and indigenous settlements and between different forms of segmentation in space, has been central to both the colonial project and its postcolonial national successors. The work of remaking these divisions is a geographical process, and one that the period of decolonization doesn't fully reckon with. Through its own divided spatial consciousness and its instruments of power, Fanon describes the iterative recreation of divided society:

> The colonial world is a world cut in two. The dividing line, the frontiers are shown by barracks and police stations. In the colonies it is the policeman and the soldier who are the official, instituted go-betweens, the spokesmen of the settler and his rule of oppression. . . .

And . . .

> This approach to the colonial world, its ordering and its geographical layout will allow us to mark out the lines on which a decolonized society will be reorganized [Fanon 2007: 38].

Mirroring this segmented spatiality, the convulsions of Rwanda's birth as a nation-state have had at their core a *split* set of narratives: a division between Tutsi dispossession, exile, and loss, and majoritarian Hutu marginalization, forced labor, and exclusion. Thus there has never been a coherent or singular narrative of the nation in the postindependence period, as much as the current RPF-led state seeks to fashion a post-genocide master narrative of the nation. The national narrative has held divergent meanings for different occupants of the postindependence house. In many ways, the spatial technique of the tabula rasa embodied in the master plan responds to this national split consciousness across time and space, attempting another national rebirth, another decolonization—an erasure of space and alternative social

FIGURE 4.1. Construction in commercial areas of old Kigali. The word "hope" is visible on a wall.

memory through a single framework that at its core is born from internal contradiction.

In this chapter I reflect on how the spatial master plan redefines and reimagines political community in the capital by way of erasure, peripheralization, and spatial redesign (figure 4.1). As master plans such as these serve to delimit who has symbolic and material rights to the polity, they demarcate and materialize the desired political community of the enfranchised.

The Master Plan as a Single Spatial Story

In the case of Kigali, there are multiple lives that underlie the single spatial story, which the master plan reconstitutes through new built space. I offer here an experiential examination of the recombination of urban space in this postconflict context. Master-planning here serves as a prism that breaks apart questions of the spatial ethics of coexistence: it highlights multiple spheres of alternative memory as the city is spatially rewritten amid the official drive for an aesthetic of order in the capital. Over time, Kigali evolved into a city of neighborhoods with different modes of dwelling, and residents from various parts of the country and farther afield. Yet, by what Chimamanda Ngozi Adichie might describe as the "dangers of the single story,"[3] the national master narrative that is physically inscribed through the spatial master plan threatens these heterogeneous ways of life and diverse forms of belonging in the capital.

Rwanda's 1994 genocide left psychic, physical, and material wounds of many types: scars running across the body of the city and evident in urban and rural landscapes. In this context, the spatial master-planning of the capital and, later, six secondary cities, which replaced old built environments with new urban aesthetics, seemed to work in tandem with the post-genocide government's broader visions for a "cleaned-up," remapped, and re-visioned Rwanda. As a nation that was spatially, narratively, and subjectively "born again" and reinvented for a new period of urbanism, the "New Rwanda," as it was called at the end of the transitional period in 2003, was recreated with a new flag, new decentralized governmental designations and mappings, and new street names in the capital that no longer honored the old Francophone postindependence period, but instead worked according to a modern grid. In this way, the urban transformation in Rwanda is "anchored in political transformation," as Antonio Tomás writes in an analysis of Luanda, Angola (2022: 195). Yet, as we see on a granular level (chapter 2), these erasures and reinventions of the old city are deeply disorienting for longer-term residents, who remember older ways of interacting with urban space. They are still conditioned by their long-standing ways of life and social memory, by daily routines and quotidian pathways worn through habit and social interaction. Many of my interlocutors say they feel lost, and express attachment to ways of life in the old city.

The science scholar Thomas Hughes (1987) conceptualizes a large technical system (LTS) as a complex infrastructural monolith that unifies technological functions such as large-scale electrical grids or other forms of standardized and networked infrastructure (as Marvin and Graham [2002] write about and complicate in their work on splintered urban network infrastructure). I extend the concept of the LTS to the spatial master plan of Kigali, itself a composite of networked infrastructures that works both above and below ground to totalize spatial planning and index the aesthetic politics of visibility in the city. The politics of spatial planning hence reveal interconnected material and social worlds that lie beneath the forms we see above ground. The master plan's totality homogenizes time and space; it puts forth certain macronarratives about the capital, and supports particular modes of livelihood sanctioned by the city's design. The city master plan is an artifact of state territorialization that reorders lifeworlds in the city and determines who can remain.

The politics of the master plan as a type of LTS are those of erasure and reinscription, of creating new memory in the aftermath of civil war and genocide that seeks to remap space and reconstitute place. In other words, in opposition to the informal livelihoods, forms of vernacular building, and multiple "heterogeneous infrastructures" (Jaglin 2014) in social and material life that have long characterized Kigali's hills, and which grew in the post-genocide period as people sought safety in cities, the master plan formalizes dwelling and space. This changing spatial organization elicits what Abdoumaliq Simone remarks on as the new "fantasies of different regimes to fix the city once and for all" (2022: 30). In this case, replacing the city wholescale in a singular sociotechnical matrix of built space above ground aims to render the city legible, controlled, and fortresslike. I suggest that sites of complex memory that are seen as "wounds" in the city can instead work as a visible urban pedagogy, bringing forth other modes of healing and conciliation. Simone reminds us that brokenness refuses the necessary "incitement to repair" as an outcome of other infrastructural trajectories in the city; this brokenness instead "suggest[s] its own courses of action without being lured into doing something about it" (29). Instead of incursions into built space intended to "fix" a broken spatial narrative, woundedness and injury in the city can also point to new pathways for action and continuities in social memory, new lines of visibility, and a reparative ethic of planning and inhabiting that forms "a reiteration of the viability *of this world*," rather than planning for the fantasy of the next (29).

SUBTERRANEAN PLANNING

The category of the "subterranean" has preoccupied scholars writing from a multiplicity of perspectives, and is generative for thinking through the lives and narratives that underlie the single spatial story in Rwanda's capital. For economists, the subterranean represents the other of formalized channels of the legally sanctioned economy "aboveground"; the extralegal, illegal, or the just informal are fraught categories that complicate normative accounts of the juridical state. As urban studies scholars have shown of planning in Indian cities, these categories are a troubled grouping: the formal predates upon the unformalized, and the law operates retroactively to regularize the sphere of the unplanned across class divides so that the state is itself rendered arbitrary and informalized through the practice of planning (Roy 2009). Rather than existing as a solitary edifice, the master plan has many layers and is constituted of its underground others—such as Holston (1989) demonstrates of the multiple informal settlements and peripheral towns that grew up around Brasilia during the construction of the modernist Brazilian capital. In psychoanalytic and narrative terms, the subterranean lives of the master plan include the trauma and injured memory and the legacies of "cleaning" (chapter 3) that haunt planning as a state practice in Rwanda today. The subterranean is hence an ambiguous and ambivalent space and narrative form, one that permits both extractivism (Emel et al. 2011) and fugitive planning (Harney and Moten 2013).

In the case of Kigali, the subterranean prods us to think through different modes of imagining urbanicity in Rwanda's capital. In opposition to the master-planned spatial reordering of the city, with its smoothing of space and the destruction of the quotidian built environment, micropractices of building and maintenance in older parts of the city are other modes of envisioning, organizing, and interacting with space. In this sense, spatial hygiene and the displacement caused by the spatial master plan reconfigure not only the visible dwellings aboveground but the subterranean infrastructures that undergird this reorganization of lifeworlds in Kigali. Sanitation infrastructures, the lines, pipes, and outflows that underpin them, and the lives, stories, and possibilities of residence that are built around these physical infrastructures present an alternative realm to that which can be seen aboveground—one that also has tangible effects on urban life and possibilities for living in shared space.

For its Millennium Development Goals (MDG) commitments, the Rwandan government set targets for access to "improved" sanitation, and was ostensibly on track to meet them: 84 percent by 2014 (including sanitation facilities shared between two or more people) according to official statistics (Tsinda and Abbott 2018), up from 54 percent in 2008 and 23 percent in 1990.[4] Under the Sustainable Development Goals (SDGs), the country aims to have 100 percent access to improved sanitation by 2030. In many ways the designation of "improved" is the catch. It refers to the "modernized" slab "toilet" facilities required by the public hygiene law and sanitation policies. In practice, approximately 90 percent of households in Kigali use pit latrines—a large but not exclusive percentage of them located in informal settlements.[5] Smaller numbers of households use septic tanks, and only a small core set of buildings in the central business district (CBD) and those with their own sanitation systems have piped, centralized sewerage.

My research in Kimisagara and Kangondo informal settlements and with sanitation providers in Kigali showed that there is now only one main pit latrine emptying service operating in the capital: Pit Vidura, which was established as an entrepreneurial start-up in 2016 (then called Pivot, it aimed to turn fecal sludge into fuel). Emptying between fifty and sixty pit latrines a month, according to its mid-2019 capacity, Pit Vidura operates as a private player to enable private residents to fulfill public, state-mandated duties. Sanitation in Rwanda remains a private duty, according to regulations (2016), which rely on "community participation" and individual initiative to build and maintain sanitation facilities and dispose of household waste.

Residents I interviewed in Kimisagara detailed how in this context they have little choice but to improvise with private means. They pay and wait for private pit latrine emptying services, construct new latrines that frequently impinge on the water table, or hire covert pit latrine emptiers from the community. Working until daybreak without personal protective equipment, and often intoxicated on drugs or alcohol to facilitate their hazardous and onerous work, covert latrine emptiers perform a service that the state fails to provide. Waste collected from pit latrines that have reached their capacity is emptied into yet other, newly dug pit latrines, storm water drains, and wetlands and marshes in the city's valleys. While officials are therefore correct to some measure in faulting informal settlement residents for polluting wetlands in the city, this occurs in the context of a very real dearth of state services.

The erasure of informal settlements and the "renewal" of lower-income areas of the old city of Kigali mean that there is a hidden subterranean infrastructure planned to underlie the aboveground edifice of the urban master plan. The Kigali Centralized Sewerage System (CSS) is currently being planned by the city of Kigali with technical consultants hired in cooperation with JICA, the Japanese technical cooperation agency. The first phase is expected to complete 89,000 connections in the CBD by 2024.[6] Accordingly, the master plan states that pit latrines will need to be phased out in the immediate future to permit the development of the CSS. Development financiers have secured ninety-six million euros (2019 value) to fund the first stages of construction, from sources such as the African Development Bank and the European Investment Bank.[7] What remains particularly salient in the context of the sanitation master plan for Kigali's CSS is that it effectively underlies the built terrain above ground: if the visible investment to modernize Kigali is the speculation in property and private investment in the built environment, then the CSS is the unseen portion of the plan to centralize and modernize the capital, integrating space and social practice along the way.

In the case of the pit latrine, the form itself is connected to pollution and death at the center of the genocide, and is dug deeply into that history. The pit latrine has a sordid history tied to the country's genocide past, as a veritable repository of remains that positions it uniquely in relation to new forms of disposal. Whereas latrine emptiers report that people throw shoes, bottles, and a miscellany of personal effects into pit latrines today, during the genocide the pit latrine became a graveyard for the disposal of the bodies and remains of those killed in the violence. Today, the pit latrine is not only an unwanted form of "unmodern" and "unhygienic" evacuation in informal and poorer areas of the city, but an enduring reminder of the aftermath of violence. Nonetheless, rather than working to include users of pit latrines in Kigali's new spatio-legal regime, the city has allowed the wholesale replacement and erasure of the latrines to reveal the limitations of the stringent municipal governance currently in force.

The elimination of pit latrines and their replacement by either CSS connections or private septic tanks means that forms of life and spatial organization in informal settlements and lower-income areas will have to go as well. Heterogeneous spatial and social infrastructures are replaced with homogeneous, segmented, and zoned spaces, both above and below the ground. These aesthetic determinations, central to the capital's reconstruction and conditioned by new environmental and planning regulations, mean that residents of settlements such as Kimisagara are no longer allowed to remain in their homes. What results is thus a restriction of the stories, emplaced epistemologies, and subject positions capable of defining change in the city; urban space is instead centralized and controlled around reticulated infrastructure as a form of spatialized master narrative.

In the next sections I examine erasure, peripheralization, and redesign as modes of urban reordering that have become predominant in the new Kigali. I focus on the informal settlement, the prison, and the market as the spatial master plan takes over as a central mode of producing space. As the older spatial order of the city is reworked, reconfiguration is a spatial technique of ordering that has implications both for social memory and for access to the city by families of prisoners, market traders, and informal workers who constitute the city's human infrastructure. I end by visiting the historic Parliament building in the center of the restructured capital to show how narratives of the past might coexist with current articulations to create a complex, palimpsestic built landscape. I argue for the significance of continuity amid rebuilding, and for a reckoning with peripheralized social memory that provides the ground for more complete forms of cohabitation, repair, and reckoning.

Erasing the Informal Settlement

As residents of informal settlements in Kigali confront displacement, their struggles over place create incremental practices of living in the changing capital that convey attachment to place and the friction of belonging and loss. Their micronarratives of continuing life—of maintaining livelihoods, accessing basic services and modes of social support, improvising water systems, helping neighbors, and sharing common fates as the city changes—and these struggles to remain and survive become small acts of resistance against the aesthetic of order imposed on the city from above. In many ways, this mode of continuing and staying against the odds creates its own affective dispositions in the city: pervasive uncertainty and waiting, shock over impending removal, and anticipation that spreads via rumor among residents.

The case of one of my interlocutors, Joyce, illustrates the precarity that characterizes provisional contemporary dwelling in the city. Joyce lives in a small house in the Kimisagara area of Kigali. She rents her one-room home from a landlord who also owns two other small houses, one of which is adjacent to Joyce's home. Part of the house next door is occupied by the landlord himself, and another part is rented out to a family that sells food from home. During my period of research, Joyce returned home one day to find a large *Towa* (Demolish) sign outside her home, and a large *X* painted in red on her exterior wall, facing the alley that connects different areas of the hilly settlement. Joyce's area is slated as a high-risk zone (HRZ). It's considered to be in environmentally hazardous terrain, a judgment made recently by the environmental and planning authorities in Kigali, who seek to protect "endangered" marshlands and enable the relocation of residents who live in areas subject to heavy rains, flooding, and landslides. Joyce and her neighbors have lived in the area for several years, but only since the advent of the city master plan have increasing numbers of homes been slated for expropriation if the residents are owners, or simply for eviction if they are tenants. Accordingly, the residents are not permitted to repair or rehabilitate their homes as they wait for formal notice to vacate. The window of time for building more stable foundations in a changing city thus closes around them as they simply wait. The master plan effectively uproots them; it renders them placeless and without urban possibilities.

Nearby in Kimisagara is the Mpazi model building project, established by a foreign planning and building firm that has partnered with the authorities in Kigali to prototype model lifestyles in this HRZ. The 8-in-1 house, as it is named, is a model home, built by design not only for visiting planning experts, foreign donors, and development partners but also as a prototyping lesson for Kimisagara residents who sit across the Mpazi creek and face its sustainably constructed brick and concrete facades. Residents like my interlocutor, Michel, a part-time mechanic and sometime joinery worker who is precariously employed in the city, can look from across the valley and creek, and reflect on everything the model house represents and wordlessly implies that they are not. The house's design indicates that it is ready to welcome a model nuclear family: kitchen, living room, dining room, bedrooms, formal bathrooms, and front garden. The house is outfitted with furniture indicative of modern domestic lifestyles. Though basic, it is appointed for inhabitants of a social class different from those who live precariously across the creek. Underemployed, mostly as casual repairmen, Michel and his friends live close to this formal, prototypical life, yet their lives and livelihoods—like those of many of Kigali's poor residents—are provisional and quotidian, measured by the week, and from one rental payment to the next.

The interaction between the model home and the residents' dwellings across the valley and channel—structures *made* "provisional" by new regulations—is one of waiting. With its visiblity countering their growing invisibility, the model house may indeed outlive the homes that face it; it is a monumental anachronism in the context of the rickety homes on the opposite hill. It represents the network of expertise and finance that fuels Kigali's moment of urban transformation. This act of looking at prototyped futures that they will not and cannot be a part of—at least not within the confines of the city, close to jobs and livelihoods—is a form of wounding in Kigali today. It signals the dearth of opportunities for a shared future as inhabitants of the capital. Residents of Kigali's "unplanned" areas do dream of a better city, and of lives uninterrupted by eviction, expropriation, and uprooting. Here, their fertile imaginative mobility in the face of growing forms of unevenness stands in contrast to the lack of a shared national social imagination.

Residents who were interviewed revealed, for example, that they had not been aware of Kimisagara's designation as an HRZ until after the genesis of the Kigali master plan. Damas, a long-term resident of the area, has spent more than twenty years there. He recounted:

> Before I was at Kabuga [in Kigali]. During the genocide I went to Congo and returned here with my brother. I got some money and bought this plot of land on the hill. They say this is an HRZ and you see this red cross that means "Move out of this place" ' [the term is *towa* in Swahili]. The problem is that they have taken a long time to inform us about this change, and they did not tell us when we have to leave or relocate us, so when your house is partly demolished you cannot renovate it. They won't give you a permit for renovating the house even if your roof is damaged or one metal sheet is loose and falls off.

They don't allow you to replace it, because you are not supposed to repair your house since you have to leave. We suffer too much. One part of our house has the "*towa*" red cross on it, and the other part doesn't have this sign and we don't know why! When we asked the reason, they don't have the answer. One day we went to the meeting where our houses were being discussed. We asked why did they allow us to construct at that place, and they don't have the answer. For sure, we are not against development, but we need compensation and money, and we will go find other affordable places. This is better instead of asking us to leave with nothing. You know the Rwandan proverb "*Inzu n'icyo uririyemo*"— the house is what you eat inside. Here you live in one side of the house, and the other side you rent it or use it as a shop, so you can gain some money to live. We know a bit about the master plan because of a meeting with the authorities, but we need to be involved in different activities that are supposed to be done for us, because you can't say it is development with unhappy people. The big challenge is living with fear of being removed, without knowing exactly when or where you will go, and you can't do anything to renovate your house.[8]

Francine, a tenant who moved to the city more recently, ties her story of possible relocation in the HRZ to other difficulties of life in the capital:

> As long as Kigali changes, life becomes more difficult. This my first year in this place [Kimisagara]. Before, I lived with my elder sister elsewhere. I got pregnant, and we decided to come here with my husband because we could find a cheap house to rent. . . .
>
> I live through informal trading and carry a basket on my head. Sometimes security stops us or takes our goods. You can pass few days in prison and get out with nothing, and you start from zero.
>
> Of course this is an HRZ area. Someone from local authority comes here and puts a red cross on each house. When we ask questions to the authorities, they tell us we are in HRZ area and we have to leave the place. It is difficult for us who don't have money to move out. First of all, we come here to search for jobs and we don't plan to return to rural areas. If it comes to leave this area, we will find another place in this city!

These testimonies from residents of the area provide insights into the constrained lifestyles of the urban poor who live with the precarity of the HRZ. Their modes of life rendered transitional by the HRZ designation, they cannot consider improved hygiene or spatial organization. The residents are also unable to upgrade or repair their dwellings in the HRZ to the extent possible given their limited means. The traditional home maintained at least partially in the informal settlement (with a single story, a threshold and entrance, and bushes separating homes where possible), as well as its resident—perceived as the "disorderly" urban migrant operating in the informal sector, and in every sense portrayed as transient to the new life of the master-planned capital—contrasts starkly with the structure and layout of the model homes prototyped in Kimisagara. The subjects of the new Kigali are reformed residents, who live according to the dictates of spatial hygiene demanded in the city under construction.

Peripheralizing the Central Prison

With roundups of suspected genocidaires after the RPF took power in July 1994, central prisons became particularly visible in the city and town centers around the country, teeming with incarcerated populations. These carceral spaces embody the contradiction between the older order of post-genocide space—what I designate as "brown"—and the "green" ecology of world-class cleanliness and renewed aesthetic order that state elites moved toward after 2003. The prison in post-genocide Rwanda is understood here as an architectural artifact and a problem space through which we can examine transitional dilemmas of the post-genocide period. The central prison is a space of contentious memory, an edifice of what might be thought of as traumatic continuity. For my interlocutors living in Muhima, near the CBD and the 1930 Kigali Central Prison, the prison conjured memories of the colonial period, when Belgian colonizers introduced incarceration. The prison and its counterpart, the communal *cachot*, or less formally organized local detention center, were spaces of incarceration and punishment infused with power and arbitrary punishment. Their persistence was a reminder of colonial rule and the central place of the prison in colonial town planning. Many of my interlocutors felt ambivalent about decommissioning or removing the central prison, a monument to contested collective memory. Some oriented themselves historically and spatially in relation to its startling edifice and the quotidian economy of informal trading that grew up around its walls.

In the aftermath of the genocide, large-scale incarceration and the visibility of prisons in the context of attempted reconciliation were especially salient as problematic spaces, particularly in urban areas. The post-genocide prison as it appears across the country poses a spatial dilemma to and contradicts the official discourse on national unity and reconciliation. Recently, central prisons have been deconcentrated and relocated out of the center of Rwanda's capital and its other main urban areas. I suggest that this is a response to the RPF-led state's need to spatially and discursively differentiate between the extraordinary violence of the genocide and the reconstruction of ordinary crime of the post-genocide period. The project of modernizing urban space—including the space of the prison—is hence also a project of respatializing a new normality through master-planning.

The advent of urban master-planning in Rwanda's capital in the early 2010s coincided with the relocation of prisons from central areas in the city. These prison relocations were the result of many factors including safety concerns and the overcrowding of central prisons. However, the correlation of the re-working of urban space and the resignification of the city's penal spaces also signals a period of moving on, marked through the built environment: a *post*-post-genocide urbanism. By decommissioning or removing prisons from the center of cities, planners, national party officials, and local government leaders made way for new tropes of master-planned urbanism. Prison removal also worked to reorganize the logic of punitive space in the city. It reconfigured pu-nitive space away from a model of spatial order in which governmental power was concentrated in centralized, visible forms of control, and toward a decen-tralized and less visible architecture of power. There are hence newer logics of visibility and space in the reorganization of Kigali, as the comprehensive urban spatial master plan produces its own forms of carceral-capitalist space.

The drive to relocate prisons out of the city center of the city and to dis-pense with the old spatial order occurred just as several prisons in Rwanda experienced fires within the span of a few years. In June 2014 the old Gi-tarama/Muhanga Central Prison was gutted by a fire of mysterious origin, which caused inmates to be relocated.[9] A few weeks later, the Rubavu Cen-tral Prison, on the border with eastern Congo, was hit by an fire that media reports blamed on the Congolese-based Hutu militia FDLR.[10] A fire in the Kigali Central Prison on December 25, 2016,[11] was followed by another fire in Kimironko Prison in Kigali in late March 2017, which affected three thousand inmates.[12] As Rwandans remained mystified by the origins of the fires,[13] the plans to relocate prisons came to fruition around the same time. Noting that most buildings in Kigali lacked proper fire safety systems, a fire insurance of-ficial working in collaboration with the government called for greater regula-tion of prisons, schools, markets, and other "high-risk" areas.[14]

As more than four thousand prisoners were relocated in February 2017 from the Kigali Central Prison—also known as the 1930 Prison, after its colonial-era founding date—to the more distant, "modernized" Mageragere Prison on the outskirts of the capital, newspaper reports chronicled mixed feelings among area residents who witnessed the relocation:

> Some residents near 1930 expressed their disappointment over relocation, but others feel comfortable. Jean Twagiramungu, 33, lives near 1930. He says business has been paralyzed and his sales have dropped. "Inmates and prison guards were potential clients coming to buy in our shops every day. We miss them. Our businesses are not doing well anymore," says Twagiramungu.

Another Kigali resident who was interviewed cited the poor hygiene standards and the push to improve the city's image as key reasons for the relocation:

"It is situated in the middle of the city with high congestion, so we had to re-locate for their safety and to ensure cleanliness of the city while abiding by the prison's international standards," he says. 1930 does not meet the standards, originally intended for only 2,000 inmates, but the number drastically increased to over 50,000 inmates following the 1994 Genocide against the Tutsi, with most of the inmates serving their sentence for their role in the genocide. The awful stench from the prison latrines has been unbearable, but due to the relocation, there is some relief. Oxygen is a little fresh.[15]

Narratives of relocation converged with interventions aimed at improved hygiene. The prison was moved out of sight, and the social networks of informal trading that families of prisoners often relied upon to feed their inmates during regular visits were in turn deemphasized.

Redesigning the Central Market

The contemporary counterpart to the central prison and its architecture of colonial power and genocide history is the urban market in older parts of Kigali. The decentralization of prison sites and the relocation of market sites are framed as modernization projects. Though usually understood to be unrelated, they can be seen as related projects that redefine the spatial organization in Rwanda's urban centers and recalibrate the post-genocide spatial order. As central spaces within key cities are reworked, old markets are closed and relocated, or modernized and kept in place—with greater regulation of informal trading.

The old market (figure 4.2) with its central location and buzzing activity has been seen as an unregulated space of informality, even disorder (*akajagari*). Plans to renew and modernize the markets that provided sustenance and livelihood to populations in older parts of Kigali, such as Nyamirambo and Muhima, thus have affected spaces of trading as well as *quartiers* of habitation. These changes have influenced the health of the old body of the city, and have torn into its social fabric. In 2014, traders in the old Biryogo market were relocated ahead of schedule to a new "modernized" market area, and this disrupted their social networks and trade associations. The market reopened as a new twenty-billion-Rwandan-franc facility named the Kigali City Market, and housed traders who had previously sold their wares in the old city's commercial zone, Quartier Matheus. The new market was then closed to require its occupants to comply with city regulations and security requirements, and reopened in early 2012. A newspaper reported: "Some of the safety

FIGURE 4.2. The old market of Biryogo, Kigali

requirements the building lacked, according to city authorities, included CCTV cameras, walk-through machines, metal detectors and car-check mirrors."[16]

In a 2014 Ministry of Commerce report on the modernization of the country's markets, the market is reconceived as a space not of sociality and trade that serves the local populace, but of display and manufactured authenticity (Republic of Rwanda 2014), much like the neovernacular of "traditional" Rwandan design in the revised master plan. The approach to the market not only is modernized, but caters to the touristic gaze rather than to the local population. Of the large Kimironko market near Remera, popular with both locals and adventurous tourists, the report says:

> We could think of Kimironko market or the market in Musanze having such mixed use. However to become popular with tourists, these markets will have to be redesigned. They should not become just big buildings like the central market in Kigali; instead they could try to emulate a market-place with a

touch of Rwandan flavor. In Mauritius, markets have been designed to emulate the traditional creole style. We could also contemplate a more *"les halles"* type of market structure [Republic of Rwanda 2014: 22–23].

As the "disordered living" of informal traders is increasingly threatened, with many traders becoming itinerant to survive and street traders (*abazungu-zayi*) forced to become mobile to evade regulation (Shearer 2020), the links between securitization and participation become apparent. The "right to the city" (Harvey 2003; Lefebvre 1996), construed as a right to participate in the city's future, is seen as a transgression rather than a norm of urban citizenship. In the process, urban citizenship and the divergent popular narratives associated with it are foreclosed.

Having two central spaces within the old space of cities—the central prison and the market—reformed by closure, relocation, and modernization, has effectively reorganized urban space and disorganized social networks (figure 4.3).

FIGURE 4.3. Traffic near the old bus station of Nyabugogo, Kigali

Patterns of information and livelihood that operated in the center of the city have also been rendered marginal. That these things occurred when the capital was being securitized and spatially reordered is likely more than coincidental. The logic of securitization played a large role in urban spatial reordering when older informal urban space was seen as a security risk.

Michelon (2016) demonstrates that about sixteen grenade attacks took place in Kigali between 2008 and 2013, mostly in older, less regulated areas of the city, including markets. The impulse to order disordered public space—the market, the prison, the informal settlement, the old city—was thus, I posit, written into the nature of post-genocide insecurity in urban areas. This imperative to create order further emphasizes the desire to recalibrate the dynamics of sociality and memory in the post-genocide city by reorganizing its very spatiality.

Preserving the Parliament Building

In its immediate postwar incarnation, post-genocide Kigali—with its ochred roads and its necro-environment strewn with artifacts and residue of genocide and the debris of war—was a "brown" ecology of postwar aftermath and disorder that nonetheless exposed truths spatially, and offered gradual pathways to coexistence. As the new RPF government has sought to reorder this post-genocide space, its focus has been on a "green" ecology of postconflict renewal—an ecology of national regeneration. The juxtaposition of multiple spatial ecologies, as we have seen in this chapter, speaks to multiple narratives in the city, and manifests itself as different orderings of space in and around the capital and its secondary towns and cities. In their green regenerative ecology, state elites reimagine the nation as a pristine space of return, a national community that can be healed and regenerated through a renewed order of space and through various other programs of renewal. I suggest that the preoccupation with security (*umutekano*) as a mode of ordering the disorderly has been central to this approach. In this final section of the chapter, I end with the Parliament building, which I present as a preserved site of complex memory that holds significance for diverse groups of Rwandans, and which endures as a singular remnant of Rwanda's storied past, an organic pedagogical milieu, and a site of cohabitation of different historic periods.

During my research, I frequently passed by the Parliament building in Kigali, and remarked on the continuity kept visible in its imposing edifice. I visited the venerable building several times for interviews, and was struck by its symbolism in bridging old and new iterations of Rwandan history, by the bullet holes preserved in one corner of its stone facade, and by the grand view of the new Kigali Convention Center complex nearby. The building hosted a permanent installation on the history of the Rwanda Patriotic Army's "war of liberation,"—an exhibition run jointly by the Institute of National Museums of Rwanda (INMR) and the National Commission for the Fight against Genocide (CNLG). On visiting the exhibition in mid-2019, I walked through its multiple rooms, taking time to consider how the war the rebel force sought to turn into national history was also perceived as an invasion and occupation in the context of the extreme Hutu nationalism of the early 1990s.

"What do they say in the museum?" my taxi driver friend asked me as we drove past the Parliament building one afternoon. "How do they tell the story of the genocide?" My friend's question could be considered in many ways. There was also much at stake in the simple act of raising this multivalent question in the midst of Kigali traffic, and in the shadow of the Parliament building, where so much of the violence had unfolded. The retelling of the past in such a contested context is necessarily an act of interpretation.

In many ways, the old Parliament building stands as Rwanda's symbolic center, connecting traumatic temporalities of this changing nation-state. The building is a reminder of the old Kigali and the RPF war of liberation during the 1994 genocide, as well as a statement of continuity between the aims of the "New Rwanda" and older forms of the nation-state. As the seat of the Conseil Nationale de Developpement (CND) from 1982 to 1994, and then the Transitional National Assembly (TNA) from 1994 to 2003, the Parliament building has witnessed several epochs of the Rwandan state's arguably uneasy relationship with representative democracy.

That the official exhibition on the RPF's war to liberate Kigali is located at the Parliament building is thus significant. The installation is narrative and pictorial. It contains audio-visual representations of the conflict, such as the sounds of artillery shelling Kigali, and the speeches of General (and later President) Paul Kagame. Letters and speeches are prominently displayed on the walls: statements of former President Habyarimana, including his apparent disparagement of the Arusha Accords (which set the basis for an end to hostilities amid the civil war between his government and the RPA, which had been ongoing since 1990); the history of hate radio in Rwanda as opposed to that of Radio Muhabura of the liberating RPF forces; the complicity of the French in militarily aiding the hardline Rwandan regime and providing a cover for the Rwandan Armed Forces (FAR); and images of foreign supporters of the RPF in exile. At the end of the exhibition, one is asked to visit the roof of the Parliament building, where there is an encased map of the strategy taken by RPF forces in the days before the capture of Kigali. I end with this example to raise the question of the persistence of divergent spatial narratives over time in a city with multiple pasts.

Rwanda's Parliament building exemplifies the preservation of aspects of older built space that maintain the grounds for a history of urban space in multiple registers. Its iconic stone facade, painted in yellow and white like a palimpsest, presents multiple narrative layers to its various publics, introducing interpretive complexity onto a landscape being erased through redevelopment.

As spaces of complex social memory are relocated and reorganized, the securitization of urban space increasingly peripheralizes modes of life and ways of remembering the past that run contrary to the official narrative. For example, the modernization of prison facilities and their relocation from central urban areas is effectively a form of peripheralization. It involves not only the space of the prison but the vast social life it supports. The prisoners' families, who are mostly poor and reliant on urban social networks for support and on popular markets for supply, are left without central social provision. An question of urban modernization and economic progress hence comes to involve post-genocide spatiality and its social entailments, as well as the peripheralization of the poor and the marginalization of their genuine right to the city, with its multiple narratives and pasts.

As this chapter has shown, top-down spatial master-planning in a context of a complex and contested postconflict history sediments and erases alternative narratives and pasts—or what the historian Ann Laura Stoler (2016) would call "occluded histories." In the next chapters I focus on the effects of dispossession and displacement on a sense of place in the city, in relation to urban transformation on still unsettled terrain. I move outward from the city's center and its informal settlements to its urban periphery and rural model villages, and contextualize the urban question in Rwanda as one that cuts across multiple scales. A local sense of place has situated urban and peri-urban residents who now struggle to remain where they are, questioning their stake in urban transformation as a shared national imaginary.

Memory and *Gacaca* in Rwanda

The *inkiko-gacaca* transitional justice courts (*gacaca* literally means "in the grass") were set up by the government of Rwanda to try lower-level crimes after the genocide in Rwanda against the country's Tutsi minority. *Gacaca* courts ran from 2002 to 2012. I wrote these three poems in 2004 while I was conducting field research in Rwanda on the *gacaca* and transitional justice system.

Silent Witnesses

In the focus of concentration sometimes, a single blade of grass can seem
Larger than the moment;
A hundred thousand green-browned moments
are silent witnesses.
In the courtroom in the grass, they are as present as
sixty bodies shifting uncomfortably on broken benches who
listen forth the proceedings of the day.

Who will bring the witnesses forward?
In memorials empty of living memory, broken bones and
Skulls laid out in bare lines that cannot speak
Are spoken for by the downturned eyes
Of yellow flowers ochred with evening's dust
and burnt out carcasses of metal strewn on winding roads;
the quietude of lake shores whose uneasy stillness
Drowns memory and sound in murky waters.
And who can silence the voice of the trees?

Only hope cannot be captured out loud
As it swings its nascent limbs from branch to branch
Forcing dulled eyes to glance up, causing commotion below.

In the Grass, Failing to Remember

I cannot forgive this woman;
Truth hangs corpse-like behind this man.
We have come too far
And go on we must
Two unfinished handshakes,
The empty anarchy of a silent crowd—
Breaths drawn in evening's fervor.

He killed my brother
My father and my husband were slain.
Too long have been the years,

Too many to pass yet ahead.
Intermingled, three hundred dusty souls.
Trees watch the ever gleaming hope of lost yesterdays
Light plays
Forgotten parodies of tomorrow

How far can we come
Before we have been too long gone?

Is this what it is to watch the theater of destiny?

Nine turned heads, gaze elegies into grassed soil
Red-ochre and consecrated
Five minutes, then ten
Two lone figures stand, one head down
One burning holes in pink perforated uniform
Sweat-laden, there opposite.

We are here, "in the grass." And listening audibly, ever present
we are the grass.
I, scribe, seemingly self-obliterating, scratch notes onto
Lined parchment and stare where
Elephants have 'ere tread.

This man, then: he will return to the prison?
I made a mistake. It was not him, but another . . .
Testimony wrapped with the incontinence of memory
flows forth to wry smiles and upturned foreheads
You lie? That is one year for you, no fifteen months.
Bring forward another. Or wait, prisoner, do you forgive?
Muffled Chinese whispers, conquered hush.
No guilt-free spectators but accomplices in drama
like billowing leaves, swaying.

Two mute silhouettes, then one silent voice flickers faintly:
I will forgive.
And You, woman, will you forgive?
I will forgive.
One partial handshake and clapping.

To re-member, to re-concile. To unearth cold bones and meaning and walk away
Into the yet unknown.

Two Generations

I cannot remember; I can't.
How does one remember?

Two figures: held together in silence, set apart by years
look at each other, beholding.
One, the worn eyelids of an aging man; the other,
son born to another, heir to a different destiny.
Après du genocide; the first fluttering of reclaimed tomorrows.

Darkness envelops outstretched hands as from prose bleeds poetry,
memory sifts through raindrops and falls down as rain
as heavily beaten corrugated tin roof and cups left out in the wet,
spill over rivulets, down stone steps
and trodden murram path, moving outwards.

Only time's arrow travels beyond the small house,
down each *colline* and up the next in a wavy nonlinearity;
Each hill dared to find space where it might stretch its back
in a nest that had not been sliced by that straight and unwavering path of grief.
Finding none.

Instead, time moves and fractures:
once at the widow's dwellings and then at that of her neighbor,
whence small arrows shoot up into the sky, merge into stars and stream once more
onto the eyes of a man full of a tarnished sense of hope,
and one younger, moving forwards whilst looking backwards.

Still sitting there, hands intertwined, trying to remember,
to carry forth the past and strip it away from history,
leaving still space for the living.

PART 2

Minor Acts

5

Political Abandonment

In February 2019 a group of residents gathered along the Kigali-Rwamagana road in the Kabuga cell of Rusororo Sector to hear the outcome of their case in the Gasabo District Court. They were part of a group of more than seven hundred property owners in the informal settlement of Bannyahe, located in Gasabo District, in the affluent locale of Nyarutarama, where their area is officially referenced as "Kangondo," its administrative designation. The case concerned the planned expropriation of their settlement and compensation to owners, who were offered the option to purchase apartments in the Busanza area of Kanombe Sector, where a project was being constructed for the relocation of property-owning households from the Bannyahe settlement. The project sits several kilometers beyond the Kigali International Airport. The first phase of construction consisted of approximately 1,040 apartments located in several three-story blocks on seven hectares of land. The remainder of the twenty-two hectares awaits future relocation projects.

Refusing to play the part of compliant citizens, these owners had argued that their possession of land title and the stipulations of the Expropriation Law (2007, revised in 2015, Government of Rwanda 2015a) entitled them to cash compensation. The Bannyahe owners had rejected relocation as an option, as well as the attendant offer to trade equivalent expropriation payments for small apartments located far from their current homes. They had taken their case to the courts. Ten months later, in December 2019, the residents would begin tearing down their houses, in a form of defiant yet compliant domicide,[1] when their case for appeal failed. In using the frontiers of place and the home as modes of localized resistance against urban displacement, they enacted a "material resistance" (Simone 2022: 131) and galvanized collective agency in seeking to remain.

FIGURE 5.1. The erstwhile Bannyahe settlement

The Bannyahe case has become contentious for owners and has captured the imagination of the local press, as well as members of the Rwandan diaspora, largely because the residents refused to capitulate to the demands of municipal government. This localized defiance marked its divergence from earlier cases of expropriation and demolition in the center of Kigali. Bannyahe had become synonymous with its designation as Kigali's largest informal settlement, a space antithetical to the utopia of orderly designs in the capital, and one that inverted this order. Administratively designated as part of the Kangondo I and II and Kibiraro I areas, the Bannyahe settlement land area slopes down from just behind the main road that used to run through Nyarutarama to the marshes of the lower Kibiraro I area (figure 5.1). At the time of my research, portions of the settlement had been designated as high risk zones (HRZs) due to the gradient and the risk of flooding and possible landslides, which also made it impossible for owners in the area to make changes to their homes while under threat of expropriation. The naming of the settlement is important to this story: the name Bannyahe—which means "Where do they go to defecate?"—has been deemed detrimental to the city's image by municipal officials. At the same time, residents of the settlement have claimed the name as a signifier to designate the lack of access to sanitation. They ask of each other, of local officials, of the municipality, and ultimately of the state:

"Where do we defecate?" Likewise, the term *akajagari* has dual valence: it is used as a signifier of disorder and disorderliness by state officials, and has been appropriated by residents of settlements across the city as a reference to urban aspirations and the absence of urban services in their areas. As a signifier of a transgressive political order that underlies Kigali's clean facade, *akajagari* thus subverts the appearance of order.

As waves of demolition and relocation moved through older parts of Kigali, residents of informal settlements often appropriated the term *akajagari* in resistance.[2] The settlement of *Kiyovu cy'abakene* (Poor People's Kiyovu), founded during the colonial period for urban workers who served in the wealthier, formal parts of the city and populated thereafter through successive waves of urbanization, was demolished in 2007 to make way for urban development that has yet to keep pace with the city's ambitions. Deemed "unplanned" by state authorities, informal settlements such as Bannyahe are visual, social, and spatial anomalies amid the aesthetics of order and the state utopia, and are increasingly endangered spaces. Housing more than 60 percent of the city's residents in 2012 (NISR 2012), Kigali's informal settlements have been formed by the various ways in which residents returned to the city after the genocide in the absence of adequate formal built space, and the increased urban migration from rural areas that has accompanied rapid urban growth since that time. Informal settlements also demonstrate the urban aspirations of lower-income Rwandans who move to the city, and the persistence of poverty in both urban and rural spaces (Michelon 2016).

In relation to umutekano, which designates the state apparatus of security in the immediate aftermath of the genocide, and the securitization of the everyday in the post-genocide period, akajagari signals a different kind of order. The "unplanned" informal settlement becomes a crucible in which questions of ordering and urban improvement are conceptualized, and it is here that the future of Kigali as a "world-class" capital is enacted through the ruptures of planning, expropriation, and displacement. I suggest in this chapter that umutekano and akajagari are intimate enemies. The fear of disorder is both spatial and social, with the informal settlement constituted as a space deemed impenetrable to the state's gaze, and to the ordering deemed necessary to keep potentially disorderly subjects in check. Insofar as the state's fear of disorder was crystallized during the post-genocide period, umutekano and akajagari are oppositional but interdependent sociopolitical metaphors of life in the changing city.

In the current phase of urban master-planning, security remains a motivating concern and is manifest in the sociospatial drive to reorder the city, with a particular focus on areas of impenetrability such as informal settlements.

Exploring the city's changing spatial order, this chapter delves into the "unplanned" informal settlement as a target of ordering and, in most cases, elimination. Urban planning in this context is not just a technology that reshapes the city's aesthetics, but one that justifies and enables security incursions into spaces deemed to be "out of place" (Douglas 2003) in the post-genocide spatial order. More than a question of security, urban evictions of "unplanned" settlements signal the abandonment of the process of urban inclusion in the city and in the reformulated polity.[3] It is ultimately this kind of political abandonment of the project of inclusion at the level of the polity that I interrogate through examining place-based politics about contention over rights to remain.

The practice of umutekano also concerns questions about who participates in the future of the city in all its stages, from planning to habitation. State security practice, generalized at this time as widespread securitization, speaks to a fundamental question about the "right to the city" as a shared space after conflict. Such a material right to shared space after conflict engages but exceeds the Lefebvrian question of the ability to circulate and re-create in urban space, and cuts to a core underlying materialist question of the role of the urban in projects of repair: the urban as material and imaginative space for the nation after conflict. In the context of the informal settlement, such engagement involves the right to remain in the city and the recognition of the role of *place* in providing affective and physical mooring for projects of repair through quotidian encounters and possibilities of longer-term engagement. As the nation's symbolic center, and as an urban commons in practice, open to different forms of habitation, spatial practice, and socioeconomic activity, the city is an important marker of the possibilities of conciliation in shared space. It is through this articulation of postconflict repair as a material project tied together through the city as its symbolic core and material terrain that I posit that repair cannot and should not be confined to spaces outside the urban. In this sense, rights to postconflict urban space require a reckoning with questions of distribution and coexistence that are bound up with the city as a material space, central to the geographic, political, and imaginative futures of the polity.

From the stabilization of acute insecurity to the quotidian policing of chronic securitization, it is in this context of urban repair that umutekano needs to be reconsidered as an operating practice and operative sociopolitical metaphor in daily urban life. Ongoing urban securitization makes crisis in the city a chronic condition, one that preempts participation in national urban futures for many as well as the coexistence of diverse sociospatial orders. The so-called unplanned settlement haunts Kigali as an animated specter that hangs over the master-planned ambitions of the capital. This idea that specters and hauntings preside over everyday urban life—present in what Simone (2010) terms "city-ness"—is an important analytic for emergent urbanism in Rwanda. Jacques Derrida's (1994) concept of "hauntology" and the spectral are useful in this regard as descriptors of the fragmentary remains of the past left on the terrain of the present. This hauntology is acutely present in Kigali today, as the old city is being dredged up through master-planning, a material tool of urban exorcism. Akajagari also haunts elite aspirations for the capital, and residents in the city's remaining informal settlements seemingly acquire new potency as agents of a transgressive urbanism as they move through the city to their "unplanned" areas, threatening disorder.

The idea of disorderliness or the "out of place" (Douglas 2003) is thus a complicated one in contemporary Kigali. Disorderliness, itinerancy, and unplanned movement can be seen as practices and performances of contestation that unsettle the disciplining order of state practice and the state's aspirations to fixed, ordered spaces and orderly citizens. If the informal settlement is a city specter, however, it is also a calculable and exploited source of stored value. As the master plan rezones urban land, it re-creates the area of the informal settlement as an attractive untapped zone for investment. The "unplanned" areas in the capital therefore become vectors for urban capitalization. In this way, the ordered renderings of umutekano are pitted against disorderly, impenetrable, and unpredictable spatial praxis in the "unplanned" settlement.

Fear of the Master Plan

At midday during an early visit to the lower part of the Bannyahe settlement (formally and formerly termed Kibiraro I) a surprising number of people were around in the vicinity of a small shop, on the small porches of a few houses, and amid the winding, uneven alleyways. I came across a group of six or seven men seated on low wooden benches on a porch, drinking sorghum beer and talking animatedly—just enough people for a natural focus group. After I bought them another round of beer, our conversation veered from the nature of their life in Bannyahe and the amount of time they had been living there, to forms of tenancy and property ownership in the area. Eventually we began to talk openly about the Kigali spatial master plan, whose spectrality loomed over the daily lives of residents in the lower reaches of the settlement. "When you got here, we thought you were from the City of Kigali and were working to remove us from this area," one of the men remarked. "We don't know much about the master plan, but we fear its results, and what it will mean for us."

As I left the gathering, I reflected upon the affective imprints of the master plan—part realized, part in blueprint form—and upon the ability of urban poor residents in settlements like Bannyahe to imagine viable futures, and the uncertainty it conjured. For many of the residents, the planning was "something done by experts and technical officials high up, not us," as another resident termed it—an exercise of performing and constructing authority with tangible effects on the affective geography of the lives and livelihoods of urban poor. The urban master plan, revised and translated into granular reality, has in its various incarnations been a documented utopia: a combination of fantasy and futurity whose slowly materializing presence in the city and in policy discourse, in the clearances of "unplanned" areas, and in investment allocations wields tangible effects on the spatial reproduction of the urban poor.

In short, the materiality of utopia still in the process of becoming has its own potent effects; it is a vivified and performative document that haunts and generates activity. Blueprints, like other planning tools, are more than objects that divide and render orderly; they possess affective potential in disordering residents' lives, particularly in areas that they render "unplanned" through assemblages of policy discourse. In her account of objects and materiality in creating affective geographies in postwar Northern Cyprus, Yael Navaro-Yashin (2012) dissects the construction of the material technologies of establishing governmental order. Maps, plans, dividing lines, practices like surveying, and generated reports leave material imprints on the terrain they seek to concretize and reestablish; these spatial practices speak to the role of objects and materiality in grounding collective memory and producing group affect in postwar terrain.

What is particularly salient for the reconstruction of Kigali is that the master plan is an affective document that produces certain suspicions, unwieldy emotions, fears, fantasies, imaginaries, and domains of authority through its conceptualization and drafting. Such talk of the master plan conditions its impeding materialization before the translation from blueprint to concretized reality has fully been realized. In the shadow of the strong authority of the central state and the municipal bureaucracy in Kigali, it is further productive to consider forms of rumor and suspicion, and their circulations among various forms of the public—for instance, urban poor in Bannyahe, who worry and plan for uncertain futures amid partial information. Faced with this asymmetry of information, there follows a game of catch-up in which incomplete and contradictory news is passed along and causes material plans to be hatched, strategies of survival to be drawn up, and rumor to circulate further. Talk of the master plan, along with material representations of planning authority, thus has affective anticipatory impact and material consequence for the personal lives of the constantly rearranged urban poor.

In the rest of this chapter, I relate the question about the spatial reproduction of the informal settlement to the idea of home and the question of the abandoned home over time. I examine the struggles of residents to remain, with particular attention to the case of the Bannyahe settlement during my field research in 2018 and 2019. I situate these struggles to remain in the city within larger questions of the political stakes of return and restitution for displacement that have operated in the post-genocide city. I focus next on the image of the abandoned home and tie it to larger questions of inclusion, repair, and recourse to political abandonment as the project of inclusion falters at the city gates. I define "political abandonment" here in terms of the abrogation of meaningful engagement with the project of recognizing complex identity and working to repair the city as a shared material space.

Situating the Abandoned Home

To understand the Bannyahe case, we first must explore earlier iterations of national history and struggles over belonging in Rwanda's capital, marked symbolically by the abandoned home, and longer genealogies of displacement and recompense in the capital. This history allows us to delve more deeply into the use of abandonment in urban struggles against displacement and dispossession today, and to understand abandonment and dispossession as a potent nexus it in the aftermath of genocide.

Internally displaced persons crowded into Rwanda's capital after the genocide, as did refugees returning from the diaspora. Many were returning to a city that lacked the capacity to hold them, with houses that had been abandoned by their owners and an urban infrastructure in disarray. The latter group of refugees—those returning from exile, termed "old caseload" refugees—comprised returnees from countries bordering Rwanda, particularly Uganda, where the RPA drew much of its core force, but also other countries in East and Central Africa, and as well as Europe and North America. Many of these old caseload returnees had been generationally exiled from Rwanda as victims or children of anti-Tutsi violence that had occurred in the late 1950s. The independence movement from 1959 to 1961 saw the advent of a Hutu-led "social revolution" (Newbury 1988) that eventually brought Gregoire Kayibanda to power as president of a majoritarian government led by his party, Parmehutu. This moment of victory and long-awaited emancipation from colonial rule and Tutsi chieftainship for the ethnic majority Hutu was equally a moment of dispossession, exile, and violence for groups of Tutsis, including Paul Kagame's family, who fled when he was an infant from Gitarama to neighboring regions in Uganda. Violence against Tutsi groups was repeated with another convulsion of the central state—the 1973 coup that saw the overthrow of the Kayibanda government and the installation of the MRND party's Juvenal Habyarimana and the Second Rwandan Republic.

These previous struggles over place and belonging can be connected to contemporary dislocations in Kigali as the central pivot of a remade Rwandan homeland. Rwandan statemaking is an ongoing, iterative, and continuous process punctuated and punctured by braided histories of liberation and loss. The country's foundational moments draw as much from ideologies of ethnic liberation and majoritarian rule as they do from narratives of loss, dispossession, and abandonment. Behind the officially imposed veneer of unity, contemporary narratives of Rwandan identity are inherently oppositional and dialectical. At the core of these layered narratives of the state are sedimented questions of return and belonging. To this end, the home forcefully vacated and left abandoned is the center of an establishment of place in the capital city. The abandoned home in this context helps us excavate analytically the ways that home constitutes place in relation to questions of abandonment, dislocation, and restitution.

Abandonment and dispossession both have historical and theoretical resonance for the post-genocide period, which is one of ongoing national transition as well as of transformation in modes of producing space for daily life for many urban residents. From its first incarnation in the form of the abandoned home of Tutsis leaving in 1959 and then in 1973 to escape from the anti-Tutsi violence that accompanied the birth of the majoritarian nation-state, abandonment threads itself through histories and questions of return, repatriation, and repair. The old caseload refugees' right of return was a central point of discussion in the Arusha Accords, signed in 1993 by a beleaguered Juvenal Habyarimana, who at the time was engaged in a protracted civil war with the exiled RPA, which was entering what was then Umutara province (and is now Northern Province, with its capital at Nyagatare). This concern about rights of return and rights over territory is seen in other conflicts; most notably, it was a key sticking point in the Israeli-Palestinian negotiations, and at stake in the aftermath of World War II.

Necropolitical questions of abandonment—in this case, leaving people to die—swirled around attenuated humanitarian discourses during the peak of the genocide in 1994 and the failure of meaningful international intervention. Medical humanitarianism shifted from failed intervention to palliation and containment as the international aid apparatus rushed to remediate the crisis of internally displaced persons and "new caseload" refugees who had largely moved toward the Zairean border with Goma, with some returning later in the decade as the RPF war in the Congo reached its peak in the early 2000s.

As returning refugees from the "new caseload" began to repopulate urban areas, claims over abandoned property became central to the reconstitution of possession in the capital. In 2004 the Rwandan Ministry of Justice was operating under a new constitutional dispensation as the Third Rwandan Republic, or the "New Rwanda." When it issued its notice on abandoned property, it not only set forth a mechanism and procedure for rehabilitating and repurposing homes, land, and buildings after the genocide, but also adjudicated what constituted "abandonment" in the built environment, establishing a statute of limitation and modes of proof. Law 28/2004, Relating to the Management of Abandoned Property, decreed that the state would manage properties determined to have been abandoned from July 19, 1994, to March 1, 2000. Coinciding with the period in which "new caseload" refugees had not yet begun their return, and with the ongoing conflict in Zaire / Democratic Republic of the Congo, abandonment of property in the capital most frequently affected Hutus who had left during the genocide and before the RPA took control of Kigali. Musahara and Huggins (2005) report on the reform of land law in this postconflict context, where abandonment and return often resulted in land-sharing requirements that in turn generated further disputes over land and property ownership:

> Land disputes are increasingly common in Rwanda, and . . . can erode social relationships. Many people consider land disputes to be at the heart of most conflicts between households. A number of organizations have estimated that between 80–95% of disputes operating at a district level reported to administrators are centered on land. The National Unity and Reconciliation Council, which conducted consultations across the country, found that land disputes are "the greatest factor hindering sustainable peace" (Musahara and Huggins 2005: 275).

This corroborates research on *gacaca* in rural Rwanda in which I participated from 2002 to 2004, which found that a large proportion of reported claims revolved around property and its restitution in various forms (Honeyman et al. 2004).

Abandonment in the material sense of a home, a building, and areas of the built environment was thus etched onto the physical landscape of the capital after its takeover by the RPA. Entwined around material abandonment is abandonment in an affective sense, involving the emotional effects of withdrawal of care and attention on Rwandans impacted by the destruction of the country's material and social infrastructures through genocide and civil war. This attritional logic of neglect has been felt powerfully inside the country, and it has been a core part of the Rwandan experience from the moment of the genocide into the present moment of urban transformation. Abandonment is hence an extended moment in the experience of loss and destruction that has characterized historical violence, communal dispossession, and the question of remedies—or the repair of what remains reparable—in the many contexts that characterize collective experience in Rwanda. To the extent that abandonment constitutes a "structure of feeling" (Williams 1977) or a national "common sense," it is an affective disposition that conditions current attempts at transformation. In turn, struggles to remain in the city embody these forms of abandonment and generate multiple politics of dispossession. I suggest that political abandonment of inclusion in the urbanizing polity signals the frontier of debates on politics and the political in Rwanda today.

Expropriation and "Planned" Relocations

It is in the "unplanned" settlement that the built sphere of the informal and the regulatory frontier of the irregular merge in the capital, with emphasis on the illegitimacy of informal dwellings in Kigali as both unmodern and irregular according to planning regulation. Urban dwellers of informal settlements must navigate both spatial and regulatory exclusions.[4] Their settlements are spaces mapped by GIS software and earmarked through master-planned zoning for expropriation and demolition. Large areas of informal settlement in Kigali have been rendered additionally problematic by the language of environmental protection and degradation, and by categorizations of risk and vulnerability made by officials (Wakhungu et al. 2010). As a result, the livelihoods of large numbers of residents in these areas who live and work in the city have been rendered precarious, with compensation uncertain for many living in HRZs. As low-income human settlements and the preservation of nature compete for legitimacy and space, the "bare life" (Agamben 2020) of urban residents living in informal settlements designated as HRZs is put at risk not only by flooding and landslides in hilly areas, but by the impulse to modernize the city through reconditioned wetland parks and urban greening.

As laws and regulations in urban areas displace and dispossess increasing numbers of low-income residents in Kigali today, many are forced to reconsider their precarious livelihood and dwelling options, and struggle to remain within the city's boundaries. Rwanda's Expropriation Law, promulgated in 2007 and revised in 2015, was first applied to the demolition of Ubumwe Cell (Kiyovu cy'abakene), where residents were given the alternative of relocation to the

Batsinda housing estate in 2007–8.[5] Of the 362 households expropriated, 120 chose to relocate to Batsinda, where the unit cost of approximately US$6,000 for a home far exceeded their expropriation compensation. In fact, Wakhungu and coauthors (2010) reported that loans offered by the Rwanda Housing Bank were difficult to accept due to their stringent terms and the relocated families' shifting, precarious options for livelihood. The distance between Ubumwe's central location and the peri-urban locale of Batsinda in Gasabo District, with its attendant travel costs and the restrictive design of its small units, also posed problems for relocated residents. However, the pace of expropriation has since been quietly questioned by developers, architects, and planners working in Kigali. Several of them remarked to me on the length of time between government expropriation of areas like Ubumwe and Kimicanga and their redevelopment by investors: "Much of Ubumwe is still lying vacant, with no development," one professional commented, adding that the city had a problem attracting investment commensurate with the pace of expropriation.

Unlike these previous cases of expropriation and demolition, the Bannyahe settlement's expropriation proved to be a limit case (or meaningful outlier) of urban contestation, testing authoritarian modes of governing the city at its margins. Sited on valuable real estate, the settlement had been earmarked to be replaced by a US$56 million high-end development by a Rwandan-Finnish investment consortium that was working according to the zoning requirements of the Kigali master plan.[6] As I visited with and interviewed residents in various parts of the Bannyahe settlement, I found that ideas of "good citizenship" were being foisted upon low-income dwellers of the city's informal settlements. They were to cooperate with the master plan's requirements so that the city might benefit from higher-value forms of use and the greater "public good." As 728 property owners in Bannyahe organized themselves and took the District of Gasabo in the City of Kigali to court from 2017 to 2019,[7] they defied norms of cooperation and compliance, and contested the means by which their expropriation had been handled by district authorities. The property owners wanted adequate compensation for expropriation, instead of relocation to an alternative site where they were given the option to purchase a share of apartments in lieu of their cash claims. In this case, the law seemed to represent an avenue of appeal through which property owners in the settlement could challenge expropriation on procedural grounds and claim to their right to remain, even if they could not openly and collectively challenge the political vision of Kigali's spatial transformation in the public realm.

I made multiple visits to the Bannyahe settlement between August 2018 and February 2019 and conducted interviews with approximately forty residents:

a mixture of property owners and tenants deliberately selected to represent all sections of the settlement (Kangondo I and II and Kibiraro I). To collect additional information on local experiences with the legal case underway, some interviews were also arranged using snowball techniques with property owners and longer-term residents of the settlement. Additional interviews were conducted with government officials, NGO workers, and development partners working on informality in Kigali. Further information was gathered from local newspapers and through attendance at sessions of the court case before it was dismissed in early 2019.

At the time of my research in 2018 and 2019, Bannyahe had more than 1,600 households (estimates ranged up to 2,300 households) and was divided into three administrative areas: Kangondo I and II, and Kibiraro I. A main set of market streets occupied the highest parts of Kangondo and then descended into medina-like mazes of small streets and alleyways with single-storied mud and concrete houses and occasional shops. The gradient grew increasingly steep toward the bottom of the area, which then linked to an access road near the portion of Bannyahe known as Kibiraro I. Wetlands and marshes were located below the boundaries of this area, and residents often fetched water from there when the water supply to communal taps was intermittent. The area contained three health posts, a number of schools, and at least two market areas, as Kibiraro I also included small market streets. Various reaches of the settlement farther out had small churches, mostly Protestant and Pentecostal. Income-generating groups, such as cooperatives, were evidence of a strong social fabric and collective life.

Most residents of Kibiraro I were tenants. Property owners held multiple dwellings in the area; some lived on site and others outside the settlement as absentee landlords. Rents ranged from less than Rwf 30,000 a month (US$32) to more than Rwf 150,000 a month (US$162) for the most expensive housing. Many residents in the lower areas of Kibiraro I were unemployed, and most were underemployed. They found it difficult to afford the rent while tending to the other expenses of trying to maintain a foothold in the city. It became apparent in the course of interviews that residents had moved to the settlement from different areas of the city and beyond: from Muhanga and Rusizi, as well as from informal settlements that had been subject to demolition and displacement of residents in earlier years. All these residents sought to remain in the city, close to existing livelihoods and employment opportunities, especially given the costs and uncertainties of moving elsewhere.

According to an organization that worked in the area, the Bannyahe community has been divided over relocation and compensation. Over the course of interviews in all three of the settlement's sections, it became apparent that most of the tenant-residents in Kibiraro I were "praying for relocation" to Busanza. So said the organization's leader, even though according to the Expropriation Law they had no legitimate claim to apartments offered in lieu of compensation by municipal authorities. Many tenants in the settlement faced precarious futures in the city due to increasing costs of living, and several had already begun to leave as the legal case progressed, leaving their empty houses behind. I chose to focus primarily on resident property owners, because they constituted the activist subpopulation in the settlement and faced the greatest potential monetary losses from the expropriation. Over the course of multiple visits, resident property owners of Kangondo I and II in the Bannyahe settlement revealed their reluctance to move because of the losses they would incur from relocation to an area far from the city center, where apartment units were smaller, which precluded or limited their rental prospects.

Claims over valuation might be characterized on the basis of my case studies and interviews as forms of circumscribed contestation, or politically feasible forms of contestation. They were enabled by the law and its procedures; in effect, the law offered an alternative to more overt forms of urban dissent that involved politics and policy. Property owners in Kangondo I and II, who had land title papers, said in interviews that they did not want to leave, but instead wanted to negotiate their claims and make their case.

Two interviews conducted in late 2018 illustrate these arguments.

CASE I: KANGONDO II

Located in a side alley down a set of steep steps, the home of Mr. K and his younger wife Mme. E was large but somewhat dilapidated, with stone floors, glass windows, and a sofa set and table in the salon. Mr. K first spoke about the history of his tenure in Kangondo: "I am from Kacyiru and have lived my whole life in Kigali; relocating is not an option for me. Where would I go?" Having lived in Kangondo for over eighty years, he was nostalgic:

> This place [Bannyahe] has changed a lot over time. It started as a place for farmers who had cattle, and this was their plot. I lived up the hill, and later on I moved farther downhill. This started as my father's plot of land and I inherited it. People started coming to this area in the 1980s, but at first there were very few. Many people started to come later on, after 1994, from different areas to buy land, as it was cheap. For Rwf 20,000 [approximately US$22] you could get a small plot here in 1994. After the genocide, a plot sold for Rwf 100,000 [US$110].

The discussion with Mr. K and Mme. E became animated as the relocation case pending with the district of Gasabo was brought up. Mme E. offered to bring her papers and legal documents to demonstrate her claims. Sifting through land titles and correspondence regarding the government determination of land value, she remarked on how the value of houses to be expropriated in this area was determined.

> We have our own house and other houses for rent on this plot of land. We are not happy with how the value was determined for our property. For example, the windows have metal frames, but they put the value as timber rather than metal. The assessors did not include metal doors and the timber roof in their calculations. This house has four rooms and a sitting room, but they did not include the full size of the house and the tiles on the floor outside, and other elements that are missing in the valuation. They valued our total property at Rwf 16 million [US$ 17,297].
>
> Before this case was launched, a private buyer came and offered us Rwf 30 million [US$32,432], but we were not interested, as this offer was too low. So we rejected it. We rent out some houses in this compound—we have six other houses on this plot—but when the valuation came out, it was for only Rwf 16 million [US$17,297]. We were told that if you are not satisfied, employ a private appraiser, produce an alternative valuation, and bring it to us.

Mme. E showed me other letters she and her husband had received, and her original land title. She showed that only two of their six houses were included in the official valuation, and that when they had written to complain, the district responded that since they had not employed a private appraiser, the government concluded that they had agreed to the official valuation. According to the district, its decision could not be changed. She showed me the national land center receipt, her land title document, and a letter from Akarere ya Gasabo (District of Gasabo).

> We were offered one house in Busanza in exchange for our plot and six houses. This apartment has three rooms and is valued at Rwf 35 million [US$37,838]. We would have to pay Rwf 19 million [US$20,541] in addition to that amount to get that house in Busanza. We don't know where to get this money, and would have to take it from them as a loan. In addition, we would have no rental properties to pay back this loan.
>
> The amounts we can charge now for rents have been reduced, because tenants have left. . . . If we have to move, we can't leave Kigali because we have lived here our whole life. We can move around Kigali and its suburbs, to farm and live.

She ended by referring to the master plan: "We don't know much about the Kigali master plan, but we are told it is in the public's interest and has to be implemented."

FIGURE 5.2. A well-kept living room in Bannyahe

CASE 2: KANGONDO I

Mrs. M has lived in the area for a long time and owns a large house with a spacious courtyard behind several shops. Her house was well-kept, with a television, plush sofa set, and carpet in the living room (figure 5.2). An adjoining dining room had a full dining table and drapes on the windows. She rented out several rooms leading off a nearby corridor. Mrs. M was born in Gacuriro, Kigali, in 1952, and got married before moving to Kangondo in 1962. Her husband was also born in Kigali. They have been living in the settlement since 1969, and were among the first families there. "There were about three households here at first," she said, "and there were only bushes in the area. First, we stayed uphill, and then we moved further down later on. There were no people here at that time."

During my visits, she continued:

People started moving to this area around 1986, and before 1994 there were only a few people here. I don't know where people came from, but plots of land here were cheap, and so people came here looking to settle and get land. At the time, around 1994, plots were between Rwf 50,000 [US$54] and Rwf 200,000 [US$216] for a small plot. The value kept increasing, and now there are no more vacant plots, but small houses can cost above Rwf 1 million [US$1,081] when they come up for sale.

Turning to the relocation situation, Mrs. M exclaimed,

> I am not happy with what they are giving us in terms of *étages* [apartments] in exchange. I want the money in exchange instead, if we have to move. How am I going to go upstairs in these *skyscrapers*? I am old now. It seems like those apartments are more chaotic than here!
>
> The case started because government officials came and told us that here there is a businessman who is going to do business here. No consultative meetings were held, or consensus developed. . . . We have been offered Rwf 30 million [US$32,432] for our houses, but we know they are worth more than this. In Busanza I was offered one house with two *chambres* [rooms] and one *salon*. Here, however, I have my own house, and sixteen houses for renting, including shops on the other side of the road.
>
> When the official appraisers came to my house, they did not take into account the total value of all the houses and the materials that were included. I believe our case will be successful. And if I have to move, I can get another house nearby if they give me money. I can't live outside the city; I am from the city and belong here.
>
> My source of income is from rental properties at the moment. Formerly, I used to farm. But now, with this situation, most of the tenants have started leaving my houses here. The banks won't accept my legal titles for the houses I own as collateral, because they think we will have to leave soon. Tenants prefer to move somewhere else, and it doesn't affect them as much, but owners of large houses are more affected.

Further information from interviewees in Kangondo II corroborated these perspectives:

> F: Our property was valued at Rwf 7 million [approx. US$7,868] by the government. As an exchange, we were offered an apartment in Busanza valued at Rwf 14 million [over US$15,135]. We would have to pay the balance of Rwf 7 million to the government through a loan to get this one house. We don't think it is a fair deal.

> P: We currently get rental income which enables us to pay school fees for the children, and if we moved to Busanza, school fees would be unaffordable, as we wouldn't have rental income there. Many tenants from Bannyahe have

moved already because of the case, and the value of the houses in terms of
rental amounts has decreased as a result.

As these interviews demonstrate, the property-owning residents' grievances against the local state included not only the inadequate consultation
over the expropriation, but the manner in which properties had been ap-
praised, and the overall lack of transparency in the process. According to
these respondents, various inconsistencies had come to light: neither were the
correct numbers of units represented on valuations, nor were improvements
such as tiles, wooden ceiling frames, and metal window casements included,
though those investments added value to the properties. As Bhan (2019) argues, a theory of Southern urban practice must take into account not just
the formal architectural, legal, and policy modalities of legitimate planning,
but also the local idioms of practice visible in informal settlements. Thus,
"repair"—one idiom of local practice differentiated from formalized vocab-
ularies of "build" and "construct," —has valence because it recognizes the
process of incremental construction undertaken by local residents as valid
means of increasing the value of space and the legitimacy of claims to specific places. These additions in Bannyahe became important through similar
mechanisms, as they enhanced place-based claims to legitimacy and the right
to remain.

Debating Relocation to Busanza

While the Expropriation Law (2015) stipulates that monetary compensation
must be available as an option to households expropriated (Article 35), the
procedural differences between law and policy were apparent on the ground.
A housing official explained that a new policy of relocation to replacement
housing had been adopted on the basis of the official valuation of the property held in the previous informal settlement. He explained, "If you compensate people, they simply move to another informal settlement in a similar
area, and you don't stop the tide of informal settlements in Kigali."[8]

Priced at Rwf 10–25 million in 2019 (approx. US$11,000–$27,000),[9] units
in Busanza have been beyond the reach of individuals in the informal sector,
thus requiring many to take out optional loans offered to cover shortfalls.
Annual market demand for affordable housing in Rwanda's urban centers far
outstripped the available supply of 22,000 units under construction at the
time of my research.[10] An earlier presentation on the Kigali housing market
estimated demand in the capital city alone at just above 450,000 dwelling
units by 2022.[11] Debates over how "affordable" the affordable housing is are

FIGURE 5.3. Construction of apartments in Busanza to house resettled residents from Bannyahe

hence even more urgent when informal-sector workers and low-income earners are actively considered.

The city's vision and its fascination with the vertical urbanism of Singapore means that the future of mass housing in Kigali lies in the construction of apartments. This vision concerns many lower-income earners, who are not used to the concept of apartment living. "Rwandans don't feel secure unless they are living in their own home, and that home has to have a yard with it, and be constructed close to the ground," commented an academic interlocutor. The traditional homestead (*urugo*) with its forecourt and back garden, fenced and located on one level, which has for generations formed the basis of a traditional sense of security, is now under threat from such vertical designs. Unsurprising, then, were the conclusions of an article in the Kinyarwanda-language newspaper *Umuseke*, which described a visit by Bannyahe residents to Busanza to view the apartments they had been allocated (figure 5.3).

Reflecting the perceived transitional character of the planned development in contrast to the lived-in spaces of their existing homes, the article reports, "Bannyahe residents visited houses being built for them at Busanza; they said that they are like a refugee camp."[12] In the midst of the fervor for planning, the specter of the "unplanned" and informal settlement hence remains an unsolved planning and policy problem as the urban poor are moved farther and farther from the city's core.

The case against the District of Gasabo began in late 2017 as a group of property owners came together to challenge the process of expropriation on the basis that the Expropriation Law (2015) was not being followed because the process did not give residents the option of monetary compensation. Although the revised law asserts the primacy of the master plan and land-use planning in determining expropriation directives in the "public's interest," Article 35 indicates that mutual agreement must be arrived at between the expropriating and expropriated parties over the form of compensation—whether in cash or in kind. In insisting that their case should go before the court, these residents bypassed traditional mediation and circumvented the power of local government leaders. The owners in Kangondo were at first eager to talk about the case. But after the first hearing date was set for November 7, 2018, in the District Court of Gasabo, they became more hesitant to speak, fearing information leaks and surveillance.

Located in the Kabuga cell of the Rusororo Sector, a few meters from the main Kigali–Rwamagana road, the District Court of Gasabo was crowded on the first hearing date, with people waiting for the trial to begin. But the residents' lawyer was missing, and the case was postponed due to procedural irregularities involving the filing of court documents. In early December the case reconvened. The proceedings this time were faster, the prosecutor arguing that the case should be broken up into separate cases for each individual litigant rather than taken as group litigation. Finally, on February 11, 2019, the case was dismissed due to procedural errors in filing the case. In effect, the court ruled in favor of the prosecution when it determined that residents could not bring a group-based case but would have to refile their cases as separate claims. At the time, many in attendance vowed to regroup and follow the procedure demanded by the court when appealing.[13] Others complained about the unfairness of being dismissed on procedural grounds when they were certain they had consulted all required national and local governmental institutions.[14] In the aftermath of the dismissal, the path forward for residents has been unclear and the momentum behind the case has dissipated, despite regular coverage in the local media. While reports indicated that a smaller group of property owners were to refile individual claims, the rejection of the group claim made them more vulnerable to dismissal and subject to individual pressures. For instance, individuals pursuing their claims were described by the media as "greedy local leaders" with whom the local government had to "deal."[15]

The court case was an occasion to pause and reflect on the site of contestation and negotiation in Kigali for residents of the "grey spaces" (Yiftachel 2009) of informal settlements. In the case of the Bannyahe settlement's legal challenge, it has proven significant that residents wanted to claim civic rights in the district-level courts rather than settle for the mediation of lower-level authorities and inevitable compromise. Nonetheless, a lack of clarity in the legal process as well as the difficulty of filing a collective lawsuit points to the limitations of making spatial claims through the law in a context where citizenship and space are differentiated in the changing city.

In December 2019, without hope of financial compensation or a chance to stay put, residents of the Bannyahe informal settlement in Gasabo District in Kigali began to destroy their own homes.[16] This trope of place-dismantling, a type of domicide, was not new. Similar forms of destruction had been reported in Rwanda's post-genocide period as the state aimed to reorganize rural populations and implement grouped settlement schemes (*imidugudu*) as well as requiring the use of corrugated metal roofing instead of thatch in Operation Bye Bye Nyakatsi, which began in 2010.[17] What was new was the form of politics that residents raised against the place annihilation mandated by the local state.

Emerging from these "unplanned" spaces in Kigali, the property owners of Bannyahe sought to stake claims in the public domain. They demonstrated that everyday questions of place are political on the capital's changing landscape. At the same time, many residents of the settlement were hesitant to openly contest master-planning as the framework of their expropriation and relocation. Although property owners expressed fear of relocation, and frustration that their tenants had begun to leave the settlement even before their case against the district had been decided, they preferred to *localize* their claims in terms of geographic scale and legal ambit, limiting contestation to questions of procedural justice over the Expropriation Law rather than larger criticisms of master-planning as the overarching concept of urban change.

Property owners hence circumscribed their contestation to appear less confrontational and not directly at odds with portrayals of good citizenship and respect for authority. They carefully delimited and localized the boundaries of contestation in multiple senses: both spatially localized and legally delimited to the procedural, unable to contest the dislocation in the larger context of the master plan as a citywide spatial plan as well as a national political vision.

"If the case fails, we don't know what we will do," one resident of Bannyahe commented. "We respect the master plan and the public's interest, but we want the process to be followed so that we can afford to move elsewhere." In a context where the capital's master plan forms part of a larger vision of national urban-led sociospatial change, localized contestation and claims centered on the scale of the neighborhood appear to represent the current limits of overt public confrontation and political claims-making in contemporary Kigali. City master-planning in Kigali today increasingly marginalizes the hybrid spatial-legal arrangement of the informal settlement, where residents struggle to retain forms of citizenship and a foothold in the city through negotiation, rights claims, and the law. Urban contention in the Bannyahe settlement serves as a limit case illustrating the possibilities and boundaries of contestation over urban redevelopment in contemporary Kigali. Such accounts of experiences of displacement in the framework of master-planning in the contemporary capital generate popular counternarratives to the overarching developmentalist master narrative of modernization-as-salvation that is currently attached to programs of transformation in Kigali.

Antina Von Schnitzler's (2017) account of the technopolitics of water infrastructure in postapartheid South Africa is also germane in analyzing the Bannyahe case. Von Schnitzler argues that local dissent after apartheid is often mundane and material, with protest toeing the line between intelligibility and dissimulation while gesturing toward earlier political forms that are now embedded in a new context. In its insistence on adequate compensation and a place in the city, the material resistance of residents in Bannyahe resonated with such micropolitics of the everyday, emplacing the registers of the home and its abandonment as contentious frontiers of localized dissent. Forms of grounded infrastructural politics permitted a particular perspective on resistance in the capital. Routing their grievances through the juridical infrastructures of the state, resident owners in Bannyahe galvanized spatial politics around place. While their dissent was grounded as material and localized, its form implicated larger spatial and societal questions: issues of the meaning of urban citizenship in the current period, and the role of the spatial master plan as dispossession's enabling framework.

Ultimately, accounts such as those of Bannyahe's residents reaffirm the significance of place in this city undergoing change from ongoing top-down spatial renovation. Struggles to remain in the city can be interpreted as the current affective enactment of a longer historical thread of abandonment and its links to place that has contemporary as well as historical relevance. Domicide, the destruction of place through dismantling the home, has happened in many guises in postindependence Rwandan history, and manifests itself in multiple stories of belonging and abandonment. Thwarted struggles to remain are hence layered and sedimented as forms of injury in the capital. The politics of repair are intimately tied to a sense of place and belonging in urban space for lower-income and unemployed Rwandan residents whose life pathways have become constricted in the city.

As the informal settlement is removed and the city morphs around it, the abandoned home stands as a political space. Its contours are retrenched as a frontier of belonging and living together in a changing, urbanizing Rwanda—one of possibility, and one of loss.

6

Peripheral Conscription

As it cuts across the snaking Akagera-Nyabarongo River, the new boundary between the city of Kigali and Bugesera District is geographically marked on the landscape. Traditionally the river has been seen as a boundary separating city and country, one that has, more conceptually, demarcated an unbridgeable divide between different modes of habitation, forms of social reproduction, and hopes for the future, in separate urban and rural space. Across time, crossing this river has been spoken and sung of in the language of impossibility and irrevocability. During the 1994 genocide, the swamps around the Akagera River were a site of massacre. Extremist *Interahamwe* Hutu militia threw bodies of their mostly Tutsi victims into the river, symbolically and morbidly aiming to harness the water's mobility to return these victims to their mythic Hamitic origins in Ethiopia, and thus positing the Tutsi as rejected foreigners (Mamdani 2020).

The old Kanzenze bridge across the Akagera River is no longer used, and the agrarian modes of life it symbolized are being replaced by a modern concrete bridge that links the capital with its former hinterland. New forms of mobility are hence enabled even as less privileged forms of life are made less viable and visible. With the changing possibilities of mobility between Kigali and Bugesera's capital, Nyamata, the periphery now indexes a new type of "affective space" (Navaro-Yashin 2012) for residents and urban speculators, and the erstwhile hinterland is thus resignified. As the city literally and figuratively moves across the bridge, the periphery has become an anticipatory zone: it is conditioned by the expectations and hopes that urbanization will bring opportunities to urban speculators looking for new forms of capitalization. At the same time, the periphery is a moving, unstable boundary that increases urban anxieties and materializes fears for low-income residents of the area, as urbanization from the capital creeps nearer and displacement looms.

As Kigali transforms from a postconflict capital to an aspiring regional model green hub through elite mobile planning expertise and transnational finance, the displacements and the imaginary that the transformation entails spill beyond the boundaries of the capital. This transformation involves the conceptual work of revisioning the capital and the practical labor of rezoning its spaces. Kigali's periphery in Bugesera District is being remade as a speculative frontier for investment capital of different forms. I consider here the various factors in the transformation, and draw together ideas of mobility, labor, and violence across space and time. I first consider the different kinds of mobilities that underpin Rwanda's urbanizing moment. Next, I examine the bureaucratic processes, as opposed to popular forms of labor, that "re-index" the periphery from being a neglected hinterland to being a speculative frontier of urbanization. I use re-indexing to encompass in one term the transformations, resignifications, and metamorphoses of spaces between different states over time (e.g., from peripherality to centrality). This reindexing is done largely through the conceptual work and administrative processes of aggregate metrics and hierarchical representations of efficiency such as the controversial and now discredited World Bank *Doing Business Report* rankings, and Rwandan bureaucratic performance contract ratings (*imihigo*).

I concentrate on the particular types of practical labor that produce this transformation in the peri-urban frontier from a disposable space of absent value to one that captures the value of the urbanizing moment, enabled by the speculative mobility of capital and expertise. What types of intervention does it take to re-index the neglected swampland of the urban periphery—a holding space to which people considered surplus to colonial and postindependence governance projects were once sent—as a new geography of city making? Who performs this labor on the city's edge, and how is value accrued and redistributed across this speculative frontier in peri-urban Bugesera District through different forms of intervention, both conceptual and practical? As seen through research on participatory planning on the capital's periphery, I suggest that the task of reproducing Kigali's urban frontier is unevenly borne. Rwanda's urban visions are produced here through participatory planning as a form of laboring for the state, as a mode of conscripted voluntarism. Those on the periphery who participate in city making as Kigali expands and as cities emerge in Bugesera carry the burden of bearing Rwanda's urban visions. However, the material dividends of the urban transformation slip through their fingers, producing instead immaterial futures tinged by affective expectation and, later, the temporal uncertainty of displacement.

Theorization of the periphery as both a method of analysis and a material aspect of urbanization has received more attention recently from scholars of urban studies. The periphery is seen as a frontier of urban warfare and capitalization in the case of Beirut (Bou Akar 2018), or as an uneven mode of city making, with "transversal logics" that occupy or produce new urban space, in São Paulo and Delhi (Caldeira 2017). Further scholarship on peripheral urban processes in cities in the Global South includes recent work on African cities and processes of accumulation by dispossession, real estate speculation, and peripheral building and dwelling in cities such as Addis Ababa, Accra, and Kampala (Follmann 2022; Gillespie 2016; Goodfellow 2022; Meth et al. 2021). Perhaps because of this scholarship that recenters the periphery as a productive area of engagement in the region, it remains important to follow opportunities to further explore deep histories of peripheralization in post-genocide Rwanda, and to examine the periphery as a space that magnifies the many intersecting interests in this specific urbanizing moment.

Histories of Mobility and Violence in Bugesera District

In 2006 the administrative boundaries in Rwanda were redrawn, following the implementation of the administrative Decentralization Policy (2000–2001, revised in 2012).[1] The country had previously comprised twelve prefectures (until 2001), renamed "provinces" under the new anglophone nomenclature. Under the new administrative mandate, the city of Kigali was enlarged, with Kicukiro District swallowing Kigali Ngali (also called Kigali Rurale) on the boundary of Bugesera District.[2] Much like the change in the capital's street names after the genocide as the city began to be spatially reordered, changes in district designations represented a spatial reorganization of national territory and political belonging. This change in spatial organization was reminiscent of pre-genocide cleavages, which had been organized on the basis of not just ethnicity but also regional factionalism (Twagilimana 2003). The drive to rename and spatially reorganize has hence been written into political geography over time, producing for the state the capacity to reorient spatial awareness and identificatory coordinates of previous historical periods.

Part of Eastern Province and one of the least hilly but also driest parts of the country, Bugesera has a historically neglected status that derives from itineraries of both human and nonhuman movement during the colonial period and in its aftermath. During the 1960s, before independence, Tutsi pastoralists from what is now Northern Province were moved to Bugesera in an attempt to order the population and space in the north of the country and subject Hutu peasants there to manual labor schemes (*paysannat*). In forcibly relocating a large Tutsi population to the marshlands and low-lying areas of Bugesera, the Belgian colonial administration didn't just reorder ways of life but subjected this population to the ravages of tsetse fly infestation.[3] In the postindependence period, forced relocations took place from Gikongoro District to Bugesera in 1963, and the Hutu-led Kayibanda government engaged in the persecution of Tutsi in the area. This period also coincides with the attempted return of displaced Tutsis to the country from neighboring Burundi.[4] Fears of "infiltration," feelings of insecurity, and environmental stagnation and stasis thus marked the marshlands as inhospitable and unwelcoming. Those unwanted in the capital, such as prisoners or opponents, were frequently exiled to this peripheral hinterland where they could safely be forgotten.[5]

Although very little has been written about this period of forced mobilities, violence, and tsetse fly infestation,[6] the relocation of large numbers of Tutsi to the district can also be inferred from the intensity of the genocidal massacres that occurred in Bugesera in 1994. Two churches stand as visceral reminders of this violence during the early part of the genocide. The Nyamata and Ntarama churches have been converted into formal genocide memorials, where the remains and belongings of those killed in 1994 are visibly displayed on church pews, skulls are lined up in extensions to the church buildings, and the clothes and formal ethnic identity passes of those massacred still lie on the floors of the central church buildings. On April 11, 1994, ten thousand Tutsi were killed in the Nyamata church, where they had flocked to seek refuge, and six thousand were massacred in Ntarama a few days later, on April 14. These curated memorials, at once moving and numbing, are an unsettling contrast to the new displays of urban speculation unfolding in Bugesera district, in both Nyamata and in the smaller town of Ntarama which sits midway to Kigali.

This brief account of the immobility of relocated populations underlies and is juxtaposed against very different forms of violence and administrative policy across time. These forms of violence and displacement are not necessarily equivalent in their qualities, but it is significant that questions of movement and stasis are central to the historical development of Bugesera as a region—redrawing zoning boundaries and rewriting local histories. These questions of movement and stasis, modernity built out of and on top of tradition, and immobility confronted by rapid mobility are guideposts to understanding the changes wrought today on the post-genocide, postcolonial landscape of urbanizing Rwanda. These histories are disappearing through the spatial reinscription produced by rapid urbanization, but they remain vital to understanding and excavating layers of political geography that lie underneath.

The Time and Cost of Competitive Urbanization

Urbanization and development in the districts bordering Kigali—not only Bugesera but also Kamonyi, Rwamagana, and Rulindo—has ruptured space and time in the lives and livelihoods of local dwellers. In the rest of this chapter, I focus primarily on urbanization and planning in Bugesera District, with its especially intense urgency to benefit from the investment spillover from Kigali. I analyze how urban competition, administrative streamlining, local governance, and centrally directed investment are remaking peripheral space. Just as capital and administrative resources flow into newly capitalizable terrain, residents in neighboring districts are peripheralized as land speculators come to their areas, looking to profit. There is a certain salience of the urban speculation taking place here on sedimented and traumatic political geography, which is all but rewritten through state-directed planning.

My conceptual framing here builds on empirical findings from field research conducted in Bugesera District in the first half of 2019, and uses interviews and observations with residents, private planners, and planning officials working in the areas of the district closest to Kigali, which are currently subject to redevelopment. As part of my research process I conducted semistructured and in-depth interviews with residents of Karumuna and Kanzenze areas that are being master-planned, asking them about their livelihoods and itineraries of movement, as well as their involvement and perceptions of the redevelopment processes underway. I further attended local participatory meetings on community-led planning that covered areas between Karumuna and Nyamata, including Kanzenze and Ntarama. At these meetings I listened to the proceedings and spoke with community representatives in charge of physical planning who were cooperating with the Bugesera District One Stop Center (OSC), which expedites permitting. I also interviewed planners and land appraisers in the private sector who work on physical plans in the area on their perceptions of and involvement in planning processes underway in Bugesera. I queried the generalization of these processes to other peripheral areas around Kigali, such as Muyumbu in Rwamagana District and Gahanga in Kicukiro District. Finally, I examined master plans, building codes, newspapers, and government documents to better understand the context of competitive urbanization and community-led urban planning on the periphery (figure 6.1).

National *imihigo* performance contract competitions and transnational rankings such as the World Bank Group (WBG) *Doing Business Report* index have helped to establish the urban periphery as Kigali's new speculative frontier.

FIGURE 6.1. Looking across the periphery in Karumuna, Bugesera District, toward Kigali

How do such performance-based index rankings get materialized on the urban periphery and center different regimes of motion and mobility? Paying special attention to the newly cemented periphery in Bugesera District, I ask fundamental questions about the cost of compliance with urbanization in and around Kigali, and the forms of labor used to operationalize it. What do trajectories of capital moving outward from Kigali and the displacement of lower-income dwellers from the city tell us about the distribution of the dividends and burdens of Rwanda's urbanizing moment?

Cost calculations and computational methods that aggregate time saved through various investment and business processes are cornerstones of the monitoring and evaluation metrics of development institutions such as the WBG. Such calculations are premised on models of competitive urbanization that rank the time saved for particular kinds of business investors in cities across the region and subnationally within a country. Metrics such as these contribute to the development of indexes that competitively rank the performance of districts, cities, and countries in attracting finance and contributing to a conducive investment climate. They privilege particular forms of consumers (propertied and formalized investors, not the informal entrepreneur or the urban poor) and prioritize specific types of governmental incentives that configure policy in favor of reducing and removing barriers to investment and facilitating speed, mobility, and interoperability across time and space, both nationally and internationally.

These practices create certain types of spaces as well: for example, the One Stop Center (OSC) housed in municipal and planning bureaucracies, is a primary invention and materialization of indexing processes. Through the OSC, business permits, construction permits, business registrations, and administrative procedures that are seen as barriers to rapid business transactions are handled more quickly and compressed. In turn, undeveloped or undercapitalized spaces are rendered more accessible. Indexes of efficiency measure success in overlapping contexts (e.g., the transnational and the subnational), and demarcate access to development funding, national prestige, and municipal reward. In excavating how these metrics aggregate performance, I examine the spaces that they affect on the periphery, as undercapitalized terrain. I suggest that while cost calculations and time savings computed for private investors during index rankings position Rwanda as a leader in efficient economic governance in the region, it is also the very speed of these planning and regulatory changes and the flows they occasion (into and out of the city) that create not only frontiers of investment but forms of dislocation and dispossession in and around the capital. The speed of mobile capital, valued preferentially over the time and lost livelihoods of former dwellers in Kigali and its peripheral zones, creates frontiers of speculative investment that aggregate the global and the local on this changing periphery.

Competitive Development on the Urban Periphery

Although Bugesera's district capital of Nyamata is not among the six secondary cities set for master-planning according to low-carbon green principles (Huye, Muhanga, Musanze, Nyagatare, Rubavu, and Rusizi), it remains one of the districts neighboring Kigali that is best positioned to reap benefits from its rapid urban growth. Bugesera District and Nyamata have become prime sites for investment with a new international "green-built" airport being constructed an hour's drive from Kigali. Additional projects include new industrial zones, bulk water supply works for Kigali, the site of a new agricultural and technological university, and a new Chinese-financed dual carriageway highway linking the capital with Nyamata. High expectations and hopes of recognition are materializing on the periphery. "Why would I want to be in one of the secondary cities?" a city official in Nyamata remarked to me. "I am much better off here in Bugesera—with so many projects coming up, we are at the center of everything!"[7]

Rwanda's decentralized governance system was reworked for implementation again in 2012, and has created increased competition over performance between districts to attract capital investment and central government approval of the local terrain. Although the decentralized framework is still heavily centralized in oversight, it contributes to districts bordering the capital competing to be the "next Kigali" in order to win favor and influence in national political circles and augment their local governments' images. In many ways, the increasingly stringent building regulations and retroactive physical planning being implemented in Bugesera's urbanizing areas are tied into nonlocal circuits of capital, expertise, and state-led urban brand building. For example, the new international airport in Bugesera, designed to replace the postindependence-era Kigali International Airport at Kanombe, is being developed at a cost of more than US$1.3 billion, with a 60 percent finance share taken by Qatar Airways. Phase 2 is expected to be complete by 2032, at which time the airport's capacity will be fourteen million passengers a year.[8] Designed using Green Mark Rating System green building technology, the country's "largest public investment" has been stewarded by the Ministries of Infrastructure and Environment in cooperation with the Singapore Building Control Authority (BCA).[9] The Government of Rwanda signed a memorandum of understanding in September 2016 with the BCA for the consolidation of the country's green building standards based on Singapore's Green Mark Scheme, one that involved bilateral finance.[10] While the government intends to extend its existing building codes and urban planning legislation to incorporate a "Rwanda Green Building Minimum Compliance Scheme," Singapore, too, sees its urban branding star rising through this collaboration. The press release from the BCA details this mutual benefit, stating that it "further augments BCA's aspiration for Singapore to become a global brand leader in green buildings with special expertise in the tropics and sub-tropics, enabling sustainable development and quality living."[11] Energy efficiency, water optimization with efficient high-technology solutions, specially sourced local and green materials to reduce waste, and regulated indoor air quality will ensure that the airport meets the highest standards of green building in the country, becoming a forerunner for similar projects in the region.[12]

The new Chinese-financed highway to the airport bypasses much of the existing urban development in Bugesera District so that international travelers, including high-profile delegates, can travel directly from the capital's green spaces to its new green-built gateway. In many ways, the competitive urbanization in Bugesera has thus capitalized on these air-hub plans through speculation, with investors from Kigali buying up land en route to the airport. This speculation is heterogeneous and involves small-time land buyers who comprise the capital's upwardly mobile bureaucratic middle class as well as higher-income and commercial developers and profiteers. Given the competitive development context at the district level and the drive to garner the esteem of the central state, it is hardly surprising that until recently, instead of working to augment Kigali's planning exercises in terms of coordination and the zoning of affordable housing, districts like Bugesera have been focusing primarily on their own economic growth. Planning exercises and capitalization of the inflow of finance and speculative buyers from Kigali have been primary preoccupations here.

With the shortage of affordable housing on Kigali's increasingly expensive land, it might make planning sense to conceive of coordinated zoning and policies for lower-income housing and local economic development between the capital and its adjacent districts. Rather than envisioning a metropolitan Kigali with planning policies coordinated between districts, however, the Kigali City master plan (Surbana 2013, revised in 2019) envisioned a self-contained world-class capital, with little joint planning with neighboring towns, at least until 2019 when directives were reportedly issued for expanded plan preparation. Bugesera, therefore, has become Kigali's speculative frontier, with residents with disposable cash and those seeking more affordable land moving across the river to areas like the district capital of Nyamata, and peripheral settlements such as Karumuna and Kanzenze.

Developmental regulation in Kigali is intimately related to the motivations that impel residents of the capital to speculate or move to Bugesera's peri-urban areas. During one of my many visits across the Akagera River, which separates Kigali and Bugesera, Charles—a relatively recent resident—explained that the stringent building regulations (published in 2015) and lack of affordable land in Kigali prompted him to move to the peripheral area of Kanzenze in 2013.[13]

> Rwandans want their own house, and in Kigali buying or constructing a home for your family is just not affordable. . . .
> When I bought land here, the price was five hundred thousand Rwandan francs for a parcel of land that was twenty-five by thirty meters in size.[14] Although my land doesn't have services like water, which is a problem in this area, its value has multiplied in just a few years. My plot of land is now worth between 4.5 and 7 million Rwandan francs. This increase is largely driven by demand, due to poor affordability in Kigali.

When asked why he did not buy in adjacent Kicukiro District, which remains part of the city of Kigali, Charles replied that the new building regulations made it financially infeasible to put up housing according to the directives of the city administration, which demands high-quality material and multiple floors of construction in certain areas.

"Rwandans are visionaries," remarked Marcel, an enthusiastic Bugesera resident with whom I spoke in March, 2019. He had bought land a few years earlier in a peripheral area of the district, and he described how the land price was rising:

> Many people buy two or three plots here in Bugesera in areas like this, and then hold onto them so that their value increases. They don't necessarily live in the area, but they benefit from the increased value of the land, and intend to sell them when the value goes higher.

Residents then use the money gained from selling their first plots of land to finance further speculation and peri-urban construction, Marcel said. Jean, another inhabitant of the area, revealed that tensions exist between long-term residents being priced off of their own land and higher-income dwellers moving to the area from Kigali. Among the new housing developments were small informal dwellings that were to be upgraded according to new physical planning directives—the expectation being that the owners would sell off their parcels to residents commuting from Bugesera to work in Kigali.[15] Hence, whereas in the pre-genocide era Bugesera District was considered an urban hinterland, housing people who could not find space, employment, and acceptance in the capital city,[16] it has fast become a repository of local municipal dreams for districts converting rural and peri-urban land to urban land and competing to become the next Kigali.

Imihigo, Live! Indexing Urban Competitiveness

To understand this urban growth on the capital's periphery I use re-indexing, which connotes both a metamorphosis that occurs over time through the re-signification of this neglected space into an urban frontier, and more recently a project operationalized through the administrative work of metrics and the state-focused urban imaginaries that these metrics represent and support. Re-indexing is, in short, a calculative practice of triaging and designating value over space and time amid various types of displacements, and now amid Rwanda's urban moment. I have already introduced some of the global metrics and transnational rankings at work in this process, such as those created by the WBG, but I begin here with local index rankings and focus on the imihigo performance contract competition in the country in relation to this fervor for subnational urban development.

The story begins at the prized One Stop Center for permitting and planning, housed in each district's offices as the hub of activity for local development. During an initial visit to the Gasabo District office in Kigali in August 2018, the lines of applicants waiting to obtain business permits, file construction permits, renew licenses, and inquire about applications were an everyday feature of the OSC office, located on the first floor of the district building. On that day in August, however, both applicants and center staff sat glued to television sets and computer screens live-streaming a national broadcast from Parliament. The results of the annual imihigo competition at the district level were being announced on live television, and officials were eagerly tracking the outcomes. Suddenly, loud cheering and clapping erupted, and district staff began to high-five, shake hands, and slap one another on the back. Their reactions made clear the importance of the imihigo competition, which the Rwandan bureaucracy proudly calls a "homegrown solution." Gasabo District had come in second place, beaten only by the adjacent Rwamagana District, located just outside Kigali and keen to attract investment spillover from the capital. The announcement ceremony was attended by top members of the government and mayors of the country's thirty districts, and was undoubtedly the highlight of the administrative year for district staff. By moving from ninth place in 2016–17 to second place in the following year's rankings (2017–18),[17] Gasabo District administrators had garnered praise, attention, and urban prestige in their efforts to streamline business permitting, investment, and development in the area.[18]

As one of Rwanda's "homegrown solutions,"[19] the institution of imihigo between different levels of decentralized bureaucracy and the central state allows for close monitoring of target-setting and delivery. Imihigo has been part of the decentralization reforms established by the central government just after the national decentralization framework came into effect in 2000 (the Decentralization Policy was revised in 2012). Officially launched in 2006, imihigo performance contracts thus allowed for greater oversight and accountability to the central state in their mandate for improved and more efficient local governance. Put forward as a key component of the competitive spirit of Rwandan culture on individual and collective levels, the competitions are described by the Rwanda Governance Board (RGB) as a revival of a precolonial institution and ethos:

> *Imihigo* is the plural Kinyarwanda word of *Umuhigo*, which means to vow to deliver. *Imihigo* also includes the concept of *Guhiganwa*, which means to

compete among one another. *Imihigo* describes the pre-colonial cultural practice in Rwanda where an individual sets targets or goals to be achieved within a specific period of time. The person must complete these objectives by following guiding principles and be determined to overcome any possible challenges that arise.[20]

Critiques of imihigo as a state reinvention of tradition are pervasive in the academic literature.[21] Ingelaere (2011) in particular defines the "vow" of imihigo as a performative act based on this reinvention of tradition and adaptation of performance-based financing (PBF) in the public sector. Writing on the renewed centralization of state oversight in the country's rural areas since 2000, Ingelaere's evidence on the state-party-controlled "parallel channels of command and control in the countryside" demonstrates that "accountability in local governance structures flows upward to central authorities, not downward to the population" (2011: 68). Citing a proverb used by one of his rural peasant interlocutors, "*Induru ntirwana n'ingoma*" (The drum is greater than the shout), Ingelaere, much like Des Forges (1986) before him, interprets the lines of the state's central control over its rural hinterland in terms of an alternative temporal order:

> By invoking this proverb, the elderly peasant sought to explain the post-genocide present in terms of the pre-colonial past—not the Rwandan Patriotic Front's (RPF's) imagined past of nonethnic harmony, but rather a past marked by the central state's political (and ethnic) domination over the periphery (Ingelaere 2011: 68).

It is in this context that we might understand imihigo as a both historical and contemporary referent of varying state orders.

Operating at a district level, imihigo has created not just greater centralized oversight but greater subnational competition over urban development and local investment by reinventing tradition and co-opting performance-based output evaluation as a principle of practice—as modeled by the "competitive performance scorecards" promoted by neoliberal governance regimes such as the WBG. Territorial reforms that heralded decentralization were followed by the comprehensive restructuring of local government, so that the pre-genocide local government structures were replaced in 2006 with new structures that coopted local leaders into the party state. At the same time, these reforms made local leaders accountable to centralized performance-based contracts, such as imihigo, with the central state. On the district level, these performance contracts are translated into commitments for enhanced delivery targets for planning and development.

In many ways, the indicators of the imihigo district competition whose results I witnessed in the Gasabo District OSC mimic the WBG's now discredited ease of doing business indicator-based evaluations. A signature product of the private-sector development initiatives of the WBG, during their prime the *Doing Business Report* rankings operated in 190 countries (2019), producing competitive scores on a range of indicators related to reduction in the time and expense required to comply with regulatory frameworks: registering property, starting a business, dealing with construction permits, and enforcing contracts, among others.[22] The rankings necessarily dealt with investors in the formal sector, both local and international, and interpret reduced time and cost input for the private sector as a key index of improved business climate and healthy economic governance. Given that Rwanda's performance contracting mechanisms are premised on precisely such indexes of economic efficiency and streamlining in the attraction of mobile capital, *Doing Business Report* rankings mattered a great deal both internally and on the international scene.

The 2019 *Doing Business Report* ranked Rwanda's performance as improved by eleven places on the global ranking, from forty-first to twenty-ninth, so that it ranked among the ten most improved countries in the region (along with Togo, Kenya, and Côte d'Ivoire), and registers second, just behind New Zealand, in ease of registering property. "It now takes only 7 days to transfer property and costs only 0.1 per cent of the property value, the same as in New Zealand," stated a newspaper article on the annual rankings.[23] Alongside the subnational district imihigo rankings, which augment central state approbation and competitive city investment generation, the international *Doing Business Report* rankings highlighted Rwanda's stellar performance on the world stage, with the city and urban development as centerpieces. Interdistrict competition for urban investment, including ease of processing business and construction permits and registering land, was undoubtedly relevant to the developments on Kigali's periphery, where urbanization has opened up a new speculative frontier.

Physical Planning and Community Voluntarism

As Bugesera urbanizes with speculative rapidity, "proper planning," as it is officially termed, has again become a metaphor for regularity, order, and marketability. Areas settled without prior formal planning on the border of Bugesera District and running up to the district capital, Nyamata, are deemed to be "unplanned" by district officials, and in need of post hoc regularization

so that formal property markets can take hold and eventually provide housing for Kigali commuters. A senior planning official explained that the area
between Karumuna, on the border with Kigali, and Nyamata were previously
rural villages (*imidugudu*) that became peri-urban areas—resettled ad hoc by
lower-income dwellers who moved out of Kigali.[24] They are now being regularized and rezoned in accordance with the area's master plan; and in order to
facilitate this, the district's OSC stopped issuing building permits in October
2018. Attempts to make the area legible to planned property development and
"higher-value uses," however, are of particular interest because of how these
endeavors are conceived and implemented. Regularization and planning processes draw on local governance structures and idioms of "community" and
"voluntarism" that hold strong valence in administering local government
nationwide.

Planning meetings held to involve local leaders and residents in participatory forms of implementation reveal how the state co-opts the local community as an instrument of development. At an initial meeting with district
officials after I arrived in Nyamata during my first month of research, key
district planner Mr. Celestin eagerly spoke to me about his ambitions for the
physical planning of the area, which he said were "innovative and impressive"
because they relied on local communities to undertake the required planning
exercises without direct intervention from the district. "This whole process
relies on voluntary work by the community," Celestin exclaimed enthusiastically. "We don't have to intervene and the communities work effectively.
Where else in the world do you see this?" The policy to form physical planning committees as adjunctive administrative structures to the local government village and cell committees at the local level sets up the "community"
(Rose 1999) as a structure of cooptation and cooperation. It is a governmental
technique that uses social approbation and approval, as much as opprobrium,
to elicit compliance.

During the planning meetings I attended, Celestin explained to gatherings of local leaders the procedure for retroactively regularizing and planning
land in the area between Karumuna and Nyamata. The procedure involves
the following sequence of steps. First, residents' committees comprised of local leaders and influential people in the area are set up and "sensitized"—that
is, given information or instruction from the government on their roles. The
designated physical planning representatives of these committees next work
with local administrative communities at cell and village levels to explain the
process to all their local residents, gaining their individual written consent on
a form to be sent to the district. These communities then themselves pay to
hire land surveying companies, which can conduct surveys of current layouts

of land parcels and ownership, and propose a plan for regularization according to minimum standards and road layouts provided by the district. These layouts are to comply with the area's centrally developed master plan for expansion. Once these plans are approved by the district and the central government (the Kigali-based Rwanda Housing Authority, or RHA), the plans go back to the community, which itself implements the regularization of land. The community is expected to allot compensation from their own means to landowners who have lost parts of their land due to the land regularization process. Finally, once each community has implemented the regularization process, individual land titles are to be reissued and the halt on building permit issuance lifted. "By involving the community we are gaining their participation and good will and also saving on time and cost," Celestin said. "The process is more efficient than if we were to do this directly ourselves. Further, residents need to be made to understand the benefits to them of this process, as their land values will triple so that they can sell at higher values once the process is completed."

These local infrastructures of compliance and conduits for governmentality at the grass roots point not just to consent and locally mediated compliance on the ground, but to the importance of *mindset change* perceived by higher authorities as central to the project of local governance and community mobilization (Thomson 2018). Alex, a planner and land surveyor in private practice in Kigali, spoke with me about the regularization of plots in Karumuna. "Many of the residents don't understand the benefits of land regularization and feel the burden of having to pay for this themselves," he said. "They don't yet see that their plot values will increase." He explained the procedures through which he had engaged with the community, and the hesitancy he encountered due to their "rural ways."[25]

Underlying this emphasis on mindset change and resident compliance is the known fact that currently instituted building codes (Government of Rwanda 2015b) mandate that G+1 (ground floor plus one floor) construction be built on regularized plots, using higher quality materials that many residents will not be able to afford. In the process of "participatory" land regularization, many residents know they will have to sell out and relocate once the new titles and building permits are issued. Many of the residents I spoke to tacitly associated planning with these mixed outcomes, which had multiple valences as "both good and bad"; as some residents envision themselves having to move farther into Bugesera's rural areas, they explicitly linked planning, as a framework of compliance and mobility, to their displacement. Lower-income residents will move, according to Fantine, a Karumuna resident, to "where planning has not yet arrived."[26] The successive process of land conversion underway on the periphery—spontaneously from rural to peri-urban, and deliberately from peri-urban to regularized and zoned urban land—follows a different logic at each step. Greatly reduced is the space for "auto-construction" and incremental improvement of individual land holdings, as are generated through land invasions and self-built settlements on the peripheries of Brazilian cities (Holston 1991). Instead, the language of planning, innovation, and best practices has taken over as an indicator of municipal improvement and a harbinger of all but inevitable displacement for others.

During another conversation, Celestin revealed that his innovative idea of bringing community-led physical planning to Bugesera drew on similar initiatives in Kicukiro District in the city of Kigali, where the formerly rural area of Gahanga was regularized. This involved community planning, and what can be termed regulatory and "market-value-based resettlement." Such endeavors have been extended to Rwamagana in the Muyumbu settlement area and are set to increase, given the efficiency of community co-optation in planning processes. Bernard, a planner in Kigali who was involved in similar processes in Gahanga in the city of Kigali, contextualized this process in relation to governmental interests: here, community land regularization formed part of a governmental strategy to extricate itself from responsibility for the direct expropriation of land and involvement in dispute resolution, including the forms of contention seen in Kigali as Kangondo and Bannyahe residents sued the district (Esmail and Corburn 2020). "It is more efficient to use the community and there is less contention that might involve the government," he said, calling to mind Celestin's earlier words: "Regularly it would cost about three hundred thousand US dollars to get this work done, but we are doing it for free and saving money while involving the local community, who are very dedicated." In a context where collective action and open defiance of directives from local government are rare, these local infrastructures of labor and mediated compliance are therefore seen as effective modes of community-based governmentality.

During a series of preparatory planning meetings I attended in March 2019 with leaders of the communities involved and district planning authorities, however, it became apparent that there were indeed contentious issues, nuanced disagreements, and a lack of clarity on the part of local leaders. One local leader charged with planning in Ntarama explained to the gathering that it would be difficult for him to execute plans for community planning without a clear understanding of the planning process, a reference land price list, and a legal mandate for conducting the land readjustment and regularization.

The gathering murmured, but largely remained silent. Later, other concerns were raised about compensation for members of the community who might lose parts of their land through the regularization processes. Another resident leader asked:

> How do we deal with parcels of land that currently have a house on them already built, but which need to be split into two, or which are designated for public use and services? How will we afford to compensate these people or decide on regularization and compensation conflicts ourselves?

District officials present at the gathering responded that it was up to local leaders to convince the community and set aside portions of the increased value of land that would be realized once new titles were issued and properties sold for delayed compensation to the affected.

Jean, a mid-level community representative, later shared his disapproval in private. "How can the local people themselves compensate their neighbors?" he said. "They may not have a common understanding of their paths. How can I compensate my neighbor? That should be a district load, not a community load!" Though subtle and constrained during the planning preparatory meetings, these expressions of discontent cast light on the varieties of disagreement with centralized planning processes and the local effects of authority. Planning in this context was both a social process infused with local politics and an expert-led endeavor, exposing socioeconomic heterogeneity and contention even as it aimed to regularize and standardize the physical landscape.

Calculating National Cost Savings

Much as *Doing Business Report* indicators measured efficiency in days and hours of time and the cost of obtaining private-sector services from national and subnational governments, these forms of calculation on the periphery in Bugesera and adjacent districts actively displaced other regimes of mobility, time, and productivity. Here, it is precisely the social immobility of lower-income, peri-urban residents that determines that they will sell their properties because they cannot comply with G+1 building codes and the requirements for improved building materials. Dislocated lower-income residents thereby free up regularized space for commuters and land speculators from Kigali. Their involuntary immobility in social and spatial terms enables the speculative flow and capital mobility drawn in by an urbanizing Kigali, with its international airport and industrial zones luring footloose capital (Goldman 2011 on "speculative urbanism" has relevance here).

Celestin's enthusiasm for his innovative community voluntarism approach to the physical planning and regularization of the Karumuna-Ntarama-Nyamata corridor is sharpened in the context of the "National Volunteerism Policy" (2012, coinciding with decentralization reforms and implementation). Deemed another "homegrown solution" by the Rwanda Governance Board (RGB)—and to some extent working in tandem with the increased emphasis on voluntarism and voluntary work by governments and communities around the world, such that voluntary labor is even quantified by the International Labor Organization (ILO)—this government by the ethos of community (Rose 1999) is actively priced and quantified as an offset to state expenditure. The "National Volunteerism Policy" (2012) is subsumed under the National Itorero Commission, designed to tie together social reeducation in the post-genocide period with "traditional" Rwandan values of courage, integrity, and self-reliance (*agaciro*). Termed *ubwitange*, which literally means a "'free will action,' performed out of self-motivation and passion," the policy ties voluntarism to traditional Rwandan values under the precolonial kingship system, ironically meshing those values with the use of contemporary terms such as "disaster relief" and "social economic community services," which belong very much to the twenty-first-century development discourse on risk and resilience (Republic of Rwanda 2012):

> The spirit of volunteerism transcended the Rwandan social structure and was relied upon by the national leadership institutions operating under the king as an effective tool of mobilizing people for national and community service activities including among others; [*sic*] security, disaster relief and other social economic community services. The volunteerism spirit was used at all levels among Rwandans to address issues confronting society at various levels.[27]

The Volunteerism Policy defines voluntary service in the context of national service to the country, using precolonial Rwanda as a referent for the contemporary nation-state, and establishing a legitimating temporal and spatial continuity in the rewriting of the country's history by the National Unity and Reconciliation Commission (NURC) (Republic of Rwanda 1999). Voluntarism in contemporary Rwanda is placed in the context of national service with the following rationale:

> Opting for National Service is mainly due to the following principal reasons: (i) Rwandans in pre-colonial Rwanda applied National Service in state rebuilding and led the Country to great achievements hence need to be re-adopted; (ii) National service is carried out by nationals and non-nationals without expecting any pay for the work accomplished unlike Volunteerism where the Volunteer expects some little pay for the work done; (iii) Nationals

and non-nationals engaged in National Service activities may later participate in Volunteerism activities as a recognition of their dedicated and committed services to their State (Republic of Rwanda 2012: 3).

Noting that there are currently thousands of volunteer officials in Rwanda, the policy *monetizes* voluntary contributions to GDP and to the public wage bill. In particular, it notes that through the 2011–12 public wage bill, the government is saving Rwf 14,633,088,710 per year in public expenditures through volunteer work and national service:

> With a conservative estimate on the current 59,368 Community Health Workers and 150,366 Local Government Officials and Committees, each of them working for an estimated 100 days in a year, 65,000 Election Process Managers each working for an estimated 15 days a year, 5,352 *Abunzi* officials, 24,000 *Gacaca* officials, and 5,000 Red Cross volunteers each working for an estimated 50 days in year, all at the rate of a token Rwf 3,000 per day (Rwf 90,000 per month), it would cost the government an estimated Rwf 70,998,000,000 per year to deliver the services that are being delivered through volunteerism. . . .
>
> It is indicative from the 2011 GDP figure of 2,540 billion francs that volunteerism contributes more than 30% to the national GDP, which is substantial. This excludes contribution by other volunteers like night patrol guards at cell level, civil servants working overtime, monthly *umuganda*, etc. . . .
>
> In the health sector at district level, the 59,368 community health workers working for 12 months at an estimated monthly salary of Rwf 90,000 would cost government Rwf 64,117,440,000 per year, while the 2,500 salaried district health personnel earning an estimated Rwf 200,000 per month for 12 months cost government Rwf 14,633,088,710 per year (MINECOFIN 2011–2012 wage bill). *This means that government is saving three times for the same work provided through volunteer effort in this sector* (Republic of Rwanda 2012; emphasis added)

These findings instantiate that state planning work has been displaced onto the citizenry, particularly the peri-urban poor, who have little in the way of speculative interests and little choice but to comply. As the Voluntarism Policy states, "government is saving three times for the same work provided through volunteer effort in this sector."

These citizen offsets echo the words of Celestin in the planning office in Bugesera. Through quantifying the labor costs of required voluntary work and the savings accrued to the state, forms of displacement—the displacement of funds, labor, and time and the cost of mobile capital and immobile livelihoods—become strikingly apparent. Here, the winners from the savings generated are the investments by the central state in projects that fund state-of-the-art green technology and urbanized investment that caters to foreign direct investment and footloose capital, all deemed as national priorities and investment generators. As the time and expense of mobile capital investment on the peripheries of Kigali gets prioritized and eased, the costs of displacement from immobile livelihoods goes up for the poor on whose labor voluntarism the local state increasingly relies.

As voluntary labor is monetized by the state, I underscore re-indexing as a calculative practice of triaging and designating value amid the displacements of Rwanda's urban moment. Such calculations bring to mind Hernando De Soto's generalized analysis of unlocking undercapitalized assets in the developing world. He writes, "By our calculation, the total value of the real estate held but not legally held by the poor of the Third World and former communist nations is at least $9.3 trillion" (De Soto 2000: 35). Amid capitalized voluntary labor and newly planned land, the formalized representational economy ploughing its way across the river and through Bugesera's hinterlands operates on sedimented political geography and in layered relational space. As the work of formalization continues in Karumuna and Kanzenze as in parts of Kigali, relational networks of former residents are severed beyond repair—producing, in turn, "dead capital" of a very different sort.

Much like the rural poor whose land has been collectivized and "freed up" to pave the way for commercialized agriculture and conservation (Cioffo et al. 2016; Gebauer 2015), leading to mass resettlements in grouped housing schemes (*imidugudu*), the urban poor in Kigali and, now, on the periphery in Bugesera District are increasingly moved around from place to place in waves of dislocation and dispossession. I term these itineraries of movement "'disorientive dispossession," not only because they dislocate and render unstable the homes and livelihoods of low-income urban residents, but because they create a literal disorientation in ways of life, modes of social reproduction, and links between personhood, place, and directions for the future. This kind of dispossession is especially disorienting for these residents at a time when the capital seeks to modernize and the Rwandan nation-state aims to reorient itself as a hub for a new era of global urbanism. To what extent do these plans include the poor in their visions of redefined urban citizenship as anything other than productive and content citizens who underpin a new elite urban order?

Speaking in peripheral Karumuna, Emmanuel relates his itinerary of dislocation:

> I moved to this area six months ago. I used to live in Kigali, but the area I lived in [an informal settlement near Gikondo] was expropriated, and we were told to leave. I was able to buy some land in Gahanga in Kicukiro district, on the border with Bugesera. The official building regulations in the city of Kigali

[issued in 2015] said that I had to either put up a high-quality multistoried residence [*étages*] or sell my land. I wasn't able to afford to construct to this level, and couldn't leave my land empty or with a smaller house, so I had to give it up. I then came to Karumuna with my family and am trying to construct a house here, but similar regulations may soon force me to move again, outward into Bugesera's rural areas.[28]

Emmanuel is fifty-seven years old, and when he asks, "How many times will I have to move?" he poses existential and experiential concerns that have grown in direct proportion to Kigali's urbanization, expanding ever outward as the capital grows, attracting investments and intensifying speculative urbanization. Other residents interviewed were divided in their assessments of urbanization and dislocation in the peripheries. "Planning in this area is both good and bad," commented shopkeeper Anne. "It will benefit those who have money and can afford to buy out more land from those who can't afford to build here. For the poor, it means they will have to move again out of this area, to a more rural place where they can afford to live."[29]

As national policy targets a 35 percent urban population by 2024 (Republic of Rwanda n.d.), the conditions of possibility for urbanization in Rwanda are being reconstituted through productive and speculative logics: the productive immobility of residents of rural areas and their presumed labor comes up against the speculative logics of mobile elites and capital flow. The twenty-first-century urbanization of this majority rural nation is best characterized as a selective endeavor, premised on the exclusivity of the population groups and spaces that are mobile, and others who are socially immobile and upon whose stasis this project to "modernize" the nation depends (Mitchell 2002). The movement from tradition to modernity, from the seemingly fixed and unchanging to the mobile and modernizing, is intertwined with stasis and flow, the opposition between varying temporalities within one nation-state, across the urban/rural divide.

Globalization—with its own rapidity of movement and selective intervention—is deeply implicated in this retrenchment of sociospatial divisions in Rwanda today. The flow of transnational funds and global expertise that makes it possible to envision the country's urban experiments does not problematize the ways in which rural and peri-urban productivity and ways of life are central to this postconflict national urbanization. Instead, it is precisely through transnational flow and circuits of expertise that rapid urbanization and green urban experiments are enabled, so that state-driven urbanization thereby seeks to bypass years of contested rural development and national catastrophe. The danger of this rapid pace is that by seeking to leap into a new urban era, Rwanda risks spatially and temporally marginalizing a majority of its populace. The speed of urbanization targeted by the state may well retrench long-standing sociospatial fissures and fractures; the ambitious developmentalism of the previous decades may have ameliorated living standards in the years after the 1994 genocide, but such splintering remains far from resolved.

Rural Imagining

On the fringes of urbanity, in the model green village, displacement has an aftermath, an affective state that I call "after dispossession."[1] The affective contours of after dispossession are rarely visible in accounts of displacement, dislocation, and exile—the feelings of nostalgia and frustration, the quiet contestation that lingers beyond enforced dislocation. In this chapter I examine the imaginative mobilities—expectations and imaginings of a better life in the city, the sentiments that accord with these longings, the unrequited watchfulness—that peripheralized rural dwellers in Bugesera District share as they seek opportunity beyond the confines of their model village or reflect nostalgically on their earlier island homes. I examine the local politics of dissent among residents who have all the trappings of sustainable green technology in their villages but find themselves stuck in place—in a state of immobility, and on display for guests of the state as object lessons of development. As residents' imaginaries in the model village make clear, the city for them is an aspirational object of imagination, and not just a physical place. For many who live in these villages and in rural areas, the city is encountered and seen from a distance. Their mobility is thwarted, in a space of untenable aspirations.[2]

The model green village of Rweru is located down a smoothly asphalted road, about an hour and a half from Bugesera's district capital of Nyamata. My inquiry here moves us farther from the capital city and its newly speculative frontier near Nyamata to areas of Bugesera that are still rural. Although many of Rwanda's roads are asphalted and well maintained, the road to Rweru is particularly so. This is partly due to a massive campaign of investment in and around the area near the model village. Reportedly, the American investor Warren Buffett has purchased large swaths of the land near Rweru and is

FIGURE 7.1. Central flagpole in the model village, Bugesera District

partnering with the Rwandan government to build a scientific and agricultural university nearby. Also visible near the farthest reaches of the village
are a mine—likely bauxite—and inhabited areas that have not been incorporated into the organizational structure of the model village. After I arrived
in Rweru, I checked in with the administrative sector head, whose office is
located near a flagpole in a central area near the village (figure 7.1), and then
I proceeded to walk over to the village itself.

During one particular visit, my interlocutors Antoine and Jessica are sitting on chairs made of fabric and wood, part of the sparse yet functional
furnishings of a model home, as we discuss details of their life in the Rweru
model green village. During my past few visits Antoine and Jessica have followed me, eavesdropping on my discussions with other settlement residents,
and rarely interjecting. I assume they belong to the network of ears who sur-
veil conversation in this model village where I am conducting research. In
their mid-twenties and educated until early secondary school, they appear
well versed in the comings and goings of the village, and could certainly provide this information to higher-ups in the village administrative structure,
which is itself attached to the tentacles of local government. The appendages
of the conjoined party and state are evident here in the model village.

The model green village is ostensibly a display of miniaturized living. Drawing on the design principles of villages in Rwanda's rural resettlement program, or *imidugudu*, it is a Potemkin village customized for the age of donor development, serving to attract green finance and functioning as a veritable museum of sustainable rural living, with low-tech strategies that involve the efficient redesign of traditional Rwandan livelihoods. The village is a self-contained exemplar of the shift by Rwanda's state bureaucracy as it repackages ideas purveyed in model villages, such as the development economist Jeffrey Sachs's Millennium Villages Project (Wilson 2017) in East Africa, for a new regime of donor finance centered around green climate financing, adaptation, and risk mitigation. According to its design handbook, the model village has a standardized layout: a form with a functional purpose, with areas zoned for specific uses (livestock, landfill, commerce, handicraft, light industries). At the center of the village are common utilities: the multipurpose hall, health post, nursery, and administration offices. The middle areas of the circular plan are devoted to grouped houses, with common pasture areas and industry located in the external areas of the village layout. Abstracted and replicated at various sites to different scales according to site location and feasibility, the model village has become a terrain for design experimentation, amalgamation, and standardization. It is a development experiment at the scale of the community, involving mobile prototypes and standardized solutions for the subjects it seeks to shape.

As I observed on my first visits, technology has overtaken human narrative, as everywhere the green ornaments of sustainable rural living are visibly planted like small monuments: biogas machinery, solar panels, and water tanks designed to conserve flow and used alternately for household consumption, animal maintenance, and irrigation. Yet to see the model green village as a whole—to see its miniaturized representations in the local administrative office, and to see its plethora of minor technological monuments and design repurposing—is to miss seeing the human infrastructure of its displaced residents that becomes apparent behind the green veneer of its rural technological reinvention. It is only a couple of visits into my research in Rweru, in Jessica and Antoine's living room with its brick walls, concrete slab floors, and pale orange and green furnishings, that I finally have the opportunity to converse with them more directly. They fidget uneasily and then break into smiles and hesitant laughter, admitting that they hope to learn of new opportunities beyond Rweru's confines, so that they can use their education and turn dreams of the city into a tangible reality, somewhere beyond the aridity of the settlement and its environs. As they look out the window onto the undulating landscape and speak of the scarce opportunities in rural Bug-esera, they call forth an imaginary of the city beyond the museumized and miniaturized rural village. Their words speak to the nature of the capital as a space that is first conjured through distant desires for mobility in all its vari-ous forms—social, economic, physical—and gradually rendered real through this combination.

This is how the city is encountered by Antoine and Jessica, and likewise by numbers of partially educated Rwandans who see the capital, often from a distance, as a space of unrealized longings and dreams of an urban future. As much as Rwanda's success stories of improved health services and social economic indicators of service delivery showcase some of the successes of the post-genocide government, narratives of thwarted mobility are everywhere evident in Rweru, and in its counterpart villages which I visited in Rwanda's north—if one digs beneath the surface. The promise of postconflict urbanism, which focuses on the city as a space of opportunity, bridge building, reconcili-ation, interaction, and imagination for shared futures—a genuine democratic "socio-technical imaginary" (Jasanoff and Kim 2015) for the population as a whole—is restricted instead to a minority class-capitalist project and an invest-ment horizon for entrenched elites. Governmental echelons in Kigali aim to create a "post"-post-genocide image of Rwanda as a green hub for the region. To achieve this, they seek to convert the capital into a "world-class" city, integrated into the aesthetic and global financial circuits of urban investment and sustain-able green expertise. This aspiration yields lifestyle choices affordable mainly to those Rwandans who have been able to capitalize on the city in transition.

Yet, in a postconflict space whose bitter contemporary pasts of genocide and contentious civil war have entrenched silent cleavages within the coun-try and beyond, the city in this postconflict context must ideally represent more than an exclusive aesthetic of order and narrowly defined economic opportunity. The city as shared space, as a tableau or Lefebvrian oeuvre for popular co-creation, is a compelling possibility in a postconflict society. Viewed from the rural fringe as Jessica and Antoine do, however, Kigali in-stead appears elusive. It embodies the loss of a jointly reimagined future and an ethnically and socioeconomically inclusive platform. The aesthetic visions for spatial planning in the capital may "zone" for an exclusive, green, and exquisitely designed city, but they also build on top of sedimented and splin-tered pasts, many narrative histories, and many stories that risk being sub-merged by a single master narrative of progress, and a master-planned built history of space. Rwanda's exclusive urbanization, attendant displacements, and thwarted mobilities imperil shared access to the city as a symbolically and materially co-created space.

As the winding Akagera River cuts across urbanizing terrain between Bugesera and the expanded domain of the city of Kigali, gradually becoming tame as it enters the confines of the capital, dreams of crossing that river and having the right to remain in the city become ever more distant possibilities. In its varied chapters, this book shows that mobile urban dreaming is increasingly estranged from material reality for the majority of Rwanda's residents: whether for the urban poor in informal settlements around the city deemed "unplanned," for peripheral dwellers pushed out of the city, or for those who gaze upon the city from the rural fringe. At a time when Rwanda has engaged extensive foreign expertise to replan its towns and cities and generate futuristic, green master-planned spatial visions for them, sustainable urban dreams for the majority of Rwandans are spectral and ephemeral. Encountering the city in the imagination of rural dwellers in Rwanda's model villages, after having encountered the city more materially throughout this book, illuminates the diminishing possibilities of shared access to this space.

Recontextualizing Rwanda's Urban Transformation

Encountering the city imaginatively as well as materially also allows us to ask how, over time, city space has marked the entrenched urban/rural division in Rwanda, which has indexed not only life chances and forms of physical and economic mobility but ethnic divides and regional allegiances that have been the currency of social division throughout the country's history. To understand Rwanda's urban transformation today requires us to consider both a "Rwandan urban question," marked by generational regional and urban/rural division, and a "postconflict urban question" of building inclusive shared futures through the space of the city.

Since the colonial period, the "urban question" in Rwanda has been one of managing a majoritarian rural population through urban power, with the country's capital as a node of centralized control. Through its various periods of dominion—colonial, postindependence, and post-genocide—Kigali's changing elite base has rendered it an urbanized node distinct and separate from rural areas. With the urbanization rate in Rwanda remaining at 5 to 8 percent urbanized from independence in 1962 (World Bank WDI statistics) to the onset of the genocide in 1994, this deeply entrenched urban/rural divide has striated popular divisions and views on reproduction and development in the nation. Most of the rural population was comprised of ethnic Hutus (approximately 85 percent of the total population in early 1994), with strongholds for Hutu elites in the south-central part of the country, and later in the north under the Second Rwandan Republic government of Juvenal Habyarimana.

The Rwandan "urban question" is hence historically configured around the distribution of population and development between rural and urban. This biopolitical question of recalibrating rurality in Rwanda during the post-genocide period of national transition and urban transformation focuses on the management of rural dwellers for whom life in Rwanda's capital is largely unattainable. In the aftermath of the RPF takeover of Kigali in July 1994 and the official end to the genocide that had unfolded from April to July of that year, the population remaining in the country was suspected of complicity and participation in genocide. Much of what I characterize as the biopolitical management of the urban/rural divide relates to this suspicion of mass participation in the genocide against the Tutsi. Mahmood Mamdani quotes an RPA army source in 1995, whose words encapsulate this complex terrain:

> Puzzling over the difference between crimes committed by a minority of state functionaries and political violence by civilians, he recalled, "When we captured Kigali, we thought we would face criminals in the state; instead, we faced a criminal population." And then, as if reflecting on the other side of the dilemma, he added, "Kigali was half empty when we arrived. It was as if the RPF was an army of occupation." His sense of ambiguity was born of the true moral and political dilemma of the genocide. Just pointing at the leadership of the genocide left the truly troubling question unanswered: How could this tiny group convince the majority to kill, or to acquiesce in the killing of, the minority? (Mamdani 2020: 7).

Living together and transforming this "criminal population" was thus at the core of the RPF's challenge as its leadership navigated between the discourse of collective responsibility on the part of all Hutus, and that of de-ethnicized unity, where all discussion of ethnicity was proscribed. The transformation of rural dwellers into "durable Rwandans" capable of resilience and quiescent to top-down governance was thus central to the problem of national transformation and urban modernization.

The Rwandan urban question also embeds competing visions of political life in the postindependence period: either majoritarian visions of state, society, and populist democracy in the early postindependence period or more narrowly defined minoritarian rule, centered on the securitization of participation in the post-genocide period. While Rwanda has never been without its elites, multiple cleavages have striated the urban/rural divide over time. These enduring ethnic and regional divides mean that an urban question in Rwanda cannot be separated from a rural-agrarian question. In turn, the RPF state's post-genocide dilemmas persist: How does the state modernize in terms of democratic participation when that participation itself would engage the ethnic majoritarian population as active agents and vote-bearing citizens? For the RPF-led state, to reimagine the spatial division between city and country is also to grapple with the challenge of reimagining participatory democracy for the population writ large. Current repressive models of rule deny the existence of ethnicity and hide the state-party and class-capitalist gains accumulated through the post-genocide political order. I suggest that the core governance challenge is not one of "creative destruction," but one of creatively deconstructing an ethnically configured urban/rural divide, and of daring to reconceptualize multiparty participatory democracy anew.

As state elites seek to leapfrog traditional "brown development" trajectories (what Rostow [1990] labels "stages of growth") through urban borrowings and "green" developmental transplantation from the East, I suggest that they are re-engaging ongoing questions of the relationship between country and city in programs of modernization and urban transformation. The differentiation between urban and rural is critical to the effort to "rebirth" and "reinvent" in this post-genocide state, but instead of recalibrating these spatial divisions, we see the retrenchment of urban/rural distributional disparities. The symbolism of the city and the management of the urban/rural divide are therefore two enduringly relevant questions as we analyze continuities and ruptures in postindependence Rwanda. The recent fervor for urbanization and the urban transformation of the physical environment of the capital— with the government of Rwanda, to recall, seeking a 35 percent urbanization rate by 2024, from its current 18–20 percent range—is remarkable not simply for its forms and models of development, but for the profound transformation of popular "mindsets" concerning urban habitation that this state project demands of its citizens.

Significantly, while urbanization seeks to structurally transform the economy of the Rwandan state into one focused more on services and manufacturing, the tightly controlled Rwandan economy has called into question the feasibility of such plans (Behuria and Goodfellow 2019; World Bank 2017). Property speculation and the attraction of mobile capital form the core of current urban growth (Goodfellow 2017, 2022), leaving a rural population still largely disenfranchised from urban aspirations of social mobility. In 2007, 60 percent of Rwanda's population lived in extreme poverty, and despite controversy over statistical measures in the past few years, at least 40 percent of Rwandans today live beneath a poverty line of two dollars a day.[3] A 2022 International Monetary Fund report further notes that unemployment and food insecurity in the country remain high, such that "35 percent of population [is] under-nourished, against the sub-Saharan average of 20 percent, [and] food insecurity concerns, due to covid-19 and high exposure to droughts, have risen as increases in fertilizer and transportation prices are constraining food supply, the bulk of which is domestically produced."[4] The planning of six secondary cities at sites of existing towns across the country (Republic of Rwanda and GGGI 2015) seeks in part to provide growth sites for the Rwandan economy and stem urban migration to the capital, where municipal anxieties over overpopulation and the potential ensuing resource crisis loom over discourses of elites and state officials. Nonetheless, demographic targets for urban migration to secondary cities to ease the pressure in Kigali remain ambitious at best (World Bank 2017), leaving questions of feasibility and logistics unanswered in national urbanization plans.

In contrast to scholarship that interprets the "urban question" (Brenner 2000; Castells 1977; Merrifield 2014) primarily as an issue of land—its boundaries and objectification, as well as its commodification and financialization—I suggest that the question in a post-genocide context such as Rwanda's is instead a *biopolitical* one (Foucault 2008). Spatial planning has a central role in this biopolitical management of the distribution of urban life. In a politically complex context such as that of post-genocide Rwanda, planning is not merely a spatial exercise with material effects, but extends into social environments that contribute in this case to the governance of urban inhabitants, their interactions with each other, and their interactions with the state.

Planning is fundamentally implicated in what one might refer to as the ongoing, iterative project of transformation that has overtaken Rwanda since the Belgian colonial period. As James Scott (1998) has shown, this transformation is taken up through the project of spatial reorientation, dislocation, and relocation, and through the remaking of individuals as "new men" for new spatial orders (on the making of "new man," see Cheng 2008). This project of transformation was written into the colonial project, reshaping subject peoples through forced labor (*corvée*) and restrictions on their movement. In the contemporary period, the project of prototyping durable, resilient, and quiescent Rwandans for new orders of post-genocide life is also a project of transformation; changing the city, redesigning space, and rearranging rural dwellers into grouped settlement schemes all work as biopolitical projects of social engineering. To reiterate what one of my interlocutors (see chapter 3) said to me in mid-2019, we must think carefully about the project of transformation and the means, motives, and meanings of "durable transformation."

Transformation is an ongoing state-led social and spatial engineering project in Rwanda which seeks to transform the basis of social order, yet retrenches the violent management of populations at each turn. The state's projects of transformation are biopolitical and necropolitical endeavors that take as their primary axis the urban/rural divide. Transformation is a state project at the intersection of violence, coercive regulation, and iterative attempts to modernize. In Rwanda, state transformation is hence an avowedly modern problematic, and is bound up with the violence of genocide and its aftermath.

Prototyping the Durable Rwandan

Returning to Rweru, the architecture of the prototype has built within it a form of everyday governance. Aside from the overall layout of the village, the model house is another site for biopolitical experimentation. The model house designed for families in the model green village operates according to a prototype; each semi-detached house is a "4-in-1" house, housing four families who share one improved latrine and biogas digester. Residents told me that they have been involved in constructing and maintaining the houses, with initial support from the authorities. At the time I studied Rweru village, several new houses were being built by residents for future occupants who were to be moved off islands nearby. There were three sets of house designs, the latest of the three constructed in redbrick with obligatory metal roofing.

The project to make villagers modern by modernizing their settlement designs and housing typologies is not a new one. Using Belgian archival records, Gaugler (2018) demonstrates that the project to transform the domesticity and dwelling of Rwandan *indigenes* through the use of more durable housing materials became more prominent in the late colonial period. From the 1940s onward, experiments with design and durability were conducted to introduce more permanent materials into Rwandan dwelling units and to revise the construction typologies used in vernacular architecture—from circular thatch houses to formalized rectangular dwellings. These changes emphasized certain visions of civilization for wealthier classes of *"evolué" indigenes* under the colonial administration, and worked in tandem with pass laws, taxation, and other restrictions on mobility to fix Rwandans to one place (Gaugler 2018: 48). Over the long term, these efforts were part of a material genealogy of the prototype or dwelling unit as a mode of governing the rural Rwandan subject.

A new period of design reform was initiated via the prototyping of grouped settlements through imidugudu and the introduction of a new program in 2009: the "bye bye nyakatsi" campaign. The campaign against *nyakatsi* (thatch) aimed to rid the country of traditional thatched roofing in favor of sheet metal roofing as a sign of modernity, but also signified governmental control over domestic space. Such top-down initiatives enforced state views of the material facets of modernity in the post-genocide period. The demand that rural populations settle in grouped housing settlements, and modernization campaigns focused on the design of individual dwellings in rural areas aligned with and augmented one another. The aim was to settle rural subjects in place, and ostensibly to regulate their movements, way of life, and possibilities for resistance. With imidugudu settlements organized spatially according to specific, regular design layouts, clearly visible in satellite imagery as congregated rectangular settlements (bearing in mind that most of the Rwandan terrain is mapped and marked out on GIS software in government records), everything that was "out of order" thus became visible and visually significant: it was detectible through spatial patterning and signaling as "matter out of place" (Douglas 2003).

Disciplining the rural Rwandan subject through environmental design and experimentation with the terrain of this intervention as the *umudugudu* or village has re-created a separation between urban citizens and rural subjects (drawing on Mamdani's [2018] theorization of colonial indirect rule): between the mobile and the modernized and those entitled only to stay in place as model subjects for state and elite versions of modernity, as circulated through sites of model villages and prototyped homes. That domestic life has been the subject of this governance by design is a significant extension of the post-genocide preoccupation with rural resistance and the enduring "peasant question" in post-genocide Rwanda. Control over spatial archetypes in the imidugudu, and the enforcement of a concept of "modernizing" subjects through sustainable infrastructures and aspirationally modern homes, enables the state to shape subjectivities on Rwanda's rural terrain. Through these spatial changes, model peasants might become, both through ideology and material culture, durable Rwandans.

Established in 2017 as part of the Rural Integrated Development Program (IDP),[5] Rweru is home to 144 families who have been living in the village since 2017. In May 2019, 140 more families were set to be relocated to the village from the nearby islands of Mazane and Charitas. These villagers have been moved from the two islands, where residents tell me they owned land, cultivated and harvested abundant food, and fished ("illegal fishing," the administrator called it as he accompanied me on my initial interviews). State authorities consider these populations to be "at risk" due to their living conditions on the island, which are deemed backward, lacking in infrastructure, and dangerous because residents need to cross over from the islands to reach health care facilities. The IDP interventions are part of the governmental programming to relocate individuals from high-risk zones and disaster-prone areas and provide support to the "vulnerable" populations in the area, defined as such because of their socioeconomic status and habitation patterns.

The IDP itself is managed by the Rwanda Environment Management Agency (REMA) which is the implementation arm of the Ministry of Environment. In this program, now supported by donor funding from the United Nations Development Program, among other contributors, the goal was to increase the number of villages in operation from forty-four in 2018 to one model green village in each of Rwanda's 416 administrative sectors by 2024.[6] The governmental narrative on the IDP villages combines climate change resilience with poverty alleviation, and draws on funding options for greening and "climate proofing" its rural development offerings. A funding proposal for the scale-up of green villages, submitted to the Global Environment Facility (GEF) in 2008 for US$8,360,000 to add to an additional US$22,360,000 over seventy-two months, describes the model green village thus:

> Green Village has a number of inter-linked components, emphasising efficient, effective, equitable and sustainable use of natural resources using technologies that optimise social, economic and environmental benefits. These include provision of water reservoirs to control run-off and ensure that it is productively utilized, control of soil erosion to reduce soil fertility loss and maintain or improve agricultural productivity and retain much of the water through terracing.[7]

The stated aim is to scale up the modes of living in these villages so that they can become 'models' in multiple senses, both exemplars for replication and miniatures for exhibition and show. From the first village established in Rubaya, Gicumbi District, in 2011 (under a policy dating to 2009), the program has gradually set up additional villages from 2012 onward based on the same prototype. Rweru is their exemplary village and the one to which officials take international leaders, dignitaries, and investors to show off Rwanda's commitment to integrated development and sustainable technologies. As a joint environment and poverty alleviation project, IDP villages both posit and tackle several problems with one integrated solution: that of the prototyped village, with prototype houses and dwelling units, and with imagined prototyped citizens willing to be on show for visitors and dignitaries, demonstrating their contribution to national development and environmental protection (Ansoms and Cioffo 2016). Rwanda's 2018 collaborative proposal with UNDP to GEF, titled "Ecosystems/Landscape Approach to Climate Proof the Rural Settlement Program of Rwanda," outlines the basic characteristics of each of the forty-four model green villages currently in operation. Each IDP village contains standardized houses and the following facilities:

> multipurpose hall, administration premises, health centres, classrooms and science laboratories and libraries, dining rooms, kitchens & stores; Early

Childhood Development Centres and playgrounds; Availing land for crops
and livestock where applicable, distribution of cows under *Girinka* program
and construction of cowsheds; Provision of Integrated Handcraft production
centre, ICT room & Installation ICT facilities; Construction of access roads,
rain water harvesting facilities, and access to clean water and electricity, including alternative energy such as biogas.[8]

In form and function, the villages combine earlier imidugudu villagization
programs, further described in the next section, with activities and elements
similar to Jeffrey Sachs's Millennium Villages Project. The villages also draw
heavily on cooperation with international development partners working in
Rwanda's rural spaces.

In addition to the Singapore model in Rwanda's urban spaces, the South
Korean model of community development has emerged as a comparably important one in Rwanda's rural spaces. Since 2006, South Korea's Saemaul Undong (SMU; translated as New Village Movement) has become influential in
developmental spheres beyond South Korea, and since 2010 has been trans-
planted to eight African countries selected as pilots for SMU transfer and implementation: Ethiopia, Rwanda, Senegal, Mozambique, Ghana, Nigeria, and
Cameroon, and the Democratic Republic of the Congo (Nauta and Lee 2017).
South Korea's narrative of its own emergence from being a developmentally
disadvantaged war-torn recipient of aid to becoming a middle-income donor
country has been attractive to developmental models of leadership, such as in
Rwanda. Accordingly, President Paul Kagame comments:

> There are things I admire, for example, about South Korea or Singapore. I ad-
> mire their history, their development, and how intensively they have invested
> in their people and technology. It was not so long ago that they were at the
> same level of development as we are. Today they are far ahead of us (in *Der
> Speigel* 2010; Nauta and Lee 2017).

SMU emerged in the 1970s in South Korea, when the developmental leader
President Park Chung-hee began to reconstruct the economy using aid
from the United States and Japan for rural development. He promoted self-
sufficiency by encouraging popular participation in infrastructure management and agricultural production at the community level. The program's three
principles still are "diligence," "self-help," and "cooperation," which resonate
deeply with Rwanda's own focus on the reformation of populations through
local participation and individual compliance with the rule of law. South Korean aid to the Rwandan government has rapidly increased to US$8 million
(Nauta and Lee 2017: 189), with the goal of a confluence of the program with
Rwanda's own Vision 2020 and National Strategy for Transformation, which

cite "the development experience of the East Asian 'Tigers' [which] proves this dream could be a reality" (Republic of Rwanda 2000: 25). Strategies to mold both individual and collective behavior, changing mindsets as well as environments, have been central to SMU and are likewise deeply woven into Rwanda's own developmental-disciplinary model.

Integrated Development and Villagization

Although it draws on modern idioms of development and green ecology, integrated development and villagization have complex genealogies of their own in Rwanda and in the larger region, which illustrates once again that global development discourse has localized meaning and valence. The grouped settlement scheme, based on villagization and the integration of populations from different areas to promote "peace building" and ensure efficient use of land and resources was implemented on a large scale from early 1997. While the predecessors of these villages (imidugudu) are the *ujamaa* villagization settlement schemes during Julius Nyerere's African Socialist government in Tanzania from 1967 onward (Lal 2015; Scott 1998), grouped rural housing schemes have had their own Rwandan incarnations since the genocide. In a 2001 report, Human Rights Watch estimated that over 225,000 households (about one million people) had been moved to imidugudu by late 1999 (Human Rights Watch 2001, Newbury 2011). The program has since been extended to the majority of Rwandan rural households. These settlement schemes change the scattered spatial layout and strong social organization that characterized rural areas in Rwanda prior to the genocide, and whose social organization also contributed to the dynamics of the genocide violence. In addition to the example of villagization in Nyerere's Tanzania, Van Leeuwen (2001) describes examples of collectivization in Mozambique and Ethiopia and writes, "Some observers perceived hidden agendas behind the policies in Mozambique and Ethiopia, where resettlement and villagization were suspected, among other things, of being designed to increase government control over farmers" (625).

Much like these earlier and largely unsuccessful attempts, which aimed to modernize and reorganize the peasantry, villagization primarily has been coerced in Rwanda, given that villagers were unwilling to give up their land and way of life (Van Leeuwen 2001: 627). Begun as a "rural resettlement program," the villagization initiative was initially designed to free up land for housing for "old caseload" returning refugees (chapter 5)—several hundred thousand families of the Tutsi diaspora who had left the country during earlier rounds of conflict or had grown up in exile. Later, it was also promoted as a means of

rational land use and better agricultural productivity. The villagization program in Rwanda has also been supported by external funders, keen to intervene in reconstruction efforts after their absence during the 1994 genocide.
Large numbers of houses were damaged or abandoned after the genocide.
While returning Tutsi refugees initially occupied those houses at the behest of
the government, the return of "new caseload" Hutu refugees from Burundi,
Tanzania, and the Congo from 1995–96 onward complicated this strategy and
created housing shortfalls for returnees (Human Rights Watch 2001).

The government of Rwanda's 1996 habitation and resettlement policy addressed the complexity of rival claims on dwelling space through imidugudu.
Particularly after 1998, many Rwandans experienced forced resettlement.
They already had their own homes, and were coerced to destroy them and to
relocate to the sparsely inhabited imidugudu settlement areas. Sources note
that after the initial settlement processes began, houses and housing material
were in short supply for later arrivals (Human Rights Watch 2001). These
later migrants to imidugudu were forced to construct their own dwellings,
often with materials salvaged from their previous destroyed homes (Gaugler
2018: 49). That coerced relocation has been a central portion of the resettlement policy is particularly problematic, contributing to the dislocation and
reorientation of rural families in ongoing "disorientive dispossession" (see
chapter 6). Writing on *ujamaa* villagization in Tanzania in the 1970s, James
Scott's (1998) interpretation of the speed and scale of forced resettlement resonates with my analysis of dislocation here. Scott surmises that

> the planners felt that the shock of lightening-quick settlement would have a
> salutary effect. It would rip the peasantry from their traditional surroundings
> and networks and would put them down in entirely new settings where, it
> was hoped, they could then be more readily remade into modern producers
> following the instructions of experts. *In a larger sense, of course, the purpose
> of forced settlement is always disorientation and then reorientation* (1998: 235;
> emphasis added).

Thus, while imidugudu was born during a period of disorder and urgency after the genocide, villagization and forced resettlement have become generic,
general modes of reorganizing populations and maintaining rural order in
the long term.

Biogas and Citizen Complaints

The model green village handbook (Government of Rwanda 2015c) goes into
great detail about the required standard templates for and maintenance of

sustainable facilities, to be replicated in each village and maintained through villager labor. Yet when local overseers accompanied me around the village and sat in on my interviews with residents, the "model villagers" interrupted the smoothly delivered explanations of the benefits of sustainable technology for villagers' lives. "The biogas isn't working for us and we need the facilities to be fixed," said one chorus of women. "We never got proper training in its maintenance, and we don't know who else will fix it." Residents in Rweru were also keen to point out their hardship due to ongoing drought conditions, which meant that rainwater harvesting wasn't an effective option. The breakdown of sustainable infrastructures in the village throws light onto the material politics of repair. Here, residents who were expected to fix broken infrastructures or endure breakdown used the opening of disrepair to enable complaint; the materiality of their environment grounded their discontent in ways that were political yet ambiguous.

Flora, an elderly resident relocated to Rweru, accompanied me and observed my visits and conversations with other residents, but was initially reticent to speak. Later, she came up to me and disclosed that she wanted to explain the nature of her distress in Rweru village:

> We have all the things here that would make our lives easier, but we prefer to go back to our old island, Mazane. There, we did not have biogas and brick houses, but we owned our own land, which was fertile, and we were able to cultivate and harvest enough food. Over here, we do not own our land and the land they have given us is too small and dry to grow crops to feed us and our cows.

Flora's statement drew approval from other residents who were listening, and contempt from the local official who was still with me. "These people don't want to change their mindsets," the official said disapprovingly. "They don't understand how much progress they have been given in the model village." A middle-aged man, Eugene, who had been a schoolteacher on the island, joined the discussion:

> It is true that it was a dangerous life on the island and we had to take the boat to get health care on the mainland, but we did have schools and we were able to provide for ourselves. We also owned our land, and here we don't even have titles to our houses. The land we have been given to cultivate is too little, and we cannot move to other places to grow crops.

Among the villagers were several young people who expressed their frustration at not being able to leave to earn money and become more economically and socially mobile. They had all the technologies of sustainability, but

FIGURE 7.2. A cattle shed and housing in Rweru

felt trapped inside the model, unable to seek greater opportunity in the city (figure 7.2).

Another green village, in northern Rwanda, was considerably smaller and more remote than Rweru. It had no asphalt road, but instead a long dirt road leading into the village, which was situated near a lake. Still, the model village had the same standardized technologies as in Rweru: biogas, rainwater harvesting, cattle sheds, land for cultivation, and standardized concrete and brick homes with modern roofing. "The biogas isn't working," one resident complained as we sat near a house, forming a spontaneous focus group of sorts. "It has been several months, and no one has come to repair it." Again, the official was exasperated, retorting that the villagers did not appreciate the benefits, like the house, and the boat provided to them for travel back to the original island home from which they had been moved. Later, in private, the villagers contradicted the official:

> We still need to go fishing to our island because we cannot cultivate enough crops here, so we asked for a boat, but the cost of the fuel for the boat is too expensive for us to afford, and we can only make a few trips every few weeks—not enough for us to gather enough food.

I asked younger residents about their lives in the village as compared to life on the island, and about their hopes and plans for the future. At first my questions elicited blank stares and a little frustrated laughter. Later, younger residents who had been moved from the island told me that the structure of housing in the village caused frustration for young men who had to live in the rigidly planned houses with the rest of their family members. "We want to get married and move on with our lives, but the houses belong to the government and we do not own them, so we have to stay with our families and cannot move out," they said. Here, state trajectories of progress explicitly contrasted with the mobile aspirations of youth, who wanted to make their own way in the village and beyond. Later, I asked the official whether the villagers could sell their houses and move to the city if they wanted to. "Where will they go?" he replied. "They can leave, but if they do, they have to give up their house to us so that we can give it to someone else to occupy—those from the risk zones."

The Texture of Local Contestation

Through state-mediated imaginaries of progress, materialized through the design of durable houses and planned settlements with the technologies of sustainability, these "green" villagers were there to be on display and to exemplify the state's programs to improve environmental management and aid to vulnerable populations. They were, in essence, trapped in service of the state as museumized populations, dubiously rescued from their hazardous living conditions on the island. Christophe, one of the men I spoke with in Rweru, had a leg amputated below the knee. Sitting below pictures and posters with religious iconography of Jesus Christ the savior, he told me that he had been attacked by a crocodile on one of his earlier crossings before moving to the island. He had been fishing on the lake, and acknowledged that the journeys he had made were not without danger. Although he is now on support from the state because of his disability, he confided that the support was not sufficient to feed his family. "I would return to the island," he said. "There, at least, we had enough food."

Contestation and claims-making constitute the terrain of the *local* in contemporary Rwanda. They situate place as a terrain of dissent, with carefully circumscribed boundaries that are at once spatially delimited to particular sites (e.g., the informal settlement, the rural model village) and by questions about specific rights and claims to place, opportunities, and livelihoods. In delimiting claims at the local level (chapter 5), it appears at first as if these displaced citizens are reluctant to contest larger issues, such as the city master plan or the imidugudu program, as contexts for their displacements. Instead, contestation within particular local boundaries both enables specific forms of dissent within Rwanda's centralized and tightly controlled public sphere, and makes that dissent potent as a set of statements that constitute local life-worlds. Such dissimulated and place-based dissent expresses specific local politics that speak to particular forms of rupture. The very localism and local terrain, of place-based politics challenges the homogenizing macronarratives of space and identity evident in state accounts of national-level change.

Here in the rural model green village, too, islanders displaced from Mazane and Charitas, and from Lake Burera in northern Rwanda, were eager to voice their dissent regarding the inadequacy of their new way of life. With their complaints about biogas and malfunctioning technology, they subverted the workings of bio-power and affirmed that, while they were subject to the state—as was manifest in the planned ordering of their daily lives—they still could express dissent and dissatisfaction locally. Compliance and complaint are two sides of the same sword; the state both needs the performance of the compliant model subject and knows that one of its transitional dilemmas is still the matter of changing rural mindsets—of reforming rural dwellers into model Rwandan citizens. As much as the state often succeeds in implementing hierarchical change, it also fails, under the surface.

Specific micropolitics of displacement and claims to place persist even as state-led planning spatially ruptures the country, from the rural model village to the urban periphery to the informal settlement in Kigali. Political claims in the contemporary moment are particularly compelling when embedded in local lifeworlds and particular places. The granular claims of rural model villagers or of displaced residents in informal settlements in Kigali over rights to remain in place constitute the terrain of the political itself in contemporary Rwanda and serve as legitimate counterweights to the state's macronarratives, such as the city master plan and the state's official history of the genocide, which assigns collective responsibility to non-Tutsis.

Top-down state planning erases, defamiliarizes, and depoliticizes these local claims to place by the use of *dis*placement, relocation, and movement; and by simultaneously thwarting possibilities for voluntary mobility in the country, including those that involve the right to the city. Through the master-planning that generalizes, and the spatial reorganization that occurs with villagization, state planning works to erase specific histories of place, particular modes of inhabiting space, and micronarratives in which memory is embedded at the local level. In other words, state planning erases tangible and material claims to alternative versions of history, and to the organic environments of memory and the social imaginaries in which they are embedded. When imagined from the rural fringe, the capital city embodies thwarted mobilities that are shared by peri-urban and rural dwellers who live in a space from which they can see the city, but where they remain far from ever crossing into urban terrain.

Conclusion

Before leaving Rwanda at the end of my research period, I revisited Nya-rubaba. I was eager to see how social space had changed in the rural sector, with the accelerated growth of a large town not too far away. I also wanted to understand how the politics of repair had been playing out in the years since I observed *gacaca* transitional justice court hearings. It was here that the material basis of the reconstruction of social relations after conflict first began to crystallize for me, as I observed *gacaca* proceedings in which neighbors and village members argued over what reconciliation and accountability meant for them.

These material politics of repair were constructed through sharing of food and beer, through physical repair of dwellings, and through reparations for lost cattle and broken roofing tiles. I have argued that these acts of exchange and the gradual integration of reciprocity are the material terrain upon which everyday life is remade, generating sociospatial relations as a form of transitional repair aimed at reintegration and the reconstruction of the quotidian. Rather than concentrating on the criteria for retributive or restorative justice for lost life, such a material terrain of repair focuses on the built environment and the shared social interactions constituted through it as an ongoing reparative fabric.

Material repair is in this context a form of micronarrative agency; it is a counterhegemonic practice of pulling together minor threads and weaving them into various sociospatial and narrative forms. Alternative modes of engaging the built environment, of cementing forms of exchange relations, and of narrating the inability to plan amid large-scale dispossession are instantiations of such antistructural agency. These minor acts in the plane of the everyday disrupt overarching narratives that consider repair as a noun—a closed state process of reconciliation and reconstruction. Instead, minor acts break through the closure of narrative form and newly planned space, inserting a tenor of incompleteness into ongoing processes of maintenance and rebuilding.

The more uneven and ongoing terrain of repair I narrate here also exposes hidden and peripheralized narratives within Rwanda's rural areas, where the quest for reconciliation and justice after genocide has been protracted and convoluted. Athanase's story is one such example, in many ways representative of the peripheralization of alternative narratives of the post-genocide transition that have been buried under the state's master narrative.[1]

The road leading to Nyarubaba was better developed upon my return, but still wound through steep and barren countryside that was often difficult to negotiate. Athanase's small home was located not far from the central sector office and flagpole. Meeting me first in Nyarubaba with a friend and translator, and then later in an outdoor bar in a nearby urban area, Athanase recollected his experiences during the genocide and afterward, up until the inception of *gacaca* in 2002: "I held an administrative position in this *cellule* [administrative division] during the genocide in 1994. It was a Sunday, and my duty was to check everyone fleeing from Bugesera, Rwisange, and Kibeho." He paused before continuing on to the changes *gacaca* and attempts at reconciliation had brought after his return: "Eventually we were obliged to flee towards Kibeho. Later, we came back to this area in 1997, and then *gacaca* started in 2002. I was also a judge of *gacaca*, but I decided to resign after people accused me of being present during the genocide."

Athanase later told of his experiences with *gacaca* and the judicial system, and the initial difficulties of resettling into the community after being accused of having been present in 1994. His experience with the court system and with iterative accusations, sentencing, and uncertainty speaks to the stark difficulties experienced by many ordinary Hutus who were present during the genocide in Rwanda in 1994 and were caught up in the chaos, fear, and disorder of the period.

Athanase's Experiences

In 2002 I was accused as someone who had participated in the roadblock; the accusation was that me and my sister looted. All four of us were found innocent in front of the *gacaca* court, that's all. In 2012, I was again accused of crimes and was put on a list of people sentenced to community work [*travaux d'interet general*, or TIG: conscripted community labor for prisoners after the genocide]. I was a teacher in the community and went to the

sector administrative office to check why I had been accused. I found there
was confusion, and they didn't have clear files on my case. I was asked to find
a lawyer, and wrote a letter to the *gacaca* chief to explain my situation. Later,
people [administrators] from Kigali came to assess my problem, and I had to
write a second letter. It took five years for the case to be resolved, and for us to
be found innocent again. The problem was that I had no files at all on my case
in the administration, so things were unclear. In 2017 all teachers were asked
to obtain a "liberation letter" indicating that they had never been sentenced
or had been in prison. I had nowhere to get the letter and I became scared, so
it [the case] then went to the normal courts, as *gacaca* was already over. As I
didn't have one [a letter], they accused me of participating in the roadblock
during the genocide all over again. Finally I went to the normal court, and the
final verdict has not yet come. I am still waiting for the letter now.

As Athanase's story shows, the ordinary lives of many in Rwanda's rural areas
are elided in state macronarratives of the genocide, and in certain regional
and international accounts of Rwanda's past. Examining local stories over
time enables one to unearth this arena as the terrain of social and material
relations, and of local politics and alternative narratives. Just as stories of reconciliation and coexistence are varied and nuanced, so are stories of participation and agency during the 1994 genocide and the civil war.

In work on the micropolitics of genocide in Rwanda, the political scientist
Lee Ann Fujii (2010) deconstructs oppositional binaries often used to explain
the violence in 1994. Rather than basing her arguments on the primordial
nature of ethnic hatred, Fujii pushes for a nuanced view of the genocidal violence as socially embedded at the local level. Her research has differentiated
between multiple categories of participants in the genocide in 1994, from national elites and local leaders to a category of participant she terms "joiners."
There was a spectrum of responses to genocide in 1994, Fujii contends, from
rescuing to resisting, witnessing, evading, pillaging, denouncing neighbors
or family members, and killing (Fujii 2010: 30). These actions were expressed
as a social script that exploded binary ideas of participation or nonparticipa-
tion in the genocide: motives and agency were conditioned at the local level
through multiple socially embedded ties and contextual local considerations.
People could play multiple roles and move between categories of participation over time.

Out of a population of more than seven million in 1990 (World Bank;
WDI), 85 percent of whom were Hutus and the majority of whom were rurally based, Scott Straus estimates that perpetrators of the genocide numbered
from 175,000 to 210,000 (Straus 2004: 94–95). Straus estimates that 90 percent

of this total were civilian perpetrators of genocidal violence, where he defines perpetration as participation in killing or injury to other civilians (87). Fujii's category of "joiners" (Fujii 2010: 6) speaks to larger conceptions of participation and lends additional perspective to the dynamics of the violence in 1994. "Joiners," for Fujii, were "'ordinary' men and women of their communities" who were "not strictly 'perpetrators'" but who took "a range of actions . . . both in support of and in defiance of the genocide" (16). Fujii uses the category of "joiners" in opposition to that of "the masses" to lend nuance to understandings of the violence and to add ambiguity and ambivalence to dissecting the motives and actions of these everyday participants (paraphrased: 13). Fujii thus locates agency at the *local* level for the range of micropolitical interactions between joiners and the groups they came to constitute. I draw attention to Fujii's analysis to articulate the local level as the terrain of micropolitical interpretation and ambivalent forms of action. Such local explanations also explain the varied experiences of ordinary Hutu Rwandans like Athanase, whose story demonstrates the ambivalence and complications of social relations and the state project of reconciliation after genocide.

A Material Peace

I began this book with the aim of parsing the political stakes of masterplanning as a form of total spatial determination, an exercise for giving shape to the community of the included in a post-genocide state, and a form of violent spatiality assumed over time in conflict-affected terrain. Questions of loss and exile, inclusion and political exclusion, and the struggle to narrate have been at the core of Rwanda's political struggles. A capture of the state involves the right to belong and inhabit, as if successive factions are competing for a single house. The stakes of these questions are critical to an urbanfocused future. They are about rights to the polity in its most specific and concrete senses: the right to remain in the material city, as well as the right of inclusion in the abstracted polity of citizenship through the nation-state.

The right to the city after conflict is about who is able to define and be counted in the community of the included, where questions of home, homeland, and belonging play across material textures of the built environment, across space and the construction and maintenance of place. Such questions of political inclusion thus have crucial sociomaterial dimensions, and can only be separated in the abstract into a dualism between political rights to citizenship and socioeconomic rights as part of the polity. The polity is hence a *tangible* entity: a composite body politic comprised of multiple bodies, a homeland where struggles over abandoned houses and the security of home are in every way material and hold high stakes because of this imbrication of the material with the political. What then does it mean to remake the polity's most symbolic and tangible space—that of the city—when questions of return, inhabitation, and dwelling are at stake in this remaking of a material space of citizenship?

Large-scale spatial recomposition is particularly devastating to existing modes of inhabiting the city as a symbolic and material space. As a form of totalization, the spatial master-planning of the city not only delimits access to the desired community of the included, but in a conflict-affected context also presents salient messages about what I call the "political abandonment" of the project of material inclusion and social belonging in a new, "reborn" Rwanda. The constriction of political discourse and the erasure of alternative means of inhabiting the city results in a very real missed opportunity to redefine the terms of inclusion in the political community—for reconfiguring meaningful terms of the "face-to-face" encounter through space and place (Levinas 1979).

In presenting an intervention on sociomaterial repair through the space of the city in this book, I have shown that repair in Rwanda is a complex web. As Rwanda's cities are remade through circulations of finance and transnational expertise, forms of relational repair (an open process operating through specific ideas of place and context) sit uneasily next to conceptions of top-down reconciliation (a large-scale project of closure). Repair in this case is more than a social process; it is also bound up with materialist considerations of distribution and access to the tangible dividends of urban space, as much as with material questions of interpersonal exchange and gradual consilience. This call for attention to a complex politics of repair centered on the city is particularly salient at the current urbanizing moment in Rwanda. Large-scale urban change in a society recovering from conflict digs up old wounds and exposes new inequalities, calling for redress and reckoning. Possibilities of repair and conciliation grow from equitable access to shared space, opening the city as a space of encounter, rather than closing it by way of exclusionary master-planning. Maintaining place as the grounds of ongoing repair and healing is central to a view of the postconflict built environment as a living and noncommodifiable spatiality. This form of repair through ongoing rebuilding and quotidian routines moves us beyond the purview of the state; such a view of repair takes us toward individual and community agency in seeking a livable consilience through existing built space.

A material politics of repair in Rwanda is an alternative spatial practice. It challenges divides that have been embedded by materialist struggle and iterative violence created through the reproduction of spatial division. Such possibilities of repair are necessarily limited—and meaningful—because they require constant rebuilding and care rather than one-stop solutions. By paying attention to what *can* be repaired and what *is* speakable amid mass atrocity and spatial division, a material politics of repair points toward tangible forms of coexistence based in the built environment and constituted through spatial fabrics. Scholarship on national reconciliation processes as "harmony ideology" (Nader 1990) calls out the state's role in enforcing an ideology of unity. As Ingelaere (2010) writes on Rwanda's reconciliation process, a type of "mise-en-scène" encodes a semblance of reconciliation, rather than representing the nuanced nature of politics on the ground with its own temporal *durée*. Focusing on the concept of "irreconciliation" (Mookherjee 2022; Wilson 2022), recent scholarly writing has conceptualized a complex conciliation that takes its own path. Against acquiescing to a simple top-down politics of forgetting, and to an acceptance of state ideologies of erasure and unity, such accounts present a more nuanced and heterogenous picture of reality on the ground.

As the burgeoning literature on social repair shows us, the conceptualizing of repair does not necessarily imply closure and a full and final settlement. Repair in Rwanda's cities is an ongoing project of rebuilding that is tinkered with over time. It is also a social and interpersonal process with multiple meanings and local instantiations, as well as possible pathways for recalibrating social relations, as Jovan Scott Lewis shows us in the context of Montego Bay, Jamaica (2020). Saliently, Simone's (2022) critique of repair points us to contexts "beyond repair," to cases where what is needed is a reckoning with and from within the present, however derelict. In thinking about the materiality of durable presents in rehabilitating *this* world, as opposed to imagining possible urban futures and alternative possibilities of other worlds, Simone is attentive to the need for reparative planning as a reworking of this present. Rather than emanating from other extractive and infrastructural projects of totality elsewhere, repair is configured through particularity. A tangible and ethical project of repair hence reinfuses value in the present, in all of its partiality and dilapidation. Such a project looks no further than the now.

Rwanda as Planning Prism

Considering Rwanda's urban processes within its wider contexts shows us that the postconflict city straddles spatial imaginaries and temporalities. In Africa, it remains an undertheorized geography. It exists between the precarity and violence of the conflict-affected state and the convivial, improvised hustle economies of the postcolonial African metropolis (Mbembe 2001 on the postcolony; Simone 2004 on improvised social infrastructure in South Africa). Using work on the city of Gulu in Uganda, Harris et al. (2022) theorize the "gendered postconflict city" as a liminal space of enduring trauma, and emphasize the need to go beyond theorization of more general forms of life in African cities and develop specific lexicons for the postconflict city.

As this book suggests, there is a certain interpersonal agency that can be harnessed to develop context-specific grassroots responses to the trauma and liminality of postconflict space. I have analyzed the phenomenology of repair as a sociomaterial sphere of minor acts that aim to make the past visible while enabling communities and survivors to build a livable present. Harris et al. (2022) reference the theoretical work of Judith Butler on "livability" in relation to conditions of precarity that circumscribe and limit lives that are worth living. In this sense, livability is "a political act because local power structures shape whose lives are livable," but it includes the necessary underpinnings of material life and "also conditions of social intelligibility, social recognition and social mattering" (Butler 2009, in Harris et al. 2022: 12). Like Butler's theorization of "dispossession" as a double-sided gesture and process of seeking encounter amid alterity and difference, such an analytic of livability points toward a concrete ethics for rebuilding the postconflict city with an understanding of how memory, place, and social difference affect life in it.

In such a complex context, state planners walk a fine line between complicity and socially conscious transformation. Professional urban planning elites and transnational development experts may think of themselves as mobile moral agents who are reconstructing a post-genocide society, but they are also the rainmakers for the new kingdom, the spatial surgeons of political terrain. Planning has long had an intimate relationship to power and politics (Bou Akar 2018; Flyvbjerg and Richardson 2002; Yiftachel 1998). It is also adept at using the "post-political" stance to "technify" its operations and render them seemingly objective (Wilson and Swyngedouw 2014). It is precisely this technical positioning in the specific context of a postconflict and post-genocide country that invites scrutiny of planning in relation to the politics of memory, as well as the social reproduction of place and community.

Looking beyond Rwanda, master-planning Kigali according to futuristic green designs imported from East Asia signals in particular ways to Rwanda's urban audiences: to global finance circuits and international governments, to climate finance and green technology investors, and to African governments in the region, which arguably have been analyzed the least (Cote-Roy and Moser 2019). With states such as Ethiopia grappling with similar dilemmas of authoritarian developmentalism and ethnic fragmentation, the green master-planned designs for urban space adopted in Rwanda serve as models within Africa, as examples of Afrofuturism, and as concrete means of bolstering specific modes of rule.

Models of urban development in Rwanda also entangle infrastructure with particular forms of political development that speak to constituencies in the capital (e.g., the Amhara in Addis Ababa, where confrontation over the growth of the city on largely Oromo land continues). In this case, urban infrastructure creates uneven territories of accelerated accumulation and dispossession, which affect populations in different ways within and beyond the urban. Finally, Rwanda's model of efficient governance and clean urbanization appeals to largely middle-class and elite citizens in other regional centers, who look askance at their own governments' inefficiencies and invoke Kigali as a foil. Here, the danger of accelerated urban renewal without democratic opening is often left inadequately examined amid widespread techno-optimism on the continent. Looking to the East as well as to the West has thus become a new solution for the problem of managing democratic opening in certain parts of the continent.

Intersecting logics characterize Rwanda's capital, Kigali, as both a model of urban transformation for other countries in the region, and an exception to prevalent characterizations of African urbanism, which largely elide a postconflict focus (Myers 2020 and 2011; Simone and Pieterse 2018). At a time of widespread ambitions for state-led urban planning or state-orchestrated private-sector development of spatial enclaves, eco-cities, and satellite towns for the wealthy in many African countries, Kigali's urban transformation has garnered increasing attention. The speed with which the Rwandan government has re-created its capital with landscaping and terracing, smoothly paved thoroughfares and sidewalks, and an emerging world-class skyline draws the envy of municipal governments and states in East and Central Africa as well as beyond. How, then, does one look beyond Kigali while still keeping it in focus?

Denizens of African cities from Lagos to Accra and from Bukavu to Nairobi post comments on social media praising President Paul Kagame as an African hero who has transformed developmental aspirations on the continent and provided a model of clean, efficient success. Rwanda has become the aesthetic capital of Africa—not only a green phoenix risen from the ashes of genocide, but the vanguard of a Pan-African image of progress on the continent. Unsurprisingly in this context, Kigali is Wakanda: the model of a "good city" and a "green city" taken form in Central Africa. Through the aesthetic and spatial reshaping of the capital, therefore, Rwandan elites appeal

to African pride amid widespread talk of "crisis" and calamity on the continent (Ferguson 2006). Much like Wakanda, their science-fiction counterpart,
Rwanda's cities harness images of green utopia to transform perceptions of
the postconflict state: from a post-genocide dystopia to a heroic wellspring of
developmental success. In this way, Kigali's transformation is as much about
the aesthetics of science fiction as it is about the concrete changes in the city,
which affect a wide range of groups, from survivors of the 1994 Rwandan
genocide to former prisoners and returning diasporic refugees.

In their potential to generate tangible effects within urban terrain to securitize space and order circulation and mobility in society, Kigali's aesthetics
demonstrate that they are more than just pleasing to the eye; they are instead
material markers of this social ordering (chapter 3). In this way the aesthetic
governs, and the biopolitical use of this aesthetic affects the material ordering
of urban society. Kigali's aesthetic of order does more than project and implement power; it serves as a transplantable genetic code for social ordering that
has been sought after by cities in the region. Study teams of municipal experts
have sought help from Kigali in regulating their cities, traveling to the Rwandan capital to seek lessons for remaking urban order at home. However, these
forms of urban transfer have varied meanings, and function differently in
their new landing places.

State and municipal leaders and ordinary citizens hence look toward
Rwanda as a paragon of urban efficiency and aesthetic order. In focusing on
Kigali as a transplantable urban "model," we can use these municipal aspirations and legitimate citizen expectations to site it in relation to other African
cities, whose citizens grow increasingly frustrated with urban governance at
home. Urban relations in cities such as Nairobi and Lagos expose inequities
in access to common urban space. Elite enclave developments, such as Eko
Atlantic in Lagos, function to "reassemble" uneven development within Nigeria's most populous city (Acey 2018), drawing stark distinctions between the
exclusive canals of the new city and the densely populated waterways of the
floating informal settlement known as Makoko, located a few kilometers away.
Violence by the military and by Nigeria's Special Anti-Robbery Squad (SARS)
has been actively protested by urban citizens, many of them youth, seeking to
symbolically "#EndSARS" during the covid-19 pandemic's lockdowns and a
period of high unemployment. Such cases point to tangible debates over rights
to the city and points of access to jobs and livelihoods in urban space as pre-
vailing themes on the continent (Hudani 2023). In many ways, these debates
resonate with the politics of access in other cities, such as Nairobi.

As much as studies of African urbanism and ongoing "accumulation by
dispossession" (Harvey 2003) similarly segment cities across the continent, I

suggest that there is a specific dynamic at play in Rwanda's urban transformation that locates it in circuits of postconflict urbanism with cities such as Phnom Penh and Sihanoukville in Cambodia. The Cambodian capital and secondary cities are being spatially replanned by expertise entrepreneurs, drawing on the green city development that is also being tailored for Rwanda's secondary cities.[2] Meanwhile, "Ream City" is being master-planned as a new urban development in the vicinity of Sihanoukville, Cambodia, by Surbana Jurong.[3]

Rwanda may be a "model" of social order and efficient governance for some on the African continent; but in this postconflict context, planning in the aftermath of mass violence also makes it an "exception" that needs to be questioned and contextualized to be understood.

On the Refusal to Plan

From my research in Bannyahe on the abandonment of the informal settlement to narratives I unearthed of not being able to upgrade housing in high-risk zones in Kimisagara and elsewhere, Rwandans I interviewed repeatedly invoked their inability to plan their lives. As state officials and planning experts halt repair and instead mandate removal in favor of better uses of the spatial master plan, residents have been caught in between. Yet while many residents were forced to reconsider their life plans, planning experts rarely consider stoppage or reversal as heuristics and circuits of action to be taken to reconsider planned trajectories. Like machineries of war, the wheels of master-planning, once started, are geared up for success, solutions, and intervention, if only with some compromise and circumvention. As manifestations of deep structural and contextual issues, obstacles to master-planned futures are often "problems" not set up to be solved. Such challenges to planning might instead point planners toward forms of *stoppage, pause,* and *reversal* on the ground. Such pause is at times the only way to address the complexity of development intervention on traumatized terrain.

I suggest that when thinking through reparative planning, we must question what success and supposed failure really mean in postconflict contexts. The temporality of gradual repair and the rapidity of policy transfer and planning solutions are often at cross-purposes. We might instead learn from scholarship in indigenous studies, which considers the nature of "refusal" as a critique of official demands and as a reconsideration of the ruse of recognition by the liberal state (Simpson 2014; Coulthard 2014). How then might we think about such "refusal" in terms of planning practice, and the pedagogy that the postconflict city demands of us? These questions have been embedded in the textures of this book as it has examined collective trauma and state intervention. Planners need to sit with the fact that, in considering reparative planning, there is often no quick or holistic solution to be found in the current frame of intervention.

Away from the closure of state forgetting, there is an alternative path: one that acknowledges the irreparability of lost life, yet seeks a material peace founded on everyday reciprocity, built incrementally through sociospatial relations for the here and now. I have put forth the argument that a material politics of repair, oriented in relation to the city as a repository of social memory and as a milieu for ongoing sociomaterial relations, offers a generative pathway for thinking through the "transitional" project of conciliation as an ongoing process. The politics of possession and dispossession after conflict focused on built space is also a fecund ground for considering the limits of such repair. As in the case of people who seek to remain in their homes in Kigali's "unplanned" settlements but are prevented from upgrading and renovating due to stringent building regulations, *disrepair*—rather than the closure of full and final reconciliation—finds its place as a heuristic for thinking through repair as something always provisional, in motion, and incomplete. In this case, the process of rebuilding is both metaphor and material reality. Through bricks, mortar, clay roof tiles, and mud and stone walls, the relations of reciprocity, exchange, and gradual conciliation can be enacted or destroyed through built space.

A pedagogy of the city is ultimately also a theory of the reconstruction of meaning and the everyday routines of sociality after the massive collapse of genocide and extended conflict. As scholars of violence and its aftermaths have recounted (Burnet 2012; Das 2006), the ordinary here becomes a compressed temporality of possibility, affected by lingering trauma and its attendant exhaustion. In such conditions, the textures of the existing city and its built spaces have become, for many of my interlocutors, tangible places in which to rebuild their routines and ways of life. What is material is orienting; it can be grasped, exchanged, and rebuilt. The material forms the architecture of quotidian recovery. In its continuities, the existing city thus forms a habitat for an "ordinary ethics" of repair (Das 2012).

As much as a material politics of repair through the built environment can anchor and orient, the erasure and recomposition of built space is also disorienting and disconnecting. Such erasure of existing built space forms a violent spatiality, a disorientive dispossession, and an extraction of locally grounded meaning. In presenting a material politics of repair exemplified through the recuperation of place in the city, this book necessarily addresses master-planning as a technique of the *collapse of meaning* in a geography afflicted by the scale and scope of existing violence. As the governmentalized project of spatial master-planning unfolds, colonizing space in and around the city, the spatial dialectics of memory interplay, rendering the built landscape a discontinuous timescape of multiple experiences and recollections. The three master plans discussed earlier in this book—the master plan of state aftermaths, the master plan of the colonial present, and the spatial master plan of postcrisis fix—layer onto and reinforce one another, if only in contradiction. Temporal landscapes in the postconflict city are dense and layered, spatial memory is thick, and careful intervention necessarily requires deep context.

I close by revisiting the idea of multiple pedagogies of postconflict rebuilding. These pedagogies are frames of encounter in relation to the built environment and spatial relations in sensitive terrain. They must be approached critically and with care. To again paraphrase one of my interlocutors on Rwanda's master-planned reconstruction, we need postconflict pedagogies to deconstruct layers of history and memory that are being destroyed by spatial planning. The built environment of the city provides the necessary medium for thinking through the materiality of questions of rebuilding and repair, where dispossession undercuts fragile acts of social reproduction in contested space.

A material politics of repair in Rwanda hence remains one of necessary incrementalism. Rather than the rapid erasure and repartitioning of built and social space, repair demands multiple pedagogies of postconflict rupture and gradual rebuilding.

Reckonings

What does it mean to reckon with the city?

As I walk down a road in Rubavu (earlier named Gisenyi) on a warm day in mid-2019, I know that this is the closest one can get to the border city of Goma, in the eastern Democratic Republic of the Congo, without passing through an official checkpoint. Between this asphalt road and the side streets that almost seamlessly connect the streets of Rwanda with those of the DRC are houses of different compositions. Some are larger and more completely built than others: more solid and sound, with more finished facades and more durable roofing sheets. "Do you see that yellow umbrella?" my interlocutor says, gesturing to his right. "That umbrella is in Congo, and here we are in Rwanda. There are Rwandan guards sitting between the borderland zones, and you can see that the houses near the umbrella are smaller and less well planned than the ones here near the Rwandan side."

Mapping borderland terrain thus comes down to the finish of roofing sheets, the size of ordinary walled structures, and the placement of a conspicuous yellow umbrella. These gradated terrains serve as extended metaphoric space for the juxtaposition between *akajagari*, the unplanned, and the planned fantasies of order operative in Kigali.

There are two main crossing points in Rubavu for workers, travelers, military convoys, and informal traders going back and forth on quotidian journeys made less regular by the militarized crossing. The first checkpoint, near the waterfront, is used by those commuting in vehicles; it involves a formal entry, a concrete structure, and armed guards on various sides of the perimeter. This entry has been mapped and demarcated—it now militates against the proximity of these sister cities that once were like conjoined twins, where informal traders, workers, and leisure seekers regularly crossed. Also crossing

here are fishermen at risk of straying into foreign waters, and Congolese people from Goma who come over to the hotels in Rubavu for weekend leisure.
The second checkpoint is farther inland, near the older parts of Rubavu town,
and is less developed and more congested; it retains a semblance of the life
that existed before development and greening began to modernize the streets
of Rubavu. Here, multitudes of brightly dressed women and younger men
cross on foot. Carrying passes, talking as they go, there is less formality, as
the border is more implicit and is frequently crossed. The explicit border of
the formal checkpoint may demarcate the boundary between these twin cities, but it also gestures toward an implicit border between the time-spaces,
experiences, and contingent livelihoods that shade what is made possible by
the multifactorial militarized presence of different natures on either side.

Visiting in 2002, I had crossed the asphalt road between Gisenyi and
Goma with relative ease; a lone barrier separated the zone of militarized
peace in Rwanda from the zone of war in the DRC. A recent volcanic erup-
tion of Mount Nyiragongo had left the city of Goma covered in dried lava.
The security guard at the border checkpoint paged through my passport and
asked me what I might bring her upon my return to Rwanda later that day.
She had a wry expression, knowing that the lava-covered city had little to
offer. The Rwandan incursions into the DRC, between 1996 and 2003, took
eastern Congo as their extractive zone and their militarized site of intervention. Along with troops from Uganda and Burundi, the intervention of
Rwandan forces and multiple militia groups make eastern Congo a site of
extreme displacement and an environment of fear (Stearns 2022). The area is
also a territory of primitive accumulation for the state parties involved, using
proxy militias under the guise of continuing to intervene against Hutu militia
from the 1994 Rwandan genocide (Wrong 2021). The porosity of the border
before 2002, and its increasing formality today, speak to graduated terrains of
formalization in the borderland zone, which is often implicitly demarcated
but heavily policed.

The City's Material Claims

This differentiation between the centrality of urban fantasies in Rwanda and
the seeming peripherality of Goma is deceptive in masking the productive
logic of disorder in Rwanda's backyard, as well as its enabling. The eastern
DRC is the region's constitutive outside, the continuing terrain of crisis amid
the postcrisis that enables and amplifies the logic of accumulation elsewhere.
Where the transforming urban landscapes in Rwanda embody the visible
tip of the accumulative iceberg—bringing formally sanctioned expertise and

financial flows together in self-validating concatenation and generating investment opportunities and spaces for recreating nationally branded futures—the
mineral wealth in the eastern DRC serves as the iceberg itself. What transformation is to Rwanda's cities, therefore, accumulation is to the militarized
extractive logics that operate across the border from Rubavu, in Goma.[1]

This border problem is not new, nor are the logics of accumulation and
peripherality operative in the Congo since the colonial period. The division
between speculative territories of urbanism and productive logics of the
hinterland has local and global dimensions in this closely stitched together
space. During the time of the Congo Free State (1885–1908), under Belgian
King Leopold II, dispossession of land and a plantation system of forced labor
and resource extraction were the logics of colonial tyranny. After Leopold's
Congo Free State collapsed in 1908, Ruanda-Urundi and the Belgian Congo
were administered as one interconnected colonial dominion. After independence in 1960, centralized infrastructures of land dispossession, forced labor,
and state violence persisted and continued to metamorphose, as postindependence governments used the contours of colonial terror to manage population and space. Well recounted and popularized by Adam Hochschild's
(1998) book on Leopold's exploits in the Congo, a colonial reckoning is only
now beginning in Brussels—the capital itself built upon the backs of selective
remembrance and the memorialization of Leopold as the country's "builder
king" (Nzongola-Ntalaja 2020). The colonial museum in Tervuren and the
numerous statues around the capital celebrating this plunder are only now
being questioned, creating apertures for reckoning and openings for claims
of repair.

The question of reparation is hence etched into the material fabric of the
metropole itself, as much as it appears regenerated through questions of postcolonial urban transformation. In this context, Rwanda's rapid urbanization
stands in contraposition to the disorder and fear across the border.

In the case of Rwanda, this postcolonial continuum included the continued
extraction of labor and the maintenance of a solidified urban/rural divide
that indexed socioeconomic privilege, geographic factionalism, and ethnic
identity. This is the border I traverse—a porous boundary—as in this book I
consider questions of state violence, terrains of accumulation, and possibilities of material repair of the contemporary city. These are material questions,
manifest in the foreclosure and zoning of the right to access urban space
and opportunity, to possess rural and urban property, and to raise questions
about the nature of reckoning through a redistribution that incorporates social justice into Rwanda's ongoing urban transformation. Reckoning is hence

a material entailment and a globally implicative problem textured in and through the city. Repairing what is materially possible in urban space is a larger ethic that works through the material fabric of the city, going beyond its aesthetic veneers and the legacies of dispossession that have emplaced them.

In this coda, I go beyond the boundaries of the nation-state in treating the problem of urban reckoning as a globally implicative problem, and one that sutures Rwanda and its post-genocide urban moment to alternately materialized presents in other parts of the world. The contexts and continuities of violence, memory and reckoning in Rwanda's urban transformation prompt us to reflect yet further. The city writ large thus brings forth temporally and spatially bounded questions: What is the debt that *is* repayable? What is the materiality of this reckoning? And what remains beyond repair, gesturing toward alter-temporalities of "debt" (Harney and Moten 2013), that assume moral, civilizational, and generational forms?

Writing Rwanda and the Planetary

Writing about Rwanda is a form of writing on planetary entanglement, a condensed spatial and social parable for these end times. Not only has the spatial texture of Rwandan towns and cities been marked by an intense and condensed heterotopia of proximity and rupture, but the Rwandan social condition in the aftermath of genocide, through civil war and its enduring aftermaths, multiplies and compounds successive periods of interruption. These successive ruptures have caused affective, aesthetic, morphological, topological, and geological traumas, positioning the Rwandan condition as an epochal portal and parable from which we might vicariously examine and reflect upon this condensed time-space of violence, transition, and re-creation. Scholars have focused attention on an "African Anthropocene," insisting that the continent remains at the core of world-structuring violence that ties together the extractive temporalities of mining in the Congo with the transatlantic slave trade (Hecht 2018; Yusoff 2018). I focus here on the terrain of the city as the space in which different forms of "debt" and accumulation are bound together at the global scale.

State elites' aims to reconstruct the image of the Rwandan nation through the portal of the aesthetic order of the city, and to thereby write Rwanda into the world, embody a mixture of aspiration and expectation that erases the locality of place and organic reckoning. But these erasures and aesthetic recompositions do more than circulate capital and reconstruct elite lineages of property and possession in Kigali. Rather, they hold up a mirror to the scale of the planetary during these misanthropic times of anthropocenic prophecy and technical fix. Rwanda's experiences with trauma and its experiments with the technopolitics of resurrection make visible in the starkest possible way the enduring entanglement between human disconnections and the "coloniality of power" that have striated the country's history as a global product (Quijano 2000). Rather than a coproduced history of violence and alternating domination, Rwanda's past is held up as the beast of a concentration of horrors: the composite of nightmares and fantasies projected onto a necropolitical Africa and reproduced iteratively therein (Mbembe 2003).

Violence and renewal, erasure and reconstruction, dystopia and utopia—these projects of opposition bring together the thematic underpinnings of a world not only in climatic crisis but in epistemic and existential crisis. These oppositional worldings bring forth the ontological crisis embedded in thinking of "planetarity" when extraction and entanglement are not just histories but facets of current world building. The continuous unfolding of violence and of violent reimagining underpins circulating forms of modernization and modernity. How do we then think of Rwanda's mass violence and spatial erasure through extraction and entanglement, through coproduction and enduring racialization, as an ongoing history? And how might we think of redemption through continuous reimagining in a minor key, through acts of reckoning without erasure, through making visible hidden memory, and through repair? Rather than an "aesthetics of order" embedded in various master plans and master narratives, what we must mandate instead is a relationality that recognizes "an aesthetics of the earth. . . . an aesthetics of disruption and intrusion . . . aesthetics of rupture and connection" (Glissant 1997: 151).[2]

The epochal violence of the genocide in Rwanda and the enduring civil war in the DRC involving M23 rebels and other armed forces has left representations of Rwanda in the world oscillating between calamity and reconstruction, apocalypse and redemption, genocidal dystopia and urbanizing utopia. Writing on Rwanda hence invokes a postcolonial history of rupture and globally coproduced violence. If the entanglement between planetarity and violence is our ongoing postcolonial predicament (Mbembe 2021), it is both an enduring warning and a portent of liberation: a reckoning as a taking of account, and a holding to account in its widest significance and yet also in its most pointed sense. For in birthing a new planetary polity that we repeatedly promise (as invocation), and for which we hold promise (as potential), if reckoning with and through Rwanda—as an epochal mirror and an ethical problematic—does not save us, then what will?

Acknowledgments

This book has materialized sooner than expected, but the larger project of which it is a part was long in incubation. Much has intervened between my first research visit to Rwanda in 2002, to study the beginnings of the *gacaca* transitional justice courts in the country, and subsequent engagement as I began to examine the larger contours of the justice and reconciliation initiatives around the country. Thinking incessantly about Rwanda became second nature as life intervened between my first research periods and my return to Rwanda for fieldwork in 2018–20. Much changed in the ordering of the city and in the spatiality of what I witnessed, while other things remained familiar.

At the time of my first research visits to Rwanda, conversations and thoughts turned deeply inward: What did it mean to reconcile after the brutality of proximate mass violence, and for people on opposite sides of ethnic and political divides to live with one another, again in close proximity? When can one say reconciliation has been achieved, and what are its signs and markers, if any? Is reconciliation when neighbors share food with one another, where favors and interpersonal bonds of trust are again forged? And what process is this, other than that of the continuous, of living amid social memory rather than enduring the rapidity of progress experienced as personal and social rupture? When is the process ever complete? If it is never complete, always a social fabric in process of being spun, what forms of erasure mark its enforced completion? I became interested in the heterotopias of disordered space that characterized the post-genocide proximity—of victim and possible perpetrator, "old caseload" returning refugees and "new caseload" internally displaced persons, the prisons and markets, the sites of massacre, the memorials, the schools, the old government offices—and the

many informal paths that crisscrossed them, on which encounters were pain-
fully necessary to the restoration of quotidian life, and were made possible
through the rhythm of daily activity.

With the master plan for Kigali taking shape on the ground, I ask what
activities are foreclosed as this spatial master narrative zones populations,
limiting the informal encounters and multiple ways of dwelling that I see
as necessary in a country that still needs the healing of quotidian life and
everyday interaction. Despite its critique of modernist planning in a rapidly
changing urban environment, this book is written in a spirit of respect for the
diverse experiences and concerns of Rwandans I encountered. It acknowledges what Chimamanda Ngozi Adichie (2009) calls "the dangers of a single
story."[1]

To the friends and research interlocutors in Rwanda who have offered their
help and support during my work, I express my gratitude and humility in
attempting to write imperfectly about the complexity of their lived contexts.

I acknowledge research funders at various stages of this project: the
Wenner-Gren Foundation's Dissertation Fieldwork Grant; the John L. Simpson Memorial Fellowship from the Institute of International Studies at the
University of California, Berkeley; and the Rocca Dissertation Research Grant
from the Center for African Studies, also at UC Berkeley. At the University
of North Carolina at Chapel Hill, I am honored to have been supported by
a faculty fellowship at the Institute for Arts and Humanities (IAH) and by a
departmental leave of absence.

I am thankful to the wonderful Susannah Engstrom at the University of
Chicago Press for her support of this project and for her patience and dedication to moving it forward. My thanks to the production staff at the Press, and
to the reviewers who read and advised on this project at various stages of the
publication process.

In enabling this continued engagement with Rwanda, I express gratitude
to a number of advisors, mentors, friends, and family members. I thank Jason
Corburn and You-tien Hsing for their irreplaceable mentoring and ongoing
encouragement of my evolving ideas over a period of time. Charisma Acey
has been an incredibly warm and welcoming presence on professional and
personal levels, and I am thankful for her support. I have benefited from Michael Watts's clearheaded advice over time, as well as his words on the importance of telling one's own story to the fullest extent possible. Khatharya Um
has been an illuminative mentor in helping me view Rwanda from a transnational perspective. I am thankful to colleagues at UNC and beyond for their

support; special appreciation goes to Eunice Sahle, Claude Clegg, and Noreen McDonald. I also thank John Pickles, Lydia Boyd, Petal Samuel, Maya Berry, Ronald Williams, Brandi Brimmer, Meenu Tewari, and other members of the Department of African, African American, and Diaspora Studies, and the Department of City and Regional Planning at UNC. Many additional thanks go to Julie Livingston, Garth Myers, Sara Smith, Yousuf Al Bulushi, Jovan Scott Lewis, David Eng, and Sayres Rudy. Others, unnamed but importantly remembered, are gratefully acknowledged for their feedback on earlier drafts.

A few precious and long-term travelers have been with me on much of this journey. Zahra Hayat has been one of my life's ongoing companions: she has offered the open door of her home, life-saving friendship, and crystal-clear advice. Sherine Ebadi has been a younger sister and a friend through the ups and downs of life through and beyond the covid-19 pandemic. Members of writing groups have been a source of intellectual support and true friendship; Lana Salman's deep insights and generous nature have nurtured me through life and work, Emma Shaw Crane's compassionate intellect and warm friendship are an inspiration, and Maira Hayat's careful reading and humor have been an important part of this journey. Shiva Amiri gave warm care and friendship from Oxford, Toronto, and the Bay Area, and Trude Renwick offered support through coffee-infused writing sessions and perambulations. I thank Ettore Santi and Bridget Martin for their generous feedback in our meetings. Abigail Cochran, Manuel Santana, and Paula Navia Pelaez have been necessary friends in Chapel Hill. A.H. was a crucial support and familial presence during my fieldwork. Also warmly present through this journey have been Sevilay Demirkesen, Alice Sverdlik, Liz Watters, Zahra Hassanali, Salima Madhany, Robin Visser, and Claudia Yaghoobi. Final thanks go to members of the IAH Spring 2023 cohort, and to members of the Department of City and Regional Planning at UC Berkeley.

Most of all, I thank my parents, whose steadfast dedication, love, and care have grounded me through the toughest of times. I offer my gratitude to them and their families.

Notes on Previously Published Work

The author acknowledges the following publications.

Sections of chapter 4 were previously published in Shakirah E. Hudani, "Carceral Urbanism: Reconstructing the Architecture of Punitive Space in Post-Genocide Rwanda," *Punishment & Society* 23 (5): 631–49 (2021).

Sections of chapter 5 were previously published as Shakirah Esmail and Jason Corburn, "Struggles to Remain in Kigali's "Unplanned" Settlements: The Case of Bannyahe," *Environment and Urbanization* 32 (1): 19–36 (2020).

Sections of chapter 6 were previously published in Shakirah E. Hudani, "The Green Masterplan: Crisis, State Transition and Urban Transformation in Post-Genocide Rwanda," *International Journal of Urban and Regional Research* 44 (4): 673–90 (2020). Published by John Wiley & Sons. © 2020 by Urban Research Publications Limited.

Appendix

Rwanda Timeline 1899–1994

COLONIAL PERIOD

1899: Germany establishes rule in "Rwanda-Urundi."

1910: Frontiers of Central African territories are fixed at conference in Brussels.

1916: Belgium takes over territory.

1930s: Process of "Tutsification" results in monopoly power of administrative and political positions. Identity cards are introduced, enabling ethnic classification and hierarchization.

1959–61: Social revolution by Hutu population with the support of Belgium and the Catholic Church. Violence against ethnic Tutsi leads to tens of thousands in exile.

INDEPENDENCE PERIOD

1962: Independence from Belgium. President Gregoire Kayibanda of Parmehutu takes power. Start of Rwanda's first republic.

1963: Tutsi attacks from Burundi. Pogroms against Tutsi in Rwanda. New wave of Tutsis flees the country.

1973: Major General Juvenal Habyarimana assumes power in a coup d'état. National Revolutionary Movement for Development (MRND) formed; beginning of the Second Republic.

1978: A new constitution sees MRND as the only political party. Habyarimana confirmed as president.

1983: Habyarimana confirmed as president.

1988: Habyarimana confirmed as president.

1988: Rwandese Alliance for National Unity (RANU) refugee front (later part of the Rwandan Patriotic Army, or RPA) is founded among Tutsis in exile.

1990: Negotiations between Rwanda, Uganda, and United Nations High Commission for Refugees (UNHCR) on refugee repatriation.

1990: Uganda-based RPA invades northern Rwanda.

1991: New constitution is promulgated, allowing for multiparty participation.

1991–April 1994: Peace talks in Arusha, ethnic violence, RPA attacks, and Hutu reprisals.

1993, October 21: Burundian president is killed, and six hundred thousand refugees flee the country, some to Rwanda.

1994, April 6: Presidents of Rwanda and Burundi are killed in plane crash in Rwandan airspace.

1994, April 7: Genocide of Tutsi in Rwanda begins.

1994, July 4: RPA wins control of Kigali, with intention to form a government.

Post-Genocide Transitional Programs, Policies, and Phases 1994–2003

Adapted from Shakirah E. Hudani, "Carceral Urbanism: Reconstructing the Architecture of Punitive Space in Post-Genocide Rwanda," *Punishment & Society* 23 (5): 631–49 (2021).

RETRIBUTIVE AND REFORMATIVE MOMENTS

- Genocide suspects are subjected to mass imprisonment
- Community *gacaca* courts for the majority of suspects occur locally between 2002 and 2012, with community service allowed for certain genocide convicts (*travaux d'interet general,* or TIG)
- First war in Zaire/Congo as RPF pursues Hutu militia in exile (1996–97). The Second Congo War takes place between 1998 and 2003, involving Rwandan support for Congolese-based militia.

RECONCILIATORY PROGRAMS

- National Unity and Reconciliation Commission (NURC) begins programs to rewrite history narrative, and establishes reeducation camps (*itorero*) and rural resettlement schemes (*imidugudu*) that revive and reform "traditional" aspects of culture while paving the way for mass population relocation
- Memorials for genocide are formalized, along with mass reburial ceremonies and commemoration events.

RESTORATIVE POLICIES

- Social protection schemes for genocide survivors
- Social and human development schemes

RECONSTRUCTIVE ACTIVITIES

- Urban and rural resettlement policies intensify as forms of spatial change, with a target of 35 percent urban population by 2024.
- Mass mapping and land titling (2012 onward)
- Capital and secondary city master-planning (2010 onward)
- Targeting of informality (2008 onward; stringent building standards implemented in 2015)
- Conservation and green growth policies (2011 onward)

Notes

Epigraphs

1. Diop 2006.
2. Levinas 1979: 43.

Introduction

1. In using the term "imaginative geographies," I invoke the work of Edward Said (2012). Writing in the late 1960s, in the midst of labor occupation of the capital city and student movements to overturn French social order, Lefebvre surmises,

> The right to the city is like a cry and a demand. . . . [It] cannot be conceived of as a simple visiting right or as a return to traditional cities. It can only be formulated as a transformed and renewed right to urban life . . . as long as the "urban" [is the] place of encounter, priority of use value, inscription in a space of a time promoted to the rank of a supreme resource among all resources (Lefebvre, 1996: 158; in Marcuse 2009).

2. The Rwandan government mandates that the genocide of 1994 be called the "Genocide against the Tutsi." I write in acknowledgement of this genocide, but place it in its wider contexts and in the frame of the civil war from 1990 onward with its multiple forms of violence. Conflict emergent from the civil war in Rwanda continues to affect eastern Congo, and demonstrates that the afterlives of violence continue in the region, in many ways unabated.

3. Https://www.csmonitor.com/2001/0118/p1s3.html (accessed January 2022).

4. Spatial reordering in socialist and postconflict countries overlaps with such postconflict reordering in interesting ways, causing ideas and modalities to travel across contexts, such as from China and the post-Soviet nations of Eastern Europe. I am, however, interested in how such reordering operates here as a singular case study in conversation with a constellation of cases, and in the effects of large-scale spatial planning on Rwanda's post-genocide social and mnemonic order.

5. In referencing the "colonial present," I draw on Derek Gregory's (2004) scholarship, but also that of Ann Laura Stoler, who writes on the durability of "a colonial *presence* that I see marking the interstices of what once was and what is, reworking both" (2016: 33).

6. The larger project of social transformation has worked through ideologies of totality since the colonial period in ways that implicate space and the meanings of access to urban areas

(chapter 3). In the current post-genocide period, master plans are modes of spatially securitizing a particular mnemonic order after genocide, shifting vision away from ongoing spaces of conflict and reorganizing sociopolitical, ethnic, and regional divides.

7. From 2002 to 2004 I conducted research in prisons in three Rwandan towns and cities—Kigali, Gitarama (now Muhanga), and Kibuye (now Karongi)—and at one rural prison encampment, Gisovu, located near tea plantations to the south of Kibuye (Karongi). During each visit I interviewed prison administrators, prison leaders, and prisoners.

Chapter 1

1. Although it doesn't consider postconflict conditions, existing urban literature on repair and maintenance includes Mattern 2018 and Millington 2019.

2. While often framed as solely privative, dispossession of personal property and relations of restitution can also be usefully framed by extending the anthropology of exchange (Mauss 2002; Malinowski 1920) as part of an interconnected web of social relations after conflict. Loss of personal property can also be viewed in aggregate as collective dispossession in the wake of large-scale eviction and displacement through the urban transformation of Kigali and urban areas in Rwanda. Work on peacebuilding in the Rwandan context includes Honeyman et al. 2004 and Staub et al. 2003.

3. Nyarubaba is a pseudonym for a synthesis of rural sectors where I conducted research between 2002 and 2004, and to which I returned in 2019.

4. For work on urban rebuilding after conflict in Colombia, see Crane 2020. For scholarship on Kosovo and Eastern Europe, see Gusic 2019. Scholarship on the Central Africa region includes Wendel and Aidoo 2015.

5. Excerpt from *Gacaca* hearing. Notes taken by group research assistant on behalf of the research group from Harvard University that visited Rwanda in 2002: Leila Chirayath, Justina Hierta, Catherine Honeyman, Shakirah Hudani, Andrew Iliff, Jens Meierhenrich, and Alfa Tiruneh.

6. Theories of dispossession are also effectively reviewed and retheorized in Nichols 2020.

7. Https://newrepublic.com/article/117398/rwanda-genocide-photos-amputees-20-years-later.

8. My discussion of "crisis capital" draws inspiration from Naomi Klein's influential discussion of "disaster capitalism," and situates it in terrains of urban remaking and postconflict accumulation; see Klein 2007.

9. Https://surbanajurong.com/corporate-information/.

10. Https://surbanajurong.com/our-history/.

11. Https://surbanajurong.com/our-history/.

12. Https://surbanajurong.com/wp-content/uploads/2021/11/SJ-Sparklers-2021.pdf (accessed November 2022).

13. Https://surbanajurong.com/wp-content/uploads/2021/11/SJ-Sparklers-2021.pdf (accessed November 2022).

14. In relation to the relationship between capitalist accumulation and violence, Rosa Luxemburg writes: "Capital knows no other solution to the problem [of the limits of accumulation] than violence, which has been a constant method of accumulation as a historical process, not merely during its emergence, but also to the present day" (Luxemburg, 2015: 267, in Tadiar 2022).

15. For further reading, see Desrosiers and Thomson 2011; Ingelaere 2010; Newbury and Newbury 2000; Purdeková and Mwambari 2022; Reyntjens 2011, 2016, and 2018; Thomson 2013; and Verwimp 2013.

16. Interview, November 2018.

17. *Ubuhake* is the term for a form of clientship operating in precolonial and colonial Rwanda, largely in the hands of Tutsi elites. Such contracts drew agricultural resources and labor from less well-off Hutu peasants in exchange for cattle and use of land. Further information in Newbury 1988.

18. Https://www.architecturaldigest.com/story/everything-need-know-about-africa-most -expensive-building (accessed August 2019).

19. Https://www.newtimes.co.rw/business/kigali-ranked-africas-2nd-most-popular-conference -destination (accessed August 2019).

20. The *mwami* was the divinely ordained king of precolonial Rwanda. The residence at the King's Palace Museum was earlier occupied by King Mutara III Rudahigwa.

21. Https://igihe.com/amakuru/u-rwanda/article/kigali-convention-center-na-city-of-dreams -manila-muri-philippines-bihuriye-he (accessed August 2019).

22. Https://www.theguardian.com/world/2020/feb/17/rwandan-gospel-star-president-critic -kizito-mihigo-dies-police-cell (accessed April 2020); Https://www.theguardian.com/world/2021 /feb/14/rwanda-kizito-mihigo-the-dove-music-united-a-national-torn-by-genocide-why-did -he-die-in-a-cell (accessed March 2021).

23. Https://www.youtube.com/watch?v=WcGC3eFuDAc (accessed April 2021).

24. As a disclaimer, please note that I do not at any point in this text deny the Genocide against the Tutsi, as it is officially named in Rwanda.

Chapter 2

1. The names of interviewees have been changed to preserve their anonymity. Interviews, October–December 2018, and January–June 2019.

2. NISR: Government of Rwanda, 2008. Https://www.statistics.gov.rw/publication/genocide -survivors-census-report-2007 (accessed March 2021).

3. According to law no. 18/2008, Rwanda criminalized "genocide ideology," which extends beyond the delimitation of the 1994 genocide as a singular "genocide against the Tutsi" to questions of intent and divisionism. The law defines genocide ideology thus: "The genocide ideology is an aggregate of thoughts characterized by conduct, speeches, documents and other acts aiming at exterminating or inciting others to exterminate people basing on ethnic group, origin, nationality, region, color, physical appearance, sex, language, religion or political opinion, committed in normal periods or during war" (Government of Rwanda, 2008). Http://www.icnl.org /research/library/files/Rwanda/Rwandageno.pdf (accessed October 2019).

4. Interview, January 2019.

5. Https://www.newtimes.co.rw/section/read/210643 (accessed March 2020).

6. Interview, June 2019.

7. Reyntjens 2016 (and in Sinalo 2018: 41).

8. Https://www.ft.com/content/a2838936–88c6-11e7-bf50-e1c239b45787 (accessed October 2019).

9. Https://www.foreignpolicyjournal.com/2015/04/27/kibeho-a-story-of-flesh-and-blood/ (accessed September 2019).

10. The social phenomenology of trauma in Rwanda has become increasingly regulated in treating what is deemed to be "legitimate" trauma and post-traumatic experience. The symptomatology of *ihahamuka* is one example of the increasingly regulated use of trauma in the country's

public sphere. *Ihahamuka*, which emerged as a symptomatology specific to post-genocide trauma experienced by survivors, is an acute affective condition that is particularly present during annual commemorations between April 7 to April 13 (commemorations take place under the term *Kwibuka Jenoside Yakorewe Abatutsi*, or "Remembering the Genocide against the Tutsi"), but which afflicts survivors of the genocide beyond that period as well (Betancourt et al. 2011). Implicated in this medicalized social phenomenology of trauma is the use of *ihahamuka* as an authenticating symptomatology of post-genocide trauma suffered by survivors, as opposed to *ihungabana*, which is a chronic manifestation of trauma seen through depression and mood volatility experienced by "non-survivor" individuals (Hagengimana and Hinton 2009). This opposition between socially validated acute *crisis* and invisible *chronicity* serves as an authenticating boundary between the Tutsi survivor of trauma and the non-Tutsi sufferer of mental illness, so that it is only *ihahamuka* through official recognition and its performativity that is seen to certify "the production of victimhood in Rwanda [which] is deeply intertwined with corporeal evidence" (Guglielmo 2015: 157). I extend the concept of *ihahamuka* as a spatialized metonym to the body of the city, suffering physical contortion and psychic displacement through the destruction of social memory and built life in its old quartiers. In this milieu, where national memory is politicized, the changing corporeal city can be seen as the metonymic extension of the body in acute crisis.

11. The "cell" or "cellule" is the lowest formal administrative unit in Rwanda's local administration. It consists of approximately one hundred households.

12. Interview, March 2019.

13. Gisimba's name has not been changed, as he is a well-known figure in Kigali and appears in the local press there.

14. Interview, March 2019.

15. Https://www.newtimes.co.rw/news/kwibuka25-gisimba-managing-largest-orphanage-during-genocide (accessed August 2019).

16. Earlier master plan accessed October 2019 at www.master plan2013.kigalicity.gov.rw.

17. Interview, March 2019.

18. Interview, April 2019.

19. *Ubudehe* is a socioeconomic classification system in contemporary Rwanda that serves as the basis for governmental support and social protection programs. It is termed a "homegrown solution" by the government, along with *gacaca* and *imihigo* performance contracts. The official Rwanda Governance Board website describes it differently: "*Ubudehe* refers to the longstanding Rwandan practice and culture of collective action and mutual support to solve problems within a community, according to a recent academic research paper. It is not known exactly when *Ubudehe* was first practiced, but it is thought to date back more than a century." Http://www.rgb.rw/index.php?id=35 (accessed October 2019).

Chapter 3

1. Interviews, May 2019 and August 2019.

2. Interviews with government environmental and municipal officials in April and May 2019.

3. Https://www.hrw.org/news/2020/01/27/rwanda-abusive-detention-street-children (accessed February 2020).

4. Rollason's (2019) perspectives on moto taxis in Kigali and what their confrontation with regulation reveals about the state is helpful in this regard.

5. Https://ktpress.rw/2018/03/kigali-the-cleanest-city-but-do-you-know-what-it-takes/ (March 4, 2018; accessed October 2019).

6. Exchange rate as of September 9, 2019: US$1 = Rwf 925.

7. Https://ktpress.rw/2018/03/kigali-the-cleanest-city-but-do-you-know-what-it-takes/ (March 4, 2018; accessed October 2019).

8. Https://www.chronicles.rw/2019/04/30/labour-day-may-1-inside-kigalis-slavery-cleaning -industry/ (April 30, 2019; accessed October 2019). Also, interview with City of Kigali official, November 2018.

9. Https://www.chronicles.rw/2019/04/30/labour-day-may-1-inside-kigalis-slavery-cleaning -industry/ (April 30, 2019: accessed October 2019).

10. Interview with sector official, March 2019.

11. Http://extwprlegs1.fao.org/docs/pdf/Rwa175367.pdf (accessed October 2019).

12. Interview with NGO leader, November 2018. Note that the definition of "marshlands" has been contentious and wide-ranging in Kigali, overlapping with questions of spaces of informal settlements.

13. Organic law no. 04/2005 of 08/04/2005, determining the modalities of protection, conservation, and promotion of environment in Rwanda (revised in 2018).

14. Interview, February 2019.

15. World Bank, 2014. *World Development Report 2015: Mind, Society, and Behavior* (World Bank Publications).

16. Cheng 2008. The theorization of "new man" in socialist and totalitarian regimes references the project of socially transforming citizens and creating new types of subjects—"new men"—for new social orders, functioning as a project of social engineering.

17. Https://www.npr.org/sections/goatsandsoda/2018/07/18/628364015/how-rwanda-tidied -up-its-streets-and-the-rest-of-the-country-too (accessed February 2020).

Chapter 4

1. Scholarship on the archive and various forms of "imperial debris" includes core work by Ann Laura Stoler (2002, 2010, 2013).

2. The Kinyarwanda term for wound or injury is *ibikomere*. The term is contested, and is sometimes used to denote enduring injuries that go beyond what can be seen on the surface, or at times is used in relation to longer histories of grievance and loss.

3. 2013 TED talk by Chimamanda Ngozi Adichie. Https://www.ted.com/talks/chimamanda _ngozi_adichie_the_danger_of_a_single_story?language=en (accessed October 2021).

4. Http://sanitationandwaterforall.org/wp-content/uploads/download-manager-files/2017%20 Rwanda%20Overview_final.pdf (accessed November 2019); Https://www.wsp.org/sites/wsp/files /publications/wsp-rwanda-sanitation-lessons.pdf (accessed November 2019).

5. Interview, March 2019.

6. Interview with engineers, Ministry of Infrastructure and City of Kigali.

7. Https://www.newtimes.co.rw/news/construction-kigali-sewerage-system-kick-june (accessed November 2019).

8. Interview, March 2019.

9. Https://www.icrc.org/en/doc/resources/documents/news-release/2014/06-12-rwanda-mu hanga-prison-emergency-aid-fire-destroyed.htm.

10. Https://www.theeastafrican.co.ke/rwanda/News/Fingers-point-at-FDLR-as-mysterious
-fires-gut-Rwanda-prisons/1433218-2381108-xl43rc/index.html (accessed October 2019).

11. Http://en.chinagate.cn/2016-12/26/content_39982186.htm (accessed October 2019).

12. Https://www.newtimes.co.rw/section/read/209963 (accessed October 2019).

13. Https://www.theeastafrican.co.ke/rwanda/News/Fires-continue-to-cause-fear-and-disquiet
-among-Rwandans-/1433218-2348138-pi3sou/index.html (accessed October 2019).

14. Https://allafrica.com/stories/201407100775.html (accessed October 2019).

15. Https://taarifa.rw/a-clean-operation-how-rwanda-relocated-thousands-of-notorious-pris
oners-broad-day-light/ (accessed July 2023).

16. Http://www.newtimes.co.rw/section/read/51853 (accessed April 18, 2021).

Chapter 5

1. The destruction of home, or domicide, by rural residents ordered to move from their
existing settlements under orders from the central government to move to grouped settlement
schemes (*imidugudu*), has also been recorded (Gaugler 2018). In this case, residents have been
able to salvage certain building materials and prevent top-down domicide of their dwellings, in
a move that is both symbolic and materially significant.

2. Interviews conducted 2018; also Shearer 2017, 2020.

3. Leshem's (2017) work on theorizing "spaces of abandonment" is useful here.

4. Bhan (2013) uses the term "planned illegalities" to describe the interaction of planning,
eviction, and the law in Delhi.

5. Wakhungu et al. 2010.

6. Oswald Niyonzima, "Has Kigali City Failed to Explain to "Bannyahe" Residents the Relocation Plan?" *KT Press*, April 17, 2018. Accessed at Http://ktpress.rw/2018/04/has-kigali-city
—failed-to-explain-to-bannyahe-residents-the-relocation-plan.

7. Case number PST raD 00020/2018/TGI/GSbO. Oswald Niyonzima, "'Bannyahe' Slam Residents Sue City of Kigali," *KT Press*, July 13, 2018. Accessed at Https://ktpress.rw/2018/07/bannyahe
-slam—residents-sue-city-of-kigali.

8. Interview, October 2018; also James Karuhanga, "Talks between Cok Officials, Slum Residents Hit Deadlock," *New Times*, January 25, 2018. Accessed at Https://www.newtimes.co.rw
/section/read/228299.

9. Exchange rate as of September 9, 2019: US$1 = Rwf 925.

10. Interview with Rwanda Housing Authority Officials, November 2018; also Ministry of
Infrastructure, *Housing Sub- Sector* (Republic of Rwanda), undated. Accessed at Http://www
.mininfra.gov.rw/index.php?id=269.

11. M. Cuevas (undated), *Housing Market Demand, Housing Finance and Housing Preferences
for the City of Kigali*, accessed at Https://housingfinanceafrica.org/app/uploads/Presentation
-kigali-housing-market-Study.pdf.

12. *Umuseke.*, "Aba 'bannyahe' basuye inzu bari kubakirwa mu busanza, ngo ni nk'inkambi,"
December 12, 2018. Accessed at Https://umuseke.rw/aba-bannyahe-basuye-inzu—bari-kubakirwa
-mu-busanza—ngo-ni-nkinkambi.html.

13. Daniel Sabiiti, "Kigali: 360 Families to be Relocated from 'Bannyahe' Slum," *KT Press*, August 29, 2019. Accessed at Https://ktpress.rw/2019/08/kigali-360—families-to-be-relocated-from
—bannyahe-slum.

14. Field notes and interviews, February 2019.

15. "Editorial: New Mayor Needs to Deal with Greedy Local Leaders in Earnest," *New Times*, August 30, 2019. Accessed at Https://www.newtimes.co.rw/opinions/editorial-new-mayor-needs —deal-greedy-local-leaders—earnest.

16. Https://www.tellerreport.com/news/2019-12-18—rwanda—in-kigali—the-inhabitants-of -bannyahe-are-standing-against-evacuations—rfi-.BkFffKwCr.html.

17. Https://www.hrw.org/news/2001/06/11/rwanda-rural-poor-forced-leave-their-homes#.

Chapter 6

1. National Decentralization Policy, Republic of Rwanda 2012; Https://www.minaloc.gov.rw /fileadmin/user_upload/Minaloc/Sector_docs/Revised_Decentralisation_Policy_for_Cabinet _30-01-2013.pdf (accessed July 2023).

2. Local governance currently operates across four tiers with 30 districts (*akarere*), 416 sectors (*imirenge*), 2,148 cells (*utugari*), and 14,837 villages (*imidugudu*) nationwide.

3. Interview with local historian, March 2019.

4. Http://www.newsoRwfanda.com/featured1/22775/genocide-flame-in-bugesera-where-tutsi -extermination-project-was-first-tested/ (accessed August 2019).

5. Interview with historian in Kigali, April 2019.

6. S. Mukasonga, *Cockroaches* (Archipelago, 2016).

7. Interview in Bugesera, January 2019.

8. Http://gggi.org/site/assets/uploads/2019/04/Certification-of-Bugesera-Airport-Fact-Sheet _FINAL.pdf (accessed April 2019); Https://www.reuters.com/article/us-rwanda-qatar-airport /qatar-airways-to-take-60-stake-in-new-rwandan-international-airport-idUSKBN1YD275 (accessed May 2020); Https://www.archdaily.com/911624/rwandas-bugesera-international-airport -to-set-records-for-sustainability (accessed August 2020).

9. Https://www.archdaily.com/911624/rwandas-bugesera-international-airport-to-set-records -for-sustainability (accessed April 2019).

10. Http://www.rha.gov.rw/fileadmin/user_upload/Documents/publications/MoU_signing_in _Singapore_-_Photo_Release.pdf (accessed April 2019).

11. Http://www.rha.gov.rw/fileadmin/user_upload/Documents/publications/MoU_signing_in _Singapore_-_Photo_Release.pdf (accessed April 2019).

12. Http://gggi.org/site/assets/uploads/2019/04/Certification-of-Bugesera-Airport-Fact-Sheet _FINAL.pdf (accessed April 2019).

13. All names of people have been changed to preserve anonymity.

14. Exchange rate as of September 9, 2019: US$1 = Rwf 925.

15. Interview in Bugesera, February, 2019.

16. Interview in Kigali, January, 2019.

17. Https://ktpress.rw/2018/08/rwamagana-retains-first-position-in-imihigo/ (accessed March 25, 2019).

18. Https://ktpress.rw/2018/08/rwamagana-retains-first-position-in-imihigo/ (accessed September 20, 2020).

19. Http://rgb.rw/home-grown-solutions/rwandas-hgs-good-practices/imihigo/ (accessed March 25, 2019).

20. Http://rgb.rw/home-grown-solutions/rwandas-hgs-good-practices/imihigo/ (accessed March 25, 2019).

21. On the "invention of tradition," in colonial Africa: E. Hobsbawm and Ranger 2012.

22. Http://www.doingbusiness.org/content/dam/doingBusiness/country/r/rwanda/RWA.pdf (accessed March 25, 2019).

23. Https://www.newtimes.co.rw/news/rwanda-jumps-11-places-world-bank-doing-business -report (accessed March 25, 2019).

24. Interview in Nyamata, March 2019.

25. Interview in Kigali, April 2019.

26. Interview in Karumuna, March 2019.

27. Https://www.minaloc.gov.rw/index.php?eID=dumpFile&t=f&f=17773&token=bfd42a4 ba0d47edc9dcfff50014662d863f6552a#:~:text=Volunteerism%20in%20Rwanda%20is%20 exhibited,(abajyanama%20b%27ubuzima)%2C (accessed July 2023).

28. Interview in Bugesera, March 2019.

29. Interview in Bugesera, March 2019.

Chapter 7

1. For an excellent study of politics *after* capitalist dispossession in India, see also Levien 2018.

2. Sommers (2012) offers a prescient analysis of the analytic of immobility in his book *Stuck*.

3. Https://www.voanews.com/africa/rwanda-accused-manipulating-poverty-statistics (accessed January 29, 2020).

4. IMF Country Report no. 22/200, June 2022: "Rwanda: Sixth Review under the Policy Coordination Instrument and Monetary Policy Consultation Clause: Press Release; Staff Report; and Statement by the Executive Director for Rwanda"; Https://www.imf.org/-/media/Files/Pub lications/CR/2022/English/1RWAEA2022002.ashx (accessed July 7, 2023).

5. IDPs have their own complex genealogies as a core part of rural development dating back to the days of postindependence rural development, and expanded by various governments on the advice on multilateral agencies during the period of structural adjustment.

6. Https://reliefweb.int/report/rwanda/green-villages-rwanda (accessed May 2020).

7. Https://www.thegef.org/sites/default/files/web-documents/10096_PIF.pdf (accessed May 2020).

8. Https://www.thegef.org/sites/default/files/web-documents/10096_PIF.pdf (accessed May 2020).

Conclusion

1. Names of people are changed to protect their anonymity.

2. Https://gggi.org/project/cambodia-green-urban-development-program/ (accessed November 2022).

3. Https://surbanajurong.com/sjconnects/developing-a-sustainable-master plan-for-cambo dia/ (accessed November 2022).

Coda

1. Rubavu is a city divided first against itself, and then against Goma. Formerly called Gisenyi, it became known as Rubavu after renaming across Rwanda took place in 2006.

2. Glissant 1997: 151; also quoted in Yusoff 2018: 10:

An aesthetics of the earth? In the half-starved dust of Africas?
In the mud of flooded Asias? In epidemics, masked forms of
exploitation, flies buzz-bombing the skeleton skins of children?
In the frozen silence of the Andes? In the rains uprooting
favelas and shantytowns? In the scrub and scree of Bantu
lands? In flowers encircling necks and ukuleles? In mud huts
crowning goldmines? In city sewers? In haggard aboriginal
wind? In red-light districts? In drunken indiscriminate consumption?
In the noose? The cabin? Night with no candle?
Yes. But an aesthetics of disruption and intrusion. Finding
the fever of passion for the ideas of "environment" (which I
call surroundings) and "ecology," both apparently such futile
notions in these landscapes of desolation. Imagining the idea
of love of the earth-so ridiculously inadequate or else frequently
the basis for such sectarian in tolerance-with all the
strength of charcoal fires or sweet syrup.
Aesthetics of rupture and connection.

Acknowledgments

1. Https://www.ted.com/talks/chimamanda_ngozi_adichie_the_danger_of_a_single_story
/transcript?language=en (accessed September 2020).

References

Acey, Charisma. 2018. "Rise of the Synthetic City: Eko Atlantic and Practices of Dispossession and Repossession in Nigeria." In *Disassembled Cities*, edited by Elizabeth L Sweet, 51–61. Routledge.

Agamben, Giorgio. 2020. *Homo Sacer: Sovereign Power and Bare Life*. Stanford University Press.

Agrawal, Arun. 2005. "Environmentality: Community, Intimate Government, and the Making of Environmental Subjects in Kumaon, India." *Current Anthropology* 46, no. 2: 161–90.

Akar, Hiba Bou. 2018. *For the War Yet to Come: Planning Beirut's Frontiers*. Stanford University Press.

Angelo, Hillary. 2019. "The Greening Imaginary: Urbanized Nature in Germany's Ruhr Region." *Theory and Society* 48 (5): 645–69.

Ansoms, An. 2009. "Re-Engineering Rural Society: The Visions and Ambitions of the Rwandan Elite." *African Affairs* 108 (431): 289–309.

Ansoms, An., and Giuseppe D. Cioffo. 2016. "The Exemplary Citizen on the Exemplary Hill: The Production of Political Subjects in Contemporary Rural Rwanda." *Development and Change* 47 (6): 1247–68.

Arendt, Hannah. 2006. *Eichmann in Jerusalem: A Report on the Banality of Evil*. Penguin.

Bakhtin, Mikhail Mikhaĭlovich. 2010. *The Dialogic Imagination: Four Essays*. University of Texas Press.

Bauman, Zygmunt. 1990. "Modernity and Ambivalence." *Theory, Culture & Society* 7 (2–3): 143–69.

Bayat, Asef. 2013. *Life as Politics: How Ordinary People Change the Middle East*. Stanford University Press.

Behuria, Pritesh, and Tom Goodfellow. 2019. "Leapfrogging Manufacturing? Rwanda's Attempt to Build a Services-Led "Developmental State." *The European Journal of Development Research*, 31 (3): 581–603.

Betancourt, Theresa S., Julia E. Rubin-Smith, William R. Beardslee, Sara N. Stulac, Ildephonse Fayida, and Steven Safren. 2011. "Understanding Locally, Culturally, and Contextually Relevant Mental Health Problems among Rwandan Children and Adolescents Affected by HIV/AIDS." *AIDS Care* 23 (4): 401–12.

Bhan, Gautam. 2013. "Planned Illegalities: Housing and the 'Failure' of Planning in Delhi: 1947–2010." *Economic and Political Weekly* 48 (24): 58–70.

————. 2014. "The Real Lives of Urban Fantasies." *Environment and Urbanization* 26 (1): 232–35.

————. 2016. *In the Public's Interest: Evictions, Citizenship, and Inequality in Contemporary Delhi*. University of Georgia Press.

————. 2019. "Notes on a Southern Urban Practice." *Environment and Urbanization* 31 (2): 639–54.

Bollen, Paige. 2022. "The (Spatial) Ties That Bind: Frequent Casual Contact, the Shadow of the Future, and Prosociality across Ethnic Divisions." Program on Governance and Local Development working paper no. 58, University of Gothenburg.

Bollens, Scott A. 2000. *On Narrow Ground: Urban Policy and Ethnic Conflict in Jerusalem and Belfast*. SUNY Press.

————. 2012. *City and Soul in Divided Societies*. Routledge.Bradshaw, York W. 1987. "Urbanization and Underdevelopment: A Global Study of Modernization, Urban Bias, and Economic Dependency." *American Sociological Review*, April: 224–39.

Brenner, Neil. 2000. "The Urban Question: Reflections on Henri Lefebvre, Urban Theory and the Politics of Scale." *International Journal of Urban and Regional Research* 24 (2): 361–78.

Burawoy, Michael. 2009. *The Extended Case Method: Four Countries, Four Decades, Four Great Transformations, and One Theoretical Tradition*. University of California Press.

Burnet, Jennie E. 2012. *Genocide Lives in Us: Women, Memory, and Silence in Rwanda*. University of Wisconsin Press.

Butler, Judith. 2009. *Frames of War: When Is Life Grievable?* Verso Books.

Butler, Judith, and Athena Athanasiou. 2013. *Dispossession: The Performative in the Political*. Polity Press.

Caldeira, Teresa P. R. 2017. "Peripheral Urbanization: Autoconstruction, Transversal Logics, and Politics in Cities of the Global South." *Environment and Planning D: Society and Space* 35 (1): 3–20.

Cardoso, Ricardo. 2016. "The Circuitries of Spectral Urbanism: Looking underneath Fantasies in Luanda's New Centralities." *Urbanisation* 1 (2): 95–113.

Castells, Manuel. 1977. *The Urban Question: A Marxist Approach*, vol. 1. Hodder Education.

Chakravarty, Anuradha. 2015. *Investing in Authoritarian Rule: Punishment and Patronage in Rwanda's Gacaca Courts for Genocide Crimes*. Cambridge University Press.

Chatterjee, Partha. 2004. *The Politics of the Governed: Reflections on Popular Politics in Most of the World*. Columbia University Press.

Cheng, Yinghong. 2008. *Creating the New Man: From Enlightenment Ideals to Socialist Realities*. University of Hawaii Press.

Corburn, Jason. 2013. *Healthy City Planning: From Neighbourhood to National Health Equity*. Routledge.

Corwin, Julia E., and Vinay Gidwani. 2022. "Repair Work as Care: On Maintaining the Planet in the Capitalocene." *Antipode*. https://doi.org/10.1111/anti.12791.

Côté-Roy, Laurence, and Sarah Moser. 2019. "'Does Africa Not Deserve Shiny New Cities?' The Power of Seductive Rhetoric around New Cities in Africa. *Urban Studies* 56 (12): 2391–2407.

Coulthard, Glen S. 2014. *Red Skin, White Masks: Rejecting the Colonial Politics of Recognition*. University of Minnesota Press.

Coward, Martin. 2008. *Urbicide: The Politics of Urban Destruction*. Routledge.

Crane, Emma Shaw. 2020. "Small Victories: Urban Politics, after War." *PoLAR*. https://polarjournal.org/2020/11/24/small-victories-urban-politics-after-war/.

Cugurullo, Federico. 2013. "How to Build a Sandcastle: An Analysis of the Genesis and Development of Masdar City." *Journal of Urban Technology* 20 (1): 23–37.

Das, Veena. 2006. *Life and Words: Violence and the Descent into the Ordinary*. University of California Press.

———. 2012. "Ordinary Ethics." In *A Companion to Moral Anthropology*, edited by Didier Fassin. 133–49. John Wiley & Sons.

Dauge-Roth, Alexandre. 2010. *Writing and Filming the Genocide of the Tutsis in Rwanda: Dismembering and Remembering Traumatic History*. Lexington Books.

De Boeck, Filip, and Marie-Françoise Plissart. 2014. *Kinshasa: Tales of the Invisible City*. Leuven University Press.

De Soto, Hernando. 2000. *The Mystery of Capital: Why Capitalism Triumphs in the West and Fails Everywhere Else*. Basic Books.

Derrida, Jacques. 1994. *Specters of Marx*. Routledge: New York.

———. 2001. *On Cosmopolitanism and Forgiveness*. Psychology Press.

———. 2004. *Dissemination*. A&C Black.

Des Forges, Alison. 1986. "'The Drum Is Greater Than the Shout': The 1912 Rebellion in Northern Rwanda." In Donald Crummey, *Banditry, Rebellion and Social Protest in Africa*, 311–31. James Currey.

———. 1999. *Leave None to Tell the Story*. Human Rights Watch.

Desrosiers, Marie-Eve. 2023. *Trajectories of Authoritarianism in Rwanda: Elusive Control before the Genocide*. Cambridge University Press.

Desrosiers, Marie Eve, and Susan Thomson. 2011. "Rhetorical Legacies of Leadership: Projections of 'Benevolent Leadership' in Pre-and Post-Genocide Rwanda." *Journal of Modern African Studies* 49 (3): 429–53.

Diop, Boubacar Boris. 2006. *Murambi: The Book of Bones*. Indiana University Press.

Douglas, Mary. 2003. *Purity and Danger: An Analysis of Concepts of Pollution and Taboo*. Routledge.

Emel, Jody, Matthew T. Huber, and Madoshi H. Makene. 2011. "Extracting Sovereignty: Capital, Territory, and Gold Mining in Tanzania." *Political Geography* 30 (2): 70–79.

Esmail, Shakirah, and Jason Corburn. 2020. "Struggles to Remain in Kigali's "Unplanned" Settlements: The Case of Bannyahe." *Environment and Urbanization* 32 (1): 19–36.

Fanon, Frantz. 2007. *The Wretched of the Earth*. Grove/Atlantic Press.

Flyvbjerg, Bent, and Tim Richardson. 2002. "Planning and Foucault." In *Planning Futures: New Directions for Planning Theory*, edited by Philip Allmendinger and Mark Tewdwr-Jones, 44–63. Routledge.

Follmann, Alexander. 2022. "Geographies of Peri-Urbanization in the Global South." *Geography Compass* 16 (7).

Foucault, Michel. 2019. *Ethics: Subjectivity and Truth: Essential Works of Michel Foucault 1954–1984*. Penguin.

Foucault, Michel, Arnold I. Davidson, and Graham Burchell. 2008. *The Birth of Biopolitics: Lectures at the Collège de France, 1978–1979*. Springer.

Fredericks, Rosalind. 2018. *Garbage Citizenship: Vital Infrastructures of Labor in Dakar, Senegal*. Duke University Press.

Fujii, Lee Ann. 2010. *Killing Neighbors*. Cornell University Press.

Gastrow, Claudia. 2017. "Aesthetic Dissent: Urban Redevelopment and Political Belonging in Luanda, Angola." *Antipode* 49 (2): 377–96.

Gaugler, Jennifer. 2018. "Modern Materials for Dwelling." *Traditional Dwellings and Settlements Review* 29 (2): 39–54.

Ghertner, D. Asher. 2010. "Calculating without Numbers: Aesthetic Governmentality in Delhi's Slums." *Economy and Society* 39 (2): 185–217.

———. 2015. *"Rule by Aesthetics": World-Class City Making in Delhi.* Oxford University Press.

Ghertner, D. Asher, and Hudson McFann. 2020. *Futureproof: Security Aesthetics and the Management of Life.* Duke University Press.

Gillespie, Tom. 2016. "Accumulation by Urban Dispossession: Struggles over Urban Space in Accra, Ghana." *Transactions of the Institute of British Geographers* 41 (1): 66–77.

Glissant, Édouard. 1997. *Poetics of Relation.* University of Michigan Press.

Goldman, Michael. 2011. "Speculative Urbanism and the Making of the Next World City." *International Journal of Urban and Regional Research* 35 (3): 555–81.

Goodfellow, Tom. 2017. "Urban Fortunes and Skeleton Cityscapes: Real Estate and Late Urbanization in Kigali and Addis Ababa." *International Journal of Urban and Regional Research* 41 (5): 786–803.

———. 2022. *Politics and the Urban Frontier: Transformation and Divergence in Late Urbanizing East Africa.* Oxford University Press.

Goodfellow, Tom, and Alyson Smith. 2013. "From Urban Catastrophe to 'Model' City? Politics, Security and Development in Post-Conflict Kigali." *Urban Studies* 50 (15): 3185–3202.

Government of Rwanda. 2015a. "Law no. 32/2015 of 11/06/2015 Relating to Expropriation in the Public Interest." https://landportal.org/library/resources/rwanda-land-lawspolicies-2/law-n° -322015-11062015-relating-expropriation-public.

Government of Rwanda. 2015b. "Ministerial Order no. 04/Cab.M/015 Of 18/05/2015 Determining Urban Planning and Building Regulations." https://bpmis.gov.rw/asset_uplds/files /Rwanda%20Building%20Code%20_Urban%20Planning%20Code.pdf.

Government of Rwanda. 2015c. "A Toolkit for the Development of Smart Green Villages in Rwanda." https://www.unpei.org/files/sites/default/files/e_library_documents/a_toolkit_for_the_de velopment_of_smart_green_villages_in_rewanda.pdf.

Government of Rwanda and Surbana. 2013. "City of Kigali Masterplan." http://www.master plan2013.kigalicity.gov.rw/Downloads/.

Graham, Steve, and Simon Marvin. 2002. *Splintering Urbanism: Networked Infrastructures, Technological Mobilities and the Urban Condition.* Routledge.

Gramsci, Antonio. 2005. *Selections from the Prison Notebooks.* Edited by Quintin Hoare and Geoffrey Nowell-Smith. Lawrence & Wishart.

Grant, Andrea M. 2021. "Public Religion after Genocide: Pentecostal Sounds and Voice in Rwanda." *Comparative Studies of South Asia, Africa and the Middle East* 41 (2): 194–204.

Gregory, Derek. 2004. *The Colonial Present: Afghanistan. Palestine. Iraq.* John Wiley & Sons.

Guglielmo, Federica. 2015. "Medicalizing Violence: Victimhood, Trauma and Corporeality in Post-Genocide Rwanda." *Critical African Studies* 7 (2): 146–63.

Gusic, I. 2019. *Contesting Peace in the Postwar City: Belfast, Mitrovica and Mostar.* Springer Nature.

Hagengimana, Athanase, and Devon E. Hinton. 2009. "'Ihahamuka,' a Rwandan Syndrome of Response to the Genocide." In Devon E. Hinton and Byron J. Good, *Culture and Panic Disorder.* Stanford University Press.

Halbwachs, Maurice. 1992. *On Collective Memory.* University of Chicago Press.

Harney, Stefano, and Fred Moten. 2013. *The Undercommons: Fugitive Planning and Black Study.* Minor Compositions Press.

Haraway, Donna. 1988. "Situated Knowledges: The Science Question in Feminism and the Privilege of Partial Perspective." *Feminist Studies* 14 (3): 575–99.

Harris, John C., Daniel Komakech, David Monk, and Maria del Guadalupe Davidson. 2023. "The Gendered Postconflict City: Possibilities for More Livable Urban Transformations in Gulu, Northern Uganda." *Journal of Urban Affairs* 45 (3): 647–64.

Harrison, Philip, and Sylvia Croese. 2022. "The Persistence and Rise of Master Planning in Urban Africa: Transnational circuits and local ambitions." *Planning Perspectives* 38 (1): 25–47.

Harvey, David. 2003. "The Right to the City." *International Journal of Urban and Regional Research*. 27 (4): 939–41.

———. 2004. *Paris, Capital of Modernity*. Routledge.

———. 2005. *The New Imperialism*. Oxford University Press.

Healey, Patsy. 1997. *Collaborative Planning*. University of British Columbia Press.

Hecht, Gabrielle. 2018. "Interscalar Vehicles for an African Anthropocene: On Waste, Temporality, and Violence." *Cultural Anthropology* 33 (1): 109–41.

Hobsbawm, Eric, and Terrence Ranger, eds. 2012. *The Invention of Tradition*. Cambridge University Press.

Hochschild, Adam. 2006. *King Leopold's Ghost: A Story of Greed, Terror, and Heroism in Colonial Africa*. Pan Macmillan.

Hoffman, Danny. 2007. "The City as Barracks: Freetown, Monrovia, and the Organization of Violence in Post-Colonial African Cities." *Cultural Anthropology* 22 (3): 400–428.

———. 2017. *Monrovia Modern: Urban Form and Political Imagination in Liberia*. Duke University Press.

Holston, James. 1989. *The Modernist City: An Anthropological Critique of Brasília*. University of Chicago Press.

———. 1991. "Autoconstruction in Working-Class Brazil." *Cultural Anthropology* 6 (4): 447–65.

Home, Robert. 2015. "Colonial Urban Planning in Anglophone Africa." In *Urban Planning in Sub-Saharan Africa*, edited by Carlos Nunes Silva, 75–88. Routledge.

Honeyman, Catherine, Shakirah Hudani, Alfa Tiruneh, Justina Hierta, Leila Chirayath, Andrew Iliff, and Jens Meierhenrich. 2004. "Establishing Collective Norms: Potentials for participatory justice in Rwanda." *Peace and Conflict* 10 (1): 1–24.

Hudani, Shakirah E. 2020. "The Green Master Plan: Crisis, State Transition and Urban Transformation in Post-Genocide Rwanda." *International Journal of Urban and Regional Research* 44 (4): 673–90.

———. 2021. "Carceral Urbanism: Reconstructing the Architecture of Punitive Space in Post-Genocide Rwanda." *Punishment & Society* 23 (5): 631–49.

———. 2023. "Gates to the City: The Meanings and Morphology of Transformation on Nairobi's Periphery." *Representations*, 162 (1): 93–108.

Hughes, Thomas. P. 1987. "The Evolution of Large Technological Systems." In *The Social Construction of Technological Systems: New Directions in the Sociology and History of Technology*, edited by Weibe E. Bijker, Thomas P. Hughes, and Thomas Pinch, 51–82. MIT Press.

Human Rights Watch. 2001. "Uprooting the Rural Poor in Rwanda." https://www.hrw.org/report/2001/05/01/uprooting-rural-poor-rwanda.

Ingelaere, Bert. 2008. "The Gacaca Courts in Rwanda." In *Traditional Justice and Reconciliation after Violent Conflict: Learning from African Experiences*, edited by Luc Huyse and Mark Salter, 25–59. International IDEA.

———. 2010. "Do We Understand Life after Genocide? Center and Periphery in the Construction of Knowledge in Postgenocide Rwanda." *African Studies Review* 53 (1): 41–59.

———. 2011. "The Ruler's Drum and the People's Shout." In *Remaking Rwanda: Statebuilding and Human Rights after Mass Violence*, edited by Scott Straus and Lars Waldorf, 67–78. University of Wisconsin Press.

———. 2016. *Inside Rwanda's Gacaca Courts: Seeking Justice after Genocide*. University of Wisconsin Press.

Jaglin, Sylvie. 2014. "Regulating Service Delivery in Southern Cities: Rethinking Urban Heterogeneity." In *The Routledge Handbook on Cities of the Global Ssouth*, edited by Susan Parnell and Sophie Oldfield, 456–69. Routledge.

Jasanoff, Sheila, and Sang-Hyun Kim. 2015. *Dreamscapes of Modernity: Sociotechnical Imaginaries and the Fabrication of Power*. University of Chicago Press.

King, Anthony D. 1977. "Exporting 'Planning': The Colonial and Neo-Colonial Experience." *Urbanism Past & Present* 5:12–22.

———. 2012. *Colonial Urban Development: Culture, Social Power and Environment*. Routledge.

Klein, Naomi. 2007. *The Shock Doctrine: The Rise of Disaster Capitalism*. Henry Holt.

Knapp, Courtney, Jocelyn Poe, and John Forester. 2022. "Repair and Healing in Planning." *Planning Theory & Practice* 23 (3): 425–58.

Kotef, Hagar. 2020. *The Colonizing Self; or, Home and Homelessness in Israel/Palestine*. Duke University Press.

Lai, Danielle. 2016. "Transitional Justice and its Discontents: Socioeconomic Justice in Bosnia and Herzegovina and the Limits of International Intervention." *Journal of Intervention and Statebuilding* 10 (3): 361–81.

Lal, Priya. 2015. *African Socialism in Post-Colonial Tanzania*. Cambridge University Press.

Lefebvre, Henri. 2009. *State, Space, World: Selected Essays*. University of Minnesota Press.

Lefebvre, Henri, Eleanore Kofman, and Elizabeth Lebas. 1996. *Writings on Cities*. Blackwell.

Lemarchand, Rene. 2009. *The Dynamics of Violence in Central Africa*. University of Pennsylvania Press.

———. 2021. *Remembering Genocides in Central Africa*. Routledge.

Leshem, Noam. 2017. "Spaces of Abandonment: Genealogies, Lives and Critical Horizons." *Environment and Planning D: Society and Space* 35 (4): 620–36.

Levien, Michael. 2018. *Dispossession without Development: Land Grabs in Neoliberal India*. Oxford University Press.

Levinas, Emmanuel. 1979. *Totality and Infinity: An Essay on Exteriority*. Martinus Nijhojf Publishers.

Lewis, Jovan Scott. 2020. *Scammer's Yard: The Crime of Black Repair in Jamaica*. University of Minnesota Press.

Long, Carol. 2013. "Transitioning Racialized Spaces." In *Race, Memory and the Apartheid Archive: Towards a Transformative Psychosocial Praxis*. Edited by Garth Stevens, Norman Duncan and Derek Hook. Palgrave Macmillan.

Longman, Timothy. 2017. *Memory and Justice in Post-Genocide Rwanda*. Cambridge University Press.

Løvgren, Rose, and Simon Turner. 2019. "'Winning Life' and the Discipline of Death at Iwawa Island." *Ethnos* 84 (1): 27–40.

Luxemburg, Rosa. 2015. *The Complete Works of Rosa Luxemburg: Volume II, Economic Writings*. Verso.

Malinowski, B. 1920. "Kula: The Circulating Exchange of Valuables in the Archipelagoes of Eastern New Guinea." *Man* 20:97–105.

Mamdani, Mahmood. 2018. *Citizen and Subject: Contemporary Africa and the Legacy of Late Colonialism*. Princeton University Press.

———. 2020. *When Victims Become Killers: Colonialism, Nativism, and the Genocide in Rwanda*. Princeton University Press.

Manirakiza, Vincent. 2014. "Promoting Inclusive Approaches to Address Urbanisation Challenges in Kigali." *African Review of Economics and Finance* 6 (1): 61–180.

———. 2015. "La Problématique de l'urbanisation spontanée face à la modernisation de la Ville de Kigali (Rwanda)." PhD diss., Universitaires de Louvain.

Marcuse, Peter, James Connolly, Johannes Novy, Ingrid Olivo, Cuz Potter, and Justin Steil, eds. 2009. *Searching for the Just City: Debates in Urban Theory and Practice*. Routledge.

Mattern, Shannon. 2018. "Maintenance and Care." *Places Journal*, November. https://doi.org /10.22269/181120.

Mauss, Marcel. 2002. *The Gift: The Form and Reason for Exchange in Archaic Societies*. Routledge.

Mbembe, Achille. 2001. *On the Postcolony*. University of California Press.

———. 2021. *Out of the Dark Night: Essays on Decolonization*. Columbia University Press.

Mbembe, J. Achille, and Libby Meintjes. 2003. "Necropolitics." *Public Culture* 15 (1): 11–40.

Meierhenrich, Jens, and Martha Lagace. 2013. "Photo Essay: Tropes of Memory." *Humanity: An International Journal of Human Rights, Humanitarianism, and Development* 4 (2): 289–312.

Merrifield, Andy. 2014. *The New Urban Question*. Pluto Press.

Meth, Paula, Tom Goodfellow, Alison Todes, and Sarah Charlton. 2021. "Conceptualizing African Urban Peripheries." *International Journal of Urban and Regional Research* 45 (6): 985–1007.

Michelon, Benjamin. 2008. "Kigali: Une urbanisation entre modernisation et réconciliation." *Urbanisme* 363: 33–38.

———. 2016. *Douala et Kigali: Villes modernes et citadins précaires en Afrique*. Karthala Press.

Millington, Nate. 2019. "Critical Spatial Practices of Repair." *Society and Space*. https://www .societyandspace.org/articles/critical-spatial-practices-of-repair

Ministry of Infrastructure. 2008. "National Urban Housing Policy for Rwanda." https://bpmis .gov.rw/asset_uplds/files/National%20Urban%20housing%20Policy.pdf.

Mitchell, Timothy. 2002. *Rule of Experts: Egypt, Techno-Politics, Modernity*. University of California Press.

Mkandawire, P. Thandika, and Charles Chukwuma Soludo, eds. 2003. *African Voices on Structural Adjustment: A Companion to Our Continent, Our Future*. Africa World Press.

Mookherjee, Nayanika. 2022. "Introduction: On Irreconciliation." *Journal of the Royal Anthropological Institute* 28 (S1): 11–33.

Mukagasana, Yolande, and Alain Kazinierakis. 2001. *Les Blessures du silence: Témoignages du génocide au Rwanda*. Actes Sud.

Mukasonga, Scholastique. 2016. *Cockroaches*. Archipelago Press.

Musahara, Herman, and Chris Huggins. 2005. "Land Reform, Land Scarcity and Post-Conflict Reconstruction: A Case Study of Rwanda." In *From the Ground Up: Land Rights, Conflict and Peace in Sub-Saharan Africa*, edited by Chris Huggins and Jenny Clover. Institute for Security Studies.

Mwambari, David. 2020. "Music and the Politics of the Past: Kizito Mihigo and Music in the Commemoration of the Genocide against the Tutsi in Rwanda." *Memory Studies* 13 (6): 1321–36.

Myers, Garth. 2011. *African Cities: Alternative Visions of Urban Theory and Practice.* Bloomsbury Publishing.

———. 2017. *Disposable Cities: Garbage, Governance and Sustainable Development in Urban Africa.* Routledge.

———. 2020. *Rethinking Urbanism: Lessons from Post-Colonialism and the Global South.* Bristol University Press.

Nader, Laura. 1990. *Harmony Ideology: Justice and Control in a Zapotec Mountain Village.* Stanford University Press.

Nauta, Wiebe, and Tae-Joo Lee. 2017. "South Korean Civic Actors in Rwanda." In *African-Asian Encounters,* edited by Arndt Graf and Azirah Hashim, 183–216. Amsterdam University Press.

Navaro-Yashin, Yael. 2012. *The Make-Believe Space: Affective Geography in a Postwar Polity.* Duke University Press.

Newbury, Catherine. 1988. *The Cohesion of Oppression: Clientship and Ethnicity in Rwanda, 1860–1960.* Columbia University Press.

———. 2011. "High Modernism at the Ground Level." In *Remaking Rwanda: State-Building and Human Rights after Mass Conflict,* edited by Scott Straus and Lars Waldorf, 223–39. University of Wisconsin Press.

Newbury, David, and Catherine Newbury. 2000. "Bringing the Peasants Back In: Agrarian Themes in the Construction and Corrosion of Statist Historiography in Rwanda." *American Historical Review,* 105 (3): 832–77.

Nguyen, Viet Thanh. 2016. *Nothing Ever Dies: Vietnam and the Memory of War.* Harvard University Press.

Nichols, Robert. 2020. *Theft Is Property! Dispossession and Critical Theory.* Duke University Press.

Njoh, Ambe. J. 2004. "The Experience and Legacy of French Colonial Urban Planning in Sub-Saharan Africa." *Planning Perspectives* 19 (4): 435–54.

———. 2009. "Urban Planning as a Tool of Power and Social Control in Colonial Africa." *Planning Perspectives* 24 (3): 301–17.

Nora, Pierre. 1989. "Between Memory and History: Les Lieux de Mémoire." *Representations* 26 (7): 24.

Nzongola-Ntalaja, Georges. 2020. "Reversing a Bloody Legacy." *Wilson Quarterly* 44 (4).

ONAPO. Republique du Rwanda. 1990. *Le Probleme demographique au Rwanda et le cadre de sa solution.* ONAPO.

Payne, Geoffrey. 2011. "Land Issues in Rwanda's Post Conflict Law Reform." In *Local Case Studies in African Land Law,* edited by Robert Home, 21–38. Pretoria University Law Press.

Poe, Jocelyn. 2002. "Theorizing Communal Trauma: Examining the Relationship between Race, Spatial Imaginaries, and Planning in the US South." *Planning Theory* 21 (1): 56–76.

Pottier, Johann. 2002. *Re-Imagining Rwanda: Conflict, Survival and Disinformation in the Late Twentieth Century.* Cambridge University Press.

Prunier, Gerard. 1997. *The Rwanda Crisis: History of a Genocide.* Columbia University Press.

———. 2008. *Africa's World War: Congo, the Rwandan Genocide, and the Making of a Continental Catastrophe.* Oxford University Press.

———. 2009. *From Genocide to Continental War: The "Congolese" Conflict and the Crisis of Contemporary Africa.* Hurst & Co.

Purdeková, Andrea. 2011. " 'Even if I Am Not Here, There Are So Many Eyes': Surveillance and State Reach in Rwanda." *Journal of Modern African Studies* 49 (3): 475–97.

———. 2012. "Civic Education and Social Transformation in Post-Genocide Rwanda: Forging the Perfect Development Subjects." In *Rwanda Fast Forward*, edited by Patrick Noack, 192–209. Springer.

———. 2015. *Making Ubumwe: Power, State and Camps in Rwanda's Unity-Building Project.* Berghahn Books.

Purdeková, Andrea, and David Mwambari. 2022. "Post-Genocide Identity Politics and Colonial Durabilities in Rwanda." *Critical African Studies* 14 (1): 19–37.

Quijano, Anibal. 2000. "Coloniality of Power and Eurocentrism in Latin America." *International Sociology* 15 (2): 215–32.

Rabinow, Paul. 1989. "Governing Morocco: Modernity and Difference." *International Journal of Urban and Regional Research* 13 (1): 32–46.

———. 1992. "France in Morocco: Technocosmopolitanism and Middling Modernism." *Assemblage* (17): 53–57.

Renan, Ernest. 2018. *What Is a Nation? and Other Political Writings.* Columbia University Press.

Republic of Rwanda. N.d. "7 Years Government Programme: National Strategy for Transformation (NST1)." http://www.minecofin.gov.rw/fileadmin/user_upload/NST1_7YGP_Final.pdf.

Republic of Rwanda. 1999. "The Unity of Rwandans." Republic of Rwanda, Office of the President of the Republic.

Republic of Rwanda. 2000. "Rwanda Vision 2020." https://faolex.fao.org/docs/pdf/rwa149721.pdf.

Republic of Rwanda. 2012. "National Volunteerism Policy." https://www.minaloc.gov.rw/index.php?eID=dumpFile&t=f&f=17773&token=bfd42a4ba0d47edc9dcfff50014662d863f6552a#:~:text=Volunteerism%20in%20Rwanda%20is%20exhibited,(abajyanama%20b%27ubuzima)%2C.

Republic of Rwanda. 2014. "Market Infrastructure Masterplan." MiniCom. https://rwandatrade.rw/media/2014%20MINICOM%20Market%20Infrastructure%20Master%20Plan.pdf.

Republic of Rwanda. 2015. "National Urbanization Policy." https://bpmis.gov.rw/asset_uplds/files/National%20Urbanization%20Policy.pdf.

Republic of Rwanda and Global Green Growth Institute. 2015. "Rwanda: National Roadmap for Green Secondary City Development." https://gggi.org/report/24716/.

Reyntjens, Filip. 2011. "Constructing the Truth, Dealing with Dissent, Domesticating the World: Governance in Post-Genocide Rwanda." *African Affairs* 110 (438): 1–34.

———. 2013. *Political Governance in Post-Genocide Rwanda.* Cambridge University Press.

———. 2018. "Understanding Rwandan Politics through the Longue Durée: From the Precolonial to the Post-Genocide era." *Journal of Eastern African Studies*, 12 (3): 514–32.

Rogaski, Ruth. 2004. *Hygienic Modernity.* University of California Press.

Rollason, Will. 2019. *Motorbike People: Power and Politics on Rwandan streets.* Lexington Books.

Rose, Nikolas. 1999. *Powers of Freedom: Reframing Political Thought.* Cambridge University Press.

Rostow, Walt Whitman. 1990. *The Stages of Economic Growth: A Non-Communist Manifesto.* Cambridge University Press.

Roy, Ananya. 2009. "Why India Cannot Plan Its Cities: Informality, Insurgence and the Idiom of Urbanization." *Planning Theory* 8 (1): 76–87.

Roy, Ananya, and Aihwa Ong, eds. 2011. *Worlding Cities: Asian Experiments and the Art of Being Global.* John Wiley & Sons.

Said, Edward W. 2012. *Culture and Imperialism.* Vintage.

Sandercock, Leonie. 2000. "When Strangers Become Neighbors: Managing Cities of Difference." *Planning Theory & Practice* 1 (1): 13–30.

Scott, James C. 1990. *Domination and the Arts of Resistance: Hidden transcripts.* Yale University Press.

———. 1998. *Seeing Like a State: How Certain Schemes to Improve the Human Condition Have Failed.* Yale University Press.

Shaw, Rosalind, Lars Waldorf, and Pierre Hazan, eds. 2010. *Localizing Transitional Justice: Interventions and Priorities after Mass Violence.* Stanford University Press.

Shearer, Samuel. 2017. "The Kigali Model: Making a 21st Century Metropolis." PhD thesis, Duke University.

———. 2020. "The City Is Burning! Street Economies and the Juxtacity of Kigali, Rwanda." *Urban Forum* 31 (3): 351–71.

Simone, AbdouMaliq. 2004. "People as Infrastructure: Intersecting Fragments in Johannesburg." *Public Culture* 16 (3): 407–29.

———. 2010. *City Life from Jakarta to Dakar: Movements at the Crossroads.* Routledge.

———. 2022. *The Surrounds: Urban Life within and beyond Capture.* Duke University Press.

Simone, AbdouMaliq, and Edgar Pieterse. 2018. *New Urban Worlds: Inhabiting Dissonant Times.* John Wiley & Sons.

Simpson, Audra. 2014. *Mohawk Interruptus: Political Life across the Borders of Settler States.* Duke University Press.

Sinalo, Caroline Williamson. 2018. *Rwanda after Genocide: Gender, Identity and Post-Traumatic Growth.* Cambridge University Press.

Sirven, Pierre. 1984. *La Sous-urbanisation et les Villes du Rwanda et du Burundi.* PhD thesis, Inist-CNRS.

Soja, Edward W. 1998. "Thirdspace: Journeys to Los Angeles and Other Real-and-Imagined Places." *Capital & Class* 22 (1): 37–139.

———. 2013. *Seeking Spatial Justice.* University of Minnesota Press.

Sommers, Marc. 2012. *Stuck: Rwandan Youth and the Struggle for Adulthood.* University of Georgia Press.

Sontag, Susan. 1978. *Illness as Metaphor.* Farrar, Straus & Giroux.

Staub, Ervin, Laurie Anne Pearlman, and Vachel Miller. 2003. "Healing the Roots of Genocide in Rwanda." *Peace Review* 15 (3): 287–94.

Stearns, Jason K. . 2022. *The War That Doesn't Say Its Name: The Unending Conflict in the Congo.* Princeton University Press.

Stoler, Ann Laura. 2002. "Colonial Archives and the Arts of Governance." *Archival Science* 2:87–109.

———. 2010. *Along the Archival Grain.* Princeton University Press.

———. 2016. *Duress: Imperial Durabilities in Our Times.* Duke University Press.

Straus, Scott. 2004. "How Many Perpetrators Were There in the Rwandan Genocide? An Estimate." *Journal of Genocide Research* 6 (1): 85–98.

Straus, Scott, and Lars Waldorf, eds. 2011. *Remaking Rwanda: State Building and Human Rights after Mass Violence.* University of Wisconsin Press.

Tadiar, Neferti X. M. 2022. *Remaindered Life.* Duke University Press.

Takeuchi, Shinichi, and Jean Marara. 2014. "Land Tenure Security in Post-Conflict Rwanda." In *Confronting Land and Property Problems for Peace,* edited by Shinichi Takeuchi, 86–108. Routledge.

Taylor, Christopher C. 1999. Sacrifice as Terror: The Rwandan Genocide of 1994. Berg.

Thomson, Susan. 2013. *Whispering Truth to Power: Everyday Resistance to Reconciliation in Post-Genocide Rwanda.* University of Wisconsin Press.

REFERENCES 233

———. 2018. *Rwanda: From Genocide to Precarious Pace*. Yale University Press.

Tomás, Antonio. 2022. *In the Skin of the City: Spatial Transformation in Luanda*. Duke University Press.

Trouillot, Michel-Rolph. 2015. *Silencing the Past: Power and the Production of History*. Beacon Press.

Tsinda, Aime, and Pamela Abbott. 2018. "Critical Water, Sanitation and Hygiene (WASH) Challenges in Rwanda." Working paper on sanitation. University of Rwanda, University of Aberdeen. https://papers.ssrn.com/sol3/papers.cfm?abstract_id=3259008.

Tsinda, Aime, Pamela Abbott, Steve Pedley, Katrina Charles, Jane Adogo, Kenan Okurut, and Jonathan Chenoweth. 2013. "Challenges to Achieving Sustainable Sanitation in Informal Settlements of Kigali, Rwanda." *International Journal of Environmental Research and Public Health* 10 (12): 6939–54.

Twagilimana, Aimable. 1996. *Manifold Annihilation: A Novel*. Rivercross Publishing.

———. 2003. *The Debris of Ham: Ethnicity, Regionalism, and the 1994 Rwandan Genocide*. University Press of America.

Van Leeuwen, Mathijs. 2001. "Rwanda's Imidugudu Programme and Earlier Experiences with Villagization and Resettlement in East Africa." *Journal of Modern African Studies* 39 (4): 623–44.

Vansina, Jan. 2005. *Antecedents to Modern Rwanda: The Nyiginya Kingdom*. University of Wisconsin Press.

Verwimp, Philip. 2000. "Development Ideology, the Peasantry and Genocide: Rwanda Represented in Habyarimana's speeches." *Journal of Genocide Research* 2 (3): 325–61.

———. 2004. "Death and Survival during the 1994 Genocide in Rwanda." *Population Studies* 58 (2): 233–45.

———. 2013. *Peasants in Power*. Springer.

Vidal, Claudine. 2001. "Les Commémorations du génocide au Rwanda." *Temps modernes* 613:1–46.

Von Schnitzler, Antina. 2017. *Democracy's Infrastructure: Techno-Politics and Protest after Apartheid*. Princeton University Press.

Wakhungu, Judi, Chris Huggins, Elvin Nyukuri, and Jane Lumumba. 2010. "Approaches to Informal Urban Settlements in Africa: Experiences from Kigali and Nairobi." Policy brief, African Center for Technology Studies, Nairobi.

Warner, Michael. 2002. "Publics and Counterpublics." *Public Culture* 14 (1): 49–90.

Watson, Vanessa. 2014. "African Urban Fantasies: Dreams or Nightmares? *Environment and Urbanization* 26 (1): 215–31.

Watts, Michael. 2003. Development and Governmentality. *Singapore Journal of Tropical Geography* 24 (1): 6–34.

Wendel, Delia D. B., and F. S. Aidoo, eds. 2015. *Spatializing Politics: Essays on Power and Place*. Harvard University Graduate School of Design.

Williams, Raymond. 1975. *The Country and the City*. Oxford University Press.

———. 1977. *Marxism and Literature*. Oxford University Press.

Wilson, Japhy. 2017. "Paradoxical Utopia: The Millennium Villages Project in Theory and Practice." *Journal of Agrarian Change* 17 (1): 122–43.

Wilson, Japhy, and Erik Swyngedouw. 2014. *The Post-Political and Its Discontents: Spaces of Depoliticisation, Spectres of Radical Politics*. Edinburgh University Press.

Wilson, Richard Ashby. 2022. "Irreconciliation, Reciprocity, and Social Change (Afterword 1)." *Journal of the Royal Anthropological Institute* 28 (S1): 95–102.

World Bank. N.d. World Development Indicators, Rwanda. https://data.worldbank. org/country
    /rwanda?view=chart.

World Bank Group. 2017. *Reshaping Urbanization in Rwanda.* World Bank.

Wright, Gwendolyn. 1987. "Tradition in the Service of Modernity: Architecture and Urbanism
    in French Colonial Policy, 1900–1930." *Journal of Modern History* 59 (2): 291–316.

Wrong, Michela. 2021. *Do Not Disturb: The Story of a Political Murder and an African Regime
    Gone Bad.* Public Affairs.

Yiftachel, Oren. 1998. "Planning and Social Control: Exploring the Dark Side." *Journal of Plan-
    ning Literature.* 12 (4): 395–406.

Yusoff, Kathryn. 2018. *A Billion Black Anthropocenes or None.* University of Minnesota Press.

Index

Page numbers in italics refer to figures.